Georg Cavallar
Failed Enlightenment?

Georg Cavallar
Failed Enlightenment?

A Philosophical Introduction

DE GRUYTER

This work has originally been published in German:
Cavallar, Georg. 2018. *Gescheiterte Aufklärung? Ein philosophischer Essay*. Stuttgart: Kohlhammer.
© Kohlhammer

ISBN 978-3-11-914291-5
e-ISBN (PDF) 978-3-11-222114-3
e-ISBN (EPUB) 978-3-11-222126-6

Library of Congress Cataloging-in-Publication Data
A CIP catalog record for this book has been applied for at the Library of Congress

Bibliographic information published by the Deutsche Nationalbibliothek
The Deutsche Nationalbibliothek lists this publication in the Deutsche Nationalbibliografie; detailed bibliographic data are available on the Internet at http://dnb.dnb.de.

© 2026 Walter de Gruyter GmbH, Berlin/Boston, Genthiner Straße 13, 10785 Berlin
Cover image: Fragonard, Jean Honoré. *Young Girl Reading*. C. 1769. Oil on canvas. 81.1 x 64.8 cm. National Gallery of Art, Washington, D.C., United States. Accession Number: 1961.16.1. Image: National Gallery of Art, Washington, D.C., CC0, https://www.nga.gov/artworks/46303-young-girl-reading.

www.degruyterbrill.com
Questions about General Product Safety Regulation:
productsafety@degruyterbrill.com

To Niko
Amor gignit amorem.

Contents

Foreword —— IX

List of Figures —— XI

Introduction
Assumptions, clichés, and narratives —— 1

Chapter 1
What was, what is, and what might the Enlightenment be? —— 20
1.1   The Concept of enlightenment and Currents of the Enlightenment —— 20
1.2   Is there really such a thing as the Enlightenment? —— 25

Chapter 2
The limits of reason: Experience, intellect, reason —— 40
2.1   How rational was the Enlightenment? —— 40
2.2   Emotions and feelings against understanding and reason —— 49
2.3   In search of the limits of reason —— 53
2.4   Contemporary relevance: Discussions about Islam —— 65

Chapter 3
Humor, cynicism, and the enlarged way of thinking —— 73
3.1   Humor, satire, parody, and cynicism —— 73
3.2   Change of perspective, the enlarged way of thinking, and a skeptical attitude —— 82
3.3   Combating Fanaticism, Prejudices, Superstition, Enthusiasm, and Dogmatism —— 89
3.4   Contemporary Context: Jihadists, Fake News, and Filter Bubbles —— 95

Chapter 4
Is there a common language of morality? Morality, ethics and law —— 99
4.1   Foundations of Morality in the Age of Enlightenment —— 101
4.2   Qualified Normative Universalism —— 107
4.3   Rule of Law and Justifications for Tolerance —— 113
4.4   Slavery, Human Rights, and Cosmopolitanism —— 129
4.5   Contemporary Relevance: Moral Relativism and Moral Universalism —— 137

Chapter 5
Faith and hope: Religion, critique of religion, and the religious Enlightenment —— 145
5.1 Hostility Toward Religion? —— **145**
5.2 Critique of Theology and State Churches, and Natural Religion —— **153**
5.3 Radical Enlightenment? Jonathan Israel and the example of Kant —— **161**
5.4 Contemporary Relevance: Between Naturalism, New Atheism, and Dogmatic Fundamentalism —— **174**

Conclusion
A failed Enlightenment? —— 177

Explanation of important terms —— 197

Select bibliography —— 200

Author Index —— 204

Subject Index —— 208

Foreword

This book is a concise introduction to the philosophy of the European Enlightenment.[1] Its main purpose is to offer a balanced view of its merits and shortcomings. The main question posed is whether the Enlightenment is still relevant or should be discarded as a relic of the past.

This is a generic introduction, not a specialized study on one specific aspect of the Enlightenment. In recent years, fascinating studies have emerged about the cultural and social history of the Enlightenment. These studies cover the emergence of public spheres or what Jürgen Habermas has called the "public realm," a culture of public debates and social interaction, the "invention" of the intellectual, the Republic of Letters, salons, and Freemasonry circles, the questioning of social hierarchies, the universities, and academies, the revolution of print, the book trade, censorship, the emergence of "Grub Street" (Robert Darnton), reading societies, and the "reading frenzy" of the 18th century. "New media" such as journals, novels, plays, pamphlets, encyclopedias, and similar materials have also been explored. Robert Darnton referred to this period as an "early information society." Some recent works delve into *how* Enlightenment ideas spread.[2] This book revolves around the more traditional question of *what* these ideas were.

---

[1] Useful introductions include Ritchie Robertson, *The Enlightenment. The Pursuit of Happiness, 1680–1790*, London: Penguin 2022, Knud Haakonssen, ed., *The Cambridge History of Eighteenth-Century Philosophy*, Cambridge, UK: Cambridge University Press 2006, Dorinda Outram, *The Enlightenment*, 4th ed., Cambridge: Cambridge University Press 2019, Steffen Martus, *Aufklärung. Das deutsche 18. Jahrhundert – ein Epochenbild*, Berlin: Rowohlt 2015, Dan Edelstein, *The Enlightenment. A Genealogy*, Chicago and London: University of Chicago Press 2010, Annette Meyer, *Die Epoche der Aufklärung*, Berlin: Akademie Verlag 2010.

[2] Here is a selection of publications focusing on these aspects: Robert Darnton, The News in Paris: An Early Information Society in: *George Washington's False Teeth. An Unconventional Guide to the Eighteenth Century*, New York: Norton 2003, 25–75, Ulrich Johannes Schneider, *Die Erfindung des allgemeinen Wissens. Enzyklopädisches Schreiben im Zeitalter der Aufklärung*, Berlin: Akademie Verlag 2013. See also Thomas Munck, *Conflict and Enlightenment. Print and Political Culture in Europe, 1635–1795*, Cambridge: Cambridge University Press 2019, Robert Darnton, *Pirating and Publishing. The Book Trade in the Age of Enlightenment*, Oxford: Oxford University Press 2021, Mark Curran, *The French Book Trade in Enlightenment Europe I. Selling Enlightenment*, London et al.: Bloomsbury Academic 2018, Simon Burrows, *The French Book Trade in Enlightenment Europe II. Enlightenment Bestsellers*, London et al.: Bloomsbury Academic 2018, Antoine Lilti, *The World of the Salons: Sociability and Worldliness in Eighteenth-Century Paris*, trans. Lydia G. Cochrane, Oxford, New York: Oxford University Press 2005, James Raven, ed., *Global Exchanges of Knowledge in the Long Eighteenth Century. Ideas and Materialities c. 1650–1850*, Woodbridge: Boydell Press 2024.

The present book does not provide a specialized examination of a single aspect of the European Enlightenment, although this is a common approach taken in many more recent works. They include studies on topics such as the Radical Enlightenment, the Catholic Enlightenment, the Scottish Enlightenment, the Black Enlightenment, the Haskalah—the Jewish Enlightenment, or the Popular Enlightenment. In addition, numerous studies focus on specific countries, like the Scottish Enlightenment, or the Enlightenment in Italy.[3] This book does not focus on one aspect of the European Enlightenment or one of its regional manifestations.[4]

A first version of this book was published in German as *Gescheiterte Aufklärung? Ein philosophischer Essay*, by Kohlhammer, Stuttgart, in 2018. This is a profoundly revised variant. Unless otherwise indicated, translations of German texts are my own.

I wish to thank Chris Laursen for valuable feedback and helpful suggestions, and the team at De Gruyter Brill for excellent support, especially Serena Pirrotta and Inga Lassen.

> This book is dedicated to my wife Niko. Thank you for everything.

> Vienna, January 2025.

---

[3] See, for example, Surya Parekh, *Black Enlightenment*, Durham and London: Duke University Press 2023, Christopher J. Berry, *Essays on Hume, Smith and the Scottish Enlightenment*, Edinburgh: Edinburgh University Press 2018.

[4] Fine examples of this category are Luisa Cifarelli and Raffaella Simili, eds., *Laura Bassi. The World's First Woman Professor in Natural Philosophy. An Iconic Physicist in Enlightenment Italy*, New York: Springer 2020 and Eva Piirimäe, *Herder and Enlightenment Politics*, Cambridge: Cambridge University Press 2023.

List of Figures

Figure 1: Willey Reveley, Plan of the *Panopticon*, 1791. Source: *The works of Jeremy Bentham*, Volume IV, 172–173, via Wikimedia Commons, Public Domain, https://commons.wikimedia.org/wiki/File:Panopticon.jpg (last accessed September 17, 2025).

Figure 2: Denis Diderot and Jean le Rond d'Alembert, *Encyclopédie ou Dictionnaire raisonné des sciences, des arts et des métiers*, published from 1751 to 1780, Volume 1, p. 1. Source: via Wikimedia Commons, Public Domain, https://commons.wikimedia.org/wiki/File:ENC_1-0001.jpg (last accessed September 17, 2025).

Figure 3: Joseph Wright of Derby, *An Experiment on a Bird in the Air Pump* (1767/68). Source: via Wikimedia Commons, Public Domain, https://commons.wikimedia.org/wiki/File:An_Experiment_on_a_Bird_in_an_Air_Pump_by_Joseph_Wright_of_Derby,_1768.jpg (last accessed September 17, 2025).

Figure 4: Daniel Nikolaus Chodowiecki (1726–1801), Series of Natural, and Affected Actions of Life, etching depicting "Sensation" (1779). Source: Albertina, Wien, Public Domain, © Albertina, Wien, https://sammlungenonline.albertina.at/?query=search=/record/objectnumbersearch=[DG2005/10352/3]&showtype=record, https://sammlungenonline.albertina.at/?query=search=/record/objectnumbersearch=[DG2005/10352/4]&showtype=record (last accessed September 17, 2025).

Figure 5: John Keenan (fl. 1791–1815), oil portrait of Mary Wollstonecraft (1759–1797), 1804, after a portrait by John Opie (1761–1807). Source: from The New York Public Library, Public Domain, https://digitalcollections.nypl.org/items/2bbe2380-0031-0130-5e34-58d385a7bc34 (last accessed September 17, 2025).

Figure 6: Maurice Quentin de La Tour (1704–1788), portrait of Jean-Jacques Rousseau (1712–1778), pastel on paper, third quarter of 18th century, after a portrait exhibited at the Salon de Paris 1753. Source: via Wikimedia Commons, Public Domain, https://commons.wikimedia.org/wiki/File:Jean-Jacques_Rousseau_(painted_portrait).jpg (last accessed September 17, 2025). Jean-Jacques Rousseau, *Du Contrat Social: ou Principes du Droit Politique*, title page, 1762. Source: via Wikimedia Commons, Public Domain, https://commons.wikimedia.org/wiki/File:Social_contract_rousseau_page.jpg (last accessed September 17, 2025).

Figure 7: Denis Diderot and Jean le Rond d'Alembert, *Encyclopédie ou Dictionnaire raisonné des sciences, des arts et des métiers*, published from 1751 to 1780, Volume 8, Plate 1, "Relieur." Source: via Wikimedia Commons, CC0 1.0, https://commons.wikimedia.org/wiki/File:Encyclop%C3%A9die,_ou_Dictionnaire_raisonn%C3%A9_des_sciences,_des_arts_et_des_m%C3%A9tiers_MET_li014_En15_Q.R.jpg (last accessed September 17, 2025).

Figure 8: J. L. Raab, after a painting by Döbler, steel engraving of Immanuel Kant, before 1899. Source: via Wikimedia Commons, Public Domain, https://commons.wikimedia.org/wiki/File:Immanuel_Kant_(portrait).jpg (last accessed September 17, 2025).

Figure 9: Francisco Rizi (1614–1685), *Auto de Fe en la plaza Mayor de Madrid*, 1683. Source: Museo del Prado, P001126, via Wikimedia Commons, Public Domain, https://commons.wikimedia.org/wiki/File:Francisco_rizi-auto_de_fe.jpg (last accessed September 17, 2025).

Figure 10: Emil Doerstling (1859–1940), Lunch at Kant's house, 1892/93. Source: via Wikimedia Commons, Public Domain, https://commons.wikimedia.org/wiki/File:Kant_doerstling2.jpg (last accessed September 17, 2025).

Figure 11: Godefroy Engelmann, after a design, *Le dragon missionnaire*, 1686. Source: via Wikimedia Commons, Public Domain, https://commons.wikimedia.org/wiki/File:Le_dragon_missionnaire.jpg (last accessed September 17, 2025).

Figure 12: T. Cook, *A credulous congregation listening to a sermon by a fiery preacher*, engraving after W. Hogarth, 1798. Source: Wellcome Collection, Public Domain, https://wellcomecollection.org/works/txdrjkcp (last accessed September 17, 2025).

Figure 13: Daniel Nikolaus Chodowiecki (1726–1801), *Jean Calas bids farewell to his family*, engraving, 1885. Source: via Wikimedia Commons, Public Domain, https://commons.wikimedia.org/wiki/File:Daniel_Chodowiecki_Calas.jpg (last accessed September 17, 2025).

Figure 14: Attributed to Louis Ferdinand Elle the Younger (1648–1717), Portrait of Pierre Bayle (1647–1706), circa 1675. Source: Château de Versailles, via Wikimedia Commons, Public Domain, https://commons.wikimedia.org/wiki/File:Pierre_Bayle_by_Louis_Ferdinand_Elle.jpg (last accessed September 17, 2025).

Figure 15: *Constitution of the United States*, September 17, 1787. Source: National Archive, 1667751, https://catalog.archives.gov/id/1667751 (last accessed September 17, 2025).

Figure 16: Henri Grégoire (1750–1831), *De la littérature des nègres*, 1808, title page. Source: via Wikimedia Commons, Public Domain, https://commons.wikimedia.org/wiki/File:Abbe_gregoire_1808.JPG (last accessed September 17, 2025).

Figure 17: Joachim Bouvet, *Etat present de la Chine*, Plate, 1697. Source: via Wikimedia Commons, Public Domain, https://commons.wikimedia.org/wiki/File:Joachim_Bouvet_Etat_present_de_la_Chine_1697.jpg (last accessed September 17, 2025).

Figure 18: Louis-Michel van Loo (1707–1771), Portrait of Denis Diderot (1713–1784), 1767. Source: Louvre Museum, Paris, via Wikimedia Commons, Public Domain, https://commons.wikimedia.org/wiki/File:Denis_Diderot_by_Louis-Michel_van_Loo.jpg (last accessed September 17, 2025).

Figure 19: Daniel Nikolaus Chodowiecki (1726–1801). Engraving in: *J. B. Basedows Elementarwerk mit den Kupfertafeln Chodowieckis u. a.*, edited by Theodor Fritzsch, Volume 3. Ernst Wiegand: Verlagsbuchhandlung Leipzig 1909. Source: via Wikimedia Commons, Public Domain, https://commons.wikimedia.org/wiki/File:Chodowiecki_Basedow_Tafel_13_a.jpg (last accessed September 17, 2025).

Figure 20: Daniel Nikolaus Chodowiecki (1726–1801), *Die aufgeklärte Weisheit als Minerva schützt die Gläubigen aller Religionen*, engraving, 1791. Source: via Wikimedia Commons, Public Domain, https://commons.wikimedia.org/wiki/File:Minerva_als_Symbol_der_Toleranz.jpg (last accessed September 17, 2025).

Figure 21: Nicolas de Largillière (1656–1746), Portrait of Voltaire (1694–1778) [at the age of twenty-four (?)], 1718–1724. Source: via Wikimedia Commons, Public Domain, https://commons.wikimedia.org/wiki/File:Atelier_de_Nicolas_de_Largilli%C3%A8re,_portrait_de_Voltaire,_d%C3%A9tail_(mus%C3%A9e_Carnavalet)_-002.jpg (last accessed September 17, 2025).

Introduction
Assumptions, clichés, and narratives

There has been some controversy surrounding the European Enlightenment in recent years. Some claim that the future of the "Enlightenment project" has become uncertain or is at risk. The achievements of the Enlightenment and modernity, it is said, need to be defended against its enemies, such as Islam, religious fundamentalism, authoritarianism, and illiberal democracy. Enlightenment is sometimes used as a polemical and bellicose term, distinguishing "us" from "them". The Enlightenment is something that others, such as Saudi Arabia, the Taliban, and Muslim-majority countries in general, do not have, or fundamentally *cannot* have. Alternatively, it is claimed that the Enlightenment has failed, together with the "unfinished project of modernity" (Jürgen Habermas). According to this narrative, the Enlightenment was the decisive era that definitively departed from tradition, heritage, and Christianity, to embark on a path that reached its peak in the 20th century and the arrival of a new Age of Darkness, namely totalitarianism, two World Wars, the Holocaust, the Gulag, and Hiroshima. These are some common narratives about the European Enlightenment.

Narratives convey meaning, values, and emotions within a particular group, serving to strengthen its identity. They reconstruct the past from a certain perspective, usually lay claim to legitimacy, and shape the way reality is perceived. Narratives help members of a group orient themselves within the past and the present and are an aid in coping with the future. There is a difference between stories and narratives. "Stories are collective or individual creations that are received individually and exist side by side in any number. A narrative, on the other hand, is aimed at a group whose story it presents from a certain perspective."[1] How do narratives about the European Enlightenment relate to the actual Enlightenment from the 1650s to around 1800?

The European Enlightenment of the late 17th and 18th centuries had only just ended when the first assumptions, clichés, and narratives about this era started to emerge. This introduction discusses and critically examines the assumptions, narratives, clichés, and assumptions about this Enlightenment.

---

[1] Aleida Assmann, Was ist ein Narrativ? Zur anhaltenden Konjunktur eines unscharfen Begriffs, in: *Merkur* 77 (2023), 88–96.

Assumption 1
Enlightenment is something that others simply cannot possess

Here, the Enlightenment is politicized, turned into a battle cry, used in political struggles, and turned into a cultural-historical category. "We" (the West, Europeans, defenders of modernity, etc.) possess this valuable Enlightenment, while others (non-Europeans, Muslims, Arabs, etc.) do not. A prominent example of this assumption in practice is the tendency to accuse countries such as Turkey or Muslim-majority countries of lacking an (European-style) Enlightenment. In the context of Turkey's potential accession to the European Union, a discussion at the beginning of this century repeatedly referred to the Enlightenment: Former German Chancellor Helmut Schmidt, for instance, remarked that, "In Islam, the crucial developments of European culture, such as the Renaissance, the Enlightenment, and the separation of spiritual and political authority, are absent. That's why Islam, despite 500 years of Ottoman expansion, couldn't establish itself in Europe."[2] Hans-Ulrich Wehler, a German historian and author of the profound five-volume *Deutsche Gesellschaftsgeschichte* (1987–2008), arrived at a similar conclusion. Like Russia or Ukraine, Turkey has "not been shaped [...] by antiquity, Roman law, the Reformation, let alone the Enlightenment."[3]

There are several objections to this narrative or perspective. Some scholars of Islamic studies point out that these arguments reflect a European view of the Islamic world which, in comparison to its own culture, identifies perceived deficits. They claim that secularization processes have also occurred (and continue to occur) in Muslim-majority societies involving a *de facto* separation of religious and political spheres.[4] Some historians emphasize that the cultural argument developed here could be a double-edged sword: Many Germans have also seen German culture opposing allegedly "Western" Enlightenment and modernity. The implicit assumptions concerning Europe in this political battle cry are constructs. It is not acceptable to "appoint oneself the world champion of values and to select from

---

2 Helmut Schmidt, Sind die Türken Europäer? Nein, sie passen nicht dazu, in: Claus Leggewie, ed., *Die Türkei und Europa. Die Positionen*, Frankfurt am Main: Suhrkamp 2004, 162–66, at 162.
3 Hans-Ulrich Wehler, Die türkische Frage. Europas Bürger müssen entscheiden, in: Leggewie, *Die Türkei und Europa*, 57–69, at 61–2.
4 See the discussions in Alexander Flores, *Islam. Zivilisation oder Barbarei?* Berlin: Suhrkamp 2015, Christopher de Bellaigue, *The Islamic Enlightenment. The Struggle Between Faith and Reason, 1798 to Modern Times*, New York: Norton 2017 and Georg Cavallar, *Islam, Aufklärung und Moderne*, Stuttgart: Kohlhammer 2017.

history—as from the supermarket—only that which one currently needs."⁵ The Enlightenment's frequently advocated "European values," such as secularization, rationality, scientific inquiry, and tolerance, have been fought for in a process spanning centuries and in competition with numerous alternative value systems. Even in Europe, they are not consistently recognized to this day.

Above all, this assumption of Enlightenment as a political battle cry does not distinguish between the Enlightenment as a historical phenomenon and enlightenment (lower case) as, firstly, the process of gaining wisdom or insight, and, secondly, (the process of) thinking for oneself (see Chapter 1). When viewed with nuance, referring to Enlightenment as something one possesses or owns, as a process a society has gone through, or as something that others do not or cannot have, becomes highly questionable.

Assumption 2
The Enlightenment corrodes, undermines, and destroys everything

Romanticism tended to portray the Enlightenment as an era of cold rationalism. The Enlightenment allegedly attempted to illuminate everything with reason, to control nature, and to destroy religion. The German poet and philosopher Georg Philipp Friedrich Freiherr von Hardenberg (1772–1801), better known by his pen name Novalis, popularized a new narrative: In the 18th century, a new faith appeared, namely the faith in reason and science. A new church with faithful members emerged. "These members were tirelessly engaged in cleansing nature, the earth, human souls, and learning of poetry, rooting out every trace of the sacred, spoiling the memory of all uplifting incidents and people through sarcastic remarks, and stripping the world of all its bright ornament. Because of its mathematical obedience and its boldness, light had become their darling."⁶ According to this narrative, the European Enlightenment had turned reason and science into new gods at the expense of feelings, poetry, faith, and tradition. They mocked everything that had previously been sacred. And they did not even realize that they

---

5 Günter Seufert, Keine Angst vor den Türken!, in: Leggewie, ed., *Türkei und Europa*, 70–5, at 71.
6 Novalis, Die Christenheit oder Europa [1799], in: *Werke*, ed. Hans-Joachim Mähl, vol. 2, München und Wien: Carl Hanser Verlag 1978, 731–50, at 741. Translated in Novalis, Christendom or Europe, in: *Philosophical Writings*, translated and edited by Margaret Mahony Stoljar, Albany: State University of New York Press 1997, 137–52, at 144–5.

had just replaced one set of beliefs with a new one. What is "enlightened" about this ideology?

The *Berlinische Monatsschrift* (Berlin Monthly), the flagship of the German Enlightenment, published several essays by Immanuel Kant (1724–1804) in their volumes, among them his famous "What is enlightenment?" in 1784. They also concluded one issue with a poem entitled, "The Monkey: A Little Fable":

> Once upon a time, a monkey set a grove
> Of cedars on fire at night,
> And greatly rejoiced, above and above,
> When he saw the world so bright.
> "Come, brothers, see what I can do;
> I – I can turn night into day!"
> The brothers came, both big and small,
> Admired the brilliance so wide,
> And all began to loudly call:
> "Long live Brother Hans with pride!
> Hans the monkey deserves renown,
> He's enlightened the entire town."[7]

Cedars are ancient and valuable trees, here probably used to symbolize tradition. The Old Testament, for example, contains numerous poetic and theological references to the cedars of Lebanon. In some passages, the cedar forests represent the Garden of Eden.[8] The poem mocks the almost childlike Enlightenment thinker who takes pride in turning night into day, refusing to see they are only causing destruction. It seems that the monkey's primary concern is its performance, being admired by others, and satisfying its own vanity, its little "self." It attempts to mimic the sun and of course fails. Its "brothers" are the other Enlightenment thinkers for whom achieving enlightenment is of the utmost importance, regardless of the cost. In 1891, the *Oxford English Dictionary* offered two definitions of "enlightenment". One related it to the pejorative German term *Aufklärerei*, or "shallow and pretentious intellectualism, unreasonable contempt for tradition, and authority, etc."[9] This definition "survived" for more than a century.

One of the editors of the *Berlin Monthly*, the publicist and popular philosopher Johann Erich Biester (1749–1816), published the fable about the ridiculous

---

7 *Berlinische Monatsschrift*, 4 (1784), 480.
8 Karl-Heinz Bernhardt, *Der alte Libanon*, Leipzig: Koehler & Amelang 1976, especially 51–57.
9 See James Schmidt, Inventing the Enlightenment: Anti-Jacobins, British Hegelians and the Oxford English Dictionary, in: *Journal of the History of Ideas*, 64/3 (2003), 421–43, at 421. Schmidt shows in his article that in Great Britain of the 1890s, enlightenment was understood as a process (of clarification) and as a project, but not yet as a historical period.

monkey explaining that the journal strove for impartiality and was willing to accept that the text could be applied against the journal itself.[10] Biester's attitude is a fine example of what I will call "the enlarged way of thinking" (see 3. 2).

Assumption 3
The European Enlightenment deified reason

It is widely understood that the Enlightenment saw reason as the absolute focus of inquiry, or uncritically established it as the ultimate standard of evaluation. One introduction to philosophy states, for example, "In 1784, Immanuel Kant demanded in his famous essay What is Enlightenment? that reason should guide life. It should no longer be superstition, religion, societal authorities, and traditions that steer the life of the individual, but rather a worldview guided by reason."[11] The narrative usually continues along the lines of Romanticism "introducing" or emphasizing the crucial role of emotions, intuitions, and feelings, as opposed to "cold" and "heartless" reason.

However, this binary opposition is suspect. Most Enlightenment thinkers sought to critically examine religions and traditions rather than to abolish them (see Chapter 5). It is debatable whether all Enlightenment thinkers advocated or promoted "reason" or the unrestricted, absolute "sovereignty of reason." Clearly, many often highlighted the finiteness, limitations, and boundaries of reason. Many Enlightenment thinkers repeatedly referred to what lies beyond reason: experience, sensitivity, feelings, sensory impressions, belief, even esoteric wisdom or a belief in spirits (see 2.1 and 2.2).

Assumption 4
The Enlightenment is synonymous with European modernity

American Historian Robert Darnton has cautioned against an "inflated" conception of the Enlightenment, in which Enlightenment is identified with "all moder-

---

10 *Berlinische Monatsschrift*, vol. 5 (1785), 337.
11 Katharina Lacina, *Das Philosophiebuch Reflexionen*, Wien: Hölder-Pichler-Tempsky 2014, 24. See also: Stefan Greif, Georg Forster – die Aufklärung und die Fremde, in: Michael Hofmann, ed., *Aufklärung. Epoche, Autoren, Werke*, Darmstadt: Wissenschaftliche Buchgesellschaft 2013, 125 – 143, at 131 – 2 and Robertson, *The Enlightenment. The Pursuit of Happiness*, 776 – 7 with the example of Isaiah Berlin, and Robertson, *The Enlightenment*, 778 with the example of German historian Friedrich Meinecke.

nity, with nearly everything subsumed under the name of Western civilization."[12] Overly generalizing concepts include "enlightened modernity" or "Enlightenment modernity". Proponents of this inflated concept include Max Horkheimer and Theodor Adorno. Writing in the shadow of National Socialism, Stalinism, the Second World War, anti-Semitism, and the Holocaust, in their *Dialectic of Enlightenment* (1944) they claimed, "We have no doubt [...] that freedom in society is inseparable from Enlightenment thinking. We believe we have perceived with equal clarity, however, that the very concept of that thinking, no less than the concrete historical forms, and the institutions of society with which it is intertwined, already contains the germ of the regression which is taking place everywhere today."[13] Adorno and Horkheimer did not reject "Enlightenment thinking" out of hand, yet they stressed that enlightenment may lead to its opposite, namely "regression."

In European cultural and intellectual history, the following suspicion and narrative can be traced back to Nietzsche: That enlightenment and violence, reason and power, science and oppression are not coincidental but perhaps necessarily intertwined. One problem with the *Dialectic of Enlightenment* is that "enlightenment thinking" coincides with the historical European Enlightenment, but also with rationalism, positivism, science, capitalism, liberalism, mass culture, modernity, and its "disenchantment of the world." The European Enlightenment is found guilty of causing many of modernity's ills. Distinctions are not made between different concepts of the Enlightenment (see Chapter 1). Horkheimer and Adorno's concept of the Enlightenment is unhistorical and oversimplified, and the book "a scattergun assault on many aspects of modernity."[14]

---

12 Robert Darnton, The Case for the Enlightenment: Georg Washington's False Teeth, in: *George Washington's False Teeth. An Unconventional Guide to the Eighteenth Century*, New York: Norton 2003, 3–24, at 11.
13 Max Horkheimer and Theodor W. Adorno, *Dialectic of Enlightenment. Philosophical Fragments* [1944], ed. Gunzelin Schmid Noerr, Stanford: Stanford University Press 2002, xvi. See also Dietmar J. Wetzel, Perspektiven der Aufklärung: zwischen Mythos und Realität – eine Einführung, in: Wetzel, ed., *Perspektiven der Aufklärung. Zwischen Mythos und Realität*, München: Wilhelm Fink 2012, 7–19, especially 9–14, Ulrich Thiele, *Verwaltete Freiheit. Die normativen Prämissen in Horkheimers Kantkritik*, Frankfurt am Main: Campus 1996 and Schneiders, *Hoffnung auf Vernunft*, 14–6.
14 Robertson, *The Enlightenment. The Pursuit of Happiness*, 775. There is a clear distinction between the Enlightenment and modernity in the writings of Bruno Latour. See Lars Gertenbach, Eine Aufklärung ohne die Moderne, in: Wetzel, ed., *Aufklärung*, 179–92. The relationship between these two concepts remains a contested issue; see, for a philosophical introduction, Matan Oram, *The Ethos of the Enlightenment and the Discontents of Modernity*, London and New York: Routledge 2022 and James Schmidt, What Enlightenment Project?, in: *Political Theory*, 28 (2000), 734–57.

Assumption 4 The Enlightenment is synonymous with European modernity — 7

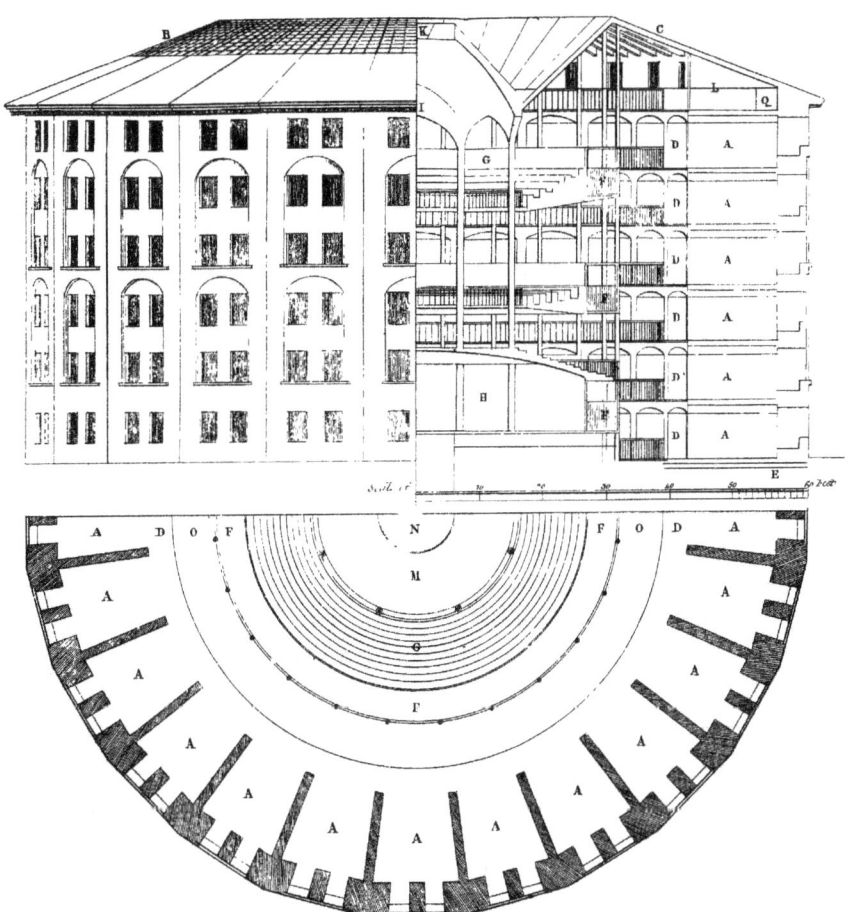

Figure 1: Willey Reveley, Plan of the *Panopticon*, 1791. The English philosopher Jeremy Bentham designed this prison so that all inmates would feel that they could be constantly observed; only one corrections officer is required. As the prisoners do not know when and how often they are watched, they are induced to regulate their own behavior. "A" indicates the prison cells. For some, the Panopticon has become a symbol of the Enlightenment and/or "Enlightenment rationality": total control, cold rationality, efficiency, subtle self-regulation, and maximum utility.

The concept of "enlightenment thinking" also tends to erase a difference which Horkheimer and Adorno themselves insisted on, namely between instrumental, and communicative reason. This difference was already recognized in the philosophical tradition with the separation of *intellectus* and *ratio*. This is one of the central distinctions of Kant's critical philosophy (see also 2.3). Horkheimer and

Adorno's criticism of the Enlightenment is not a critique of "the" Enlightenment as such, but rather of its being reduced to the natural sciences and so-called positivism: Reality is reduced to sensory perception, to means-end relations and physical causality, and reason is narrowed down to mere understanding or intellect and prudence.

Damien Tricoire even argues that the Enlightenment was not a break with the past, but rather very different from secular modernity. According to Tricoire, the key concepts of mainstream Enlightenment philosophy go back to a cluster of ideas rooted in Aristotle, medieval scholasticism, and Renaissance humanism. While distancing itself from Platonism and Augustinianism, Enlightenment anthropology and worldview followed the scholastic concept of a natural order of things, guaranteed by God.[15]

The concept of the "Counter-Enlightenment" is also problematic, as is any inflated understanding of the European Enlightenment. Isaiah Berlin applied this term to a group of late 18th century thinkers who favored authentic feelings over reason. According to Berlin, this Counter-Enlightenment has inspired the greatest evils of the 19th and 20th centuries, namely "nationalism, imperialism, and finally, in their most violent, and pathological form, Fascist, and totalitarian doctrines."[16] Italian philosopher Giambattista Vico (1668–1744) and German Lutheran theologian Johann Georg Hamann (1730–1788) are seen as key Founding Fathers of this tradition of an irrational and particularistic Counter-Enlightenment. However, Berlin distinguishes between *critics* of the Enlightenment such as philosopher and poet Johann Gottfried von Herder (1744–1803), and its *enemies*, such as Savoyard writer Joseph de Maistre (1753–1821).[17]

In recent decades, Berlin's nuanced assessment has given way to a simpler mindset, narrative, or way of thinking, like that associating the Enlightenment with modernity. In this case, an essentially morally superior and authentic Enlightenment (rational, secular, progressive, scientific) faces a demonized Counter-Enlightenment. Again, the Enlightenment becomes a polemical concept and a battle cry. Completely different currents, whether Romanticism, conservatism, nationalism, Fascism, Nazism, and totalitarianism, or contemporary Islamism, re-

---

15 Tricoire, *Die Aufklärung*, 41–2, 99–129 and 247.
16 Isaiah Berlin, The Counter-Enlightenment, in: *The Proper Study Of Mankind. An Anthology of Essays*, ed. Henry Hardy and Roger Hausheer, London: Random House 1998, 243–68, at 268.
17 Isaiah Berlin, Reply to Hans Aarsleff, Vico and Berlin, in: *London Review of Books*, vol. 20, 3 (Nov. 1981), 7–8. Piirimäe, *Herder and Enlightenment Politics* offers a recent and sophisticated interpretation of Herder's complex moral and political philosophy. See Piirimäe, *Herder and Enlightenment*, viii and 8–12 and Eva Piirimäe, Herder, Berlin and the Counter-Enlightenment, *Eighteenth-Century Studies*, 49 (2015), 71–6 on the misleading label "Counter-enlightener".

ligious fundamentalism, neoconservatism, and postmodernism are lumped together and attacked under the label "Counter-Enlightenment." Again, simplifications, exaggerations, black-and-white thinking, ball-park generalizations, and sweeping judgments prevail over a nuanced view.[18]

A simplified concept of the Counter-Enlightenment overlooks how criticism of the Enlightenment can sometimes be part of the Enlightenment itself. Rousseau is perhaps the most prominent example (see 2.3). German philosopher Friedrich Heinrich Jacobi (1743–1819) can also serve as an illustration.[19] He warned against the rule or hegemony of reason as well as of the Enlightenment. According to Jacobi, the supposedly natural "light of reason" is normatively charged and legitimizes itself through the struggle against the powers of darkness. With this binary opposition, Jacobi argues, there is a danger of self-immunization of any Enlightenment "project." Furthermore, violence can be employed to enforce the hegemony of reason. Initially, it may start as moral violence, then as the violence of public opinion. Eventually, it may resort to political means. "The great mass of our thinking heads [...] wants to see the essential truth and the essential good spread – *by force*, and *by force* every error suppressed." They want to "enlighten *elsewhere than in the understanding* (*Verstand*), because it takes too long for them there; extinguish the lights, full of childish impatience, *so that it becomes day*." This may lead to despotism, "violence and subjugation."[20] Jacobi's examples are

---

18 See Robert E. Norton, The Myth of the Counter-Enlightenment, *Journal of the History of Ideas*, 68 (2007), 635–58, Theo Jung, Gegenaufklärung: Ein Begriff zwischen Aufklärung und Gegenwart, in: Wetzel, ed., *Aufklärung*, 87–100, especially 96–99 and Meyer, *Die Epoche der Aufklärung*, 171–82 on the concept. Useful monographs are Graeme Garrard, *Counter-Enlightenments. From the eighteenth century to the present*, New York: Routledge 2006 and Darrin M. McMahon, *Enemies of the Enlightenment. The French Counter-Enlightenment and the Making of Modernity*, Oxford: Oxford University Press 2001. In my opinion, an inflated concept of Counter-Enlightenment prevails in Zeev Sternhell, *The Anti-Enlightenment Tradition*, translated by David Maisel, New Haven and London: Yale University Press 2010 and Ingo Elbe, *Gestalten der Gegenaufklärung. Untersuchungen zu Konservatismus, politischem Existentialismus und Postmoderne*, 2. Aufl., Würzburg: Königshausen und Neumann 2021.
19 Walter Jaeschke, Eine Vernunft, welche nicht die Vernunft ist. Jacobis Kritik der Aufklärung, in: Jaeschke and Birgit Sandkaulen, eds., *Friedrich Heinrich Jacobi. Ein Wendepunkt der geistigen Bildung der Zeit*, Hamburg: Meiner 2004, 199–216, Jaeschke, Aufklärung Gegen Aufklärung. Friedrich Heinrich Jacobis Kampf gegen die Herrschaft der Vernunft, in: Richard Faber and Brunhilde Wehinger, eds., *Aufklärung in Geschichte und Gegenwart*, Würzburg: Königshausen & Neumann 2010, 231–43.
20 Friedrich Heinrich Jacobi, Etwas das Lessing gesagt hat. Ein Commentar zu den Reisen der Päpste nebst Betrachtungen von einem Dritten [1782], in: *Werke. Gesamtausgabe*, ed. Klaus Hammacher and Walter Jaeschke, vol. 4, 1, Hamburg: Meiner 2006, 301–46, at 305.

evidently the enlightened despotism or absolutism of Emperor Joseph II. of Austria (1741–1790) and, after 1789, the French Revolution.

Jacobi's criticism of the European Enlightenment is also enlightenment about the Enlightenment. The struggle against all forms of fanaticism and misunderstood enthusiasm is one of the fundamental themes of the European Enlightenment (see 3.3). And there may be some truth in Jacobi's accusation that some forms of the Enlightenment are prone to fanaticism and misguided enthusiasm. It would be unreasonable to deny reasonable elements in Jacobi's critique.

In short, it is evident that brands of Counter-Enlightenment are incompatible with the scientific model of the Enlightenment. Yet this does not imply that *some* currents of the Counter-Enlightenment are indeed part of the overall European Enlightenment. In addition, it can be argued that these strands are a form of Enlightenment, trying to enlighten their fellow human beings "about the flaws of *one* particular conception of enlightenment (that which prevailed in eighteenth century Europe and America), not enlightenment in general."[21]

Counter-Enlightenment and its various brands remains a useful concept, if Isiah Berlin's distinction between friendly *critics* of the European Enlightenment such as Rousseau and Herder and its *enemies*, such as de Maistre, is maintained.[22] The critics are still part of the Enlightenment because they adhere to its core features (see 1.1).

Assumption 5
The European Enlightenment was many things, but not enlightened

In a polemical exaggeration, the Enlightenment is described as racist, androcentric, and Eurocentric, legitimizing colonialism, and imperialism. An author summarizes the criticism of the human rights concepts of the European Enlightenment with the following words: "Critics argue that the Enlightenment human rights legacy represents little more than an imperialist masquerade aimed at subduing the rest of the world under the pretense of promoting universality."[23] Focus-

---

21 Garrard, Tilting at Counter-Enlightenment Windmills, 80.
22 Isaiah Berlin, Reply to Hans Aarsleff, Vico and Berlin, in: *London Review of Books*, vol. 20, 3 (Nov. 1981), 7–8.
23 Micheline R. Ishay, *The History of Human Rights*, Berkeley und Los Angeles: University of California Press 2008, 8. See also the examples in Claudia Honegger, Die Aufklärung der Gegenwart, in: Wetzel, *Aufklärung*, 73–85, at 73.

ing on environmental destruction, the former British heir to the throne, Prince Charles (now King Charles III.), accused the Enlightenment of having an unenlightened and exploitative attitude toward nature. "We cannot go on like this, just imagining that the principles of the Enlightenment still apply now. I don't believe they do."[24]

What does talk of the unenlightened Enlightenment suggest? It could mean that the Enlightenment itself was contradictory: Its proponents proclaimed ideals or norms to which they themselves did not adhere. Alternatively, the Enlightenment might be criticized for its lack of self-reflection. It merely replaced one worldview or ideology with another, without critically questioning the new one. There are certainly examples of an unenlightened Enlightenment; one famous instance is a footnote by the Scottish empiricist and skeptic David Hume (1711–1776), who suggested that Africans were naturally inferior to whites because there were "[n]o ingenious manufacturers among them, no arts, no sciences."[25] In this particular instance, Hume ignored both his empiricist approach and his skeptical attitude (this does not necessarily imply that his philosophy *tout court* is without merit).

Objections to this view of the Enlightenment can be quickly identified. Once again, it is a sweeping statement about "the Enlightenment." Secondly, every critique of the Enlightenment "has become possible only through the Enlightenment."[26] In the 18th century, Hume's racism could and was critiqued with enlightened arguments: Empirical evidence such as examples of cultured, civilized, and rational Africans contradicted his thesis. The absence of "ingenious manufacturers" was explained by other factors, such as climate (see also assumption 8). Thus, Hume was dogmatic, not skeptical, in his causal explanation of a phenomenon. Criticism of the European Enlightenment is not necessarily a version of Counter-Enlightenment, but perhaps, in some cases, an attempt at a better or more reflective Enlightenment. This might be understood as "metacritique" or "meta-enlightenment," meaning it is a critique of the critique, an attempt to enlighten (elements of) the European Enlightenment. Historically, the beginnings

---

24 Valentine Low, Prince Charles declares war on … the Enlightenment, *The Times*, 4. February 2010. See Parekh, *Black Enlightenment* and Nicholas Hudson, ed., *A Cultural History of Race in the Reformation and Enlightenment*, London et al.: Bloomsbury Academic 2022 for the accusation of the European Enlightenment being racist.
25 See Georg Cavallar, *The Rights of Strangers: Theories of international hospitality, the global community, and political justice since Vitoria*, Aldershot: Ashgate 2002, 246 with references, and Parekh, *Black Enlightenment*, 24–7 for the broader context.
26 Werner Schneiders, *Das Zeitalter der Aufklärung.* 3rd ed., München: Beck 2005, 132.

of this form of self-reflective Enlightenment can be traced back to thinkers like Rousseau, Herder, or Kant (see 1.1 for more information).

Thirdly, it can be argued that key Enlightenment thinkers like Charles-Louis de Secondat, Baron de la Brède et de Montesquieu, commonly known as Montesquieu (1689–755), Voltaire (1694–1778) or Denis Diderot (1723–1784) practiced what Matthew Sharpe calls "self-estranging" or "self-othering." They tried to imagine how European customs and practices would appear through the eyes of members of other cultures. For example, in the case of Montesquieu, they were Persians visiting Paris, American Indians in the case of Voltaire, and Tahitians for Diderot. This change of perspective had the function of challenging what Kant would call logical egoism.[27] It is *not* obvious that they all failed in these endeavors (see 3.2).

Fourthly, it is true that proponents of the Enlightenment *might* also regress into dogmatism, prejudice, or irrationalism. However, the same can apply to Enlightenment criticism, especially when it lacks self-reflection. Therefore, critical questions are necessary in this context: Can "the ideals of the Enlightenment" accurately be described as a disguised ideology of European imperialism? Can we really hold "the Enlightenment" responsible for the ills of modernity or the destruction of our planet, as King Charles III. suggested? Would not modernity, industrialization, globalization, or capitalism be better scapegoats (if we need them at all)? Perhaps we should first define umbrella terms like "modernity" or "capitalism?"

Finally, narratives such as "the European Enlightenment inevitably leads to totalitarianism and the destruction of the environment" should be challenged because causal relationships are unclear. There may be cases of unintended consequences. Enlightenment philosophers probably intended results that were different from, or completely opposed to, the actual outcomes. A related phenomenon is what Graeme Garrard calls "the inversion thesis of the Enlightenment." This is "the unforeseen reversal that occurs when human actions unexpectedly produce the very opposite of their author's intentions, with tragic consequences, as in ancient Greek drama."[28] Moderate mainstream enlighteners, for example, would have been shocked by the French Reign of Terror (1793–1794), yet enemies of the European Enlightenment have claimed that these enlighteners *in toto* were directly responsible for it. These moderate enlighteners would have protested that the mass murder of the *terreur* had never been their intention, or an integral

---

27 Matthew Sharpe, *The Other Enlightenment. Self-Estrangement, Race, and Gender*, Lanham, Boulder, New York, London: Rowman & Littlefield Publishers 2023, especially 109–33.
28 Garrard, *Counter-Enlightenments*, 14.

part of their "projects." In fact, most enlighteners might not have rallied to the cause of the French Revolution at all, since they often supported enlightened despotism, favored reform over revolution, cherished ordered freedom, and were suspicious of the masses or the "mob."[29]

Critics or enemies of the Enlightenment should at least maintain the argumentative and self-reflective level that they find lacking in the Enlightenment itself—a level that some European enlighteners also did not achieve. Criticisms of the Enlightenment usually contain implicit definitions of this movement: Self-reflective, consistent, critical, universal, humanistic, secular. Yet it remains open to debate whether these implicit definitions coincide with the core features of the European Enlightenment (see 1.2).

Assumption 6
The European Enlightenment was hostile to religion

Religion is defined here as the thought and belief in a comprehensive framework of meaning that transcends the narrow confines of immediate experience, or a mere biological understanding of existence. In this understanding, religion is seen as a "final binding or re-binding of human existence" to something or someone, appearing in various forms.[30] This re-binding transcends sensory perception and is, in that sense, "transcendent" in terms of going beyond the realm of experience.

The alleged Enlightenment hostility toward religion and its atheism had already been criticized in a poem by the German Romantic poet Karoline von Günderrode (1780–1806) at the beginning of the Romantic era:

> But everything has now become quite different,
> Heaven has fallen, the abyss has been filled,
> And comfortably covered with reason, easy to walk upon.

---

29 Garrard, *Counter-Enlightenments*, 125–6.
30 Thomas Luckmann, *The Invisible Religion. The Problem of Religion in Modern Society* [1963], ed. by Tom Kaden and Bernt Schnettler, London and New York: Routledge 2023, 34, 45. See also Thomas Luckmann, *Die unsichtbare Religion* [1967], 3rd ed., Frankfurt am Main: Suhrkamp 1996, 90, Frank-Michael Kuhlemann, Mentalitätsgeschichte. Theoretische und methodische Überlegungen am Beispiel der Religion im 19. und 20. Jahrhundert, in: Wolfgang Hardtwig and Hans-Ulrich Wehler eds., *Kulturgeschichte Heute*, Göttingen: Vandenhoeck & Ruprecht 1996, 182–211, at 185 and Anne Conrad, Umschwebende Geister und aufgeklärter Alltag. Esoterik als Religiosität der Spätaufklärung, in: Monika Neugebauer-Wölk and Holger Zaunstöck, eds., *Aufklärung und Esoterik*, Hamburg: Felix Meiner 1999, 397–415, at 399–400.

> The heights of faith are now demolished.
> And on the flat earth, intellect strides,
> And measures everything, by fathoms, and by feet.[31]

This is a familiar accusation: According to the Enlightenment thinkers, especially the French *philosophes*, nature should be measured, and turned into an object of scientific inquiry with the help of the intellect, which acknowledges only experience. There is no longer any room for religious faith amidst a multitude of "facts and figures." The thesis that the European Enlightenment was hostile to religion and itself atheistic can also be found in unexpected places. One example is the first volume of *Winnetou* (1893), a novel by bestseller author Karl May (1842–1912). In one episode, Klekih-petra, Winnetou's teacher from Germany, says of his past: "In me, the ideas of the Enlightenment had taken root. My goddess was Reason. My greatest pride was to be a freethinker, to have dethroned God, and to be able to prove, down to the last dot, that belief in God was nonsense." He had fought against secular authorities in 1848 and then atoned for his sins among the Indians. The first two sentences were later added to the Bamberg edition. The cliché endorsed here is evident: The Enlightenment is destructive and subversive, and it fights against religion and state authority.[32]

This assumption and narrative has also established itself as part of Enlightenment historiography through to the present day. For instance, the German-American historian Peter Gay (1923–2015) claimed that despite all their differences, the Enlightenment thinkers were united by a single passion, namely "the passion to cure the spiritual malady that is religion, the germ of ignorance, barbarity, filth, and the basest self-hatred."[33] Gay erroneously extrapolated from a group of radical atheists and materialists to the movement as a whole. This portrayal does not do justice to the actual heterogeneity of the European Enlightenment. Positions cover deism, skepticism, agnosticism, pantheism, atheism, Neology, and the Catholic Enlightenment as well as apologetic literature. The French atheist materialists were a small group that were criticized by other, more mainstream Enlightenment thinkers. Most Enlightenment thinkers opposed religious fanaticism and intolerance, dogmatic attitudes, fanaticism, and denominational polemics. However, this did not imply a wholesale rejection of religion or Christianity as

---

31 Karoline von Günderrode, *Der Schatten eines Traumes. Gedichte, Prosa, Briefe, Zeugnisse*, ed. Christa Wolf, Darmstadt et al.: Luchterhand 1981, 56.
32 Peter Pütz, *Die deutsche Aufklärung*, Darmstadt: Wissenschaftliche Buchgesellschaft 1978, 58 with all relevant quotations.
33 Peter Gay, *The Enlightenment: An Interpretation*, vol. 1: *The Rise of Modern Paganism*, New York: Norton 1966, 373.

a whole. Most Enlightenment thinkers aimed for religious reform, trying to overcome denominational differences through the concepts of "natural religion" or a "religion of reason." They often rejected established and external forms of religion in favor of religious inner experience and individualization. They advocated tolerance and emphasized the moral content of religions, particularly Christianity. In the words of Robert Louden, "Most Enlightenment intellectuals were convinced that religion, if properly reformed, could, and should serve as a progressive force for the transformation of moral and social life—specifically, as a primary contributing factor in the formation of a more cosmopolitan moral community."[34] Prominent examples include representatives of Neology, a theological current which aimed at an enlightened religiosity and a Christian religion compatible with modernity (see Chapter 5 for a detailed discussion).

Assumption 7
There is a good and a bad Enlightenment

This assumption is also popular in some academic circles (although one would expect them to be more sophisticated). One example is Gertrude Himmelfarb's book entitled *The Roads to Modernity: The British, French, and American Enlightenments* (2004). The book's key thesis is that there were three fundamentally different forms of European Enlightenment: the British, the French, and the American. Other currents such as the German Enlightenment, the Enlightenment in Latin America, Italy, or the Habsburg Empire are not even mentioned in the study. Himmelfarb uses very broad templates to describe the three alleged "traditions" of Enlightenment. The British Enlightenment stands for "the sociology of virtue," the French *lumières* for "the ideology of reason," and the American Enlightenment for "the politics of liberty."[35] The French Enlightenment is described as one-sidedly rational, deifying reason (see Assumption 3). This ideology led to the French Revolution, the Terror of 1793, and Napoleon's military dictatorship. The only truly good and desirable Enlightenment, according to Himmelfarb, is the American version. It combined the positive elements of the British Enlightenment, namely common sense, and virtue, with the politics of freedom. In today's France,

---

34 Robert B. Louden, *The World We Want: How and Why the Ideals of the Enlightenment Still Elude Us*, Oxford: Oxford University Press 2007, 16. See also Steffen Martus, *Aufklärung. Das deutsche 18. Jahrhundert – ein Epochenbild*, Berlin: Rowohlt 2015, 771.
35 Gertrude Himmelfarb, *The Roads to Modernity. The British, French and American Enlightenments*, New York: Knopf 2004, 23, 147 and 189. There are some critical remarks in Claudia Honegger, Die Aufklärung der Gegenwart, in: Wetzel, *Aufklärung*, 73–85, at 75–77.

the author claims, the Enlightenment is practically dead, but in the United States, it has triumphed. "In America today, the Enlightenment is alive, and well."[36]

For similar reasons, Jonathan Israel's studies are also unconvincing. His ideological orientation is diametrically opposed to Himmelfarb's. Himmelfarb champions US neoconservatism, while Israel prefers the materialistic, atheistic Enlightenment over an allegedly deficient "moderate Enlightenment." Nevertheless, Israel's thought patterns resemble Himmelfarb's, albeit with different content: There is a good Enlightenment (atheist, secular, materialist, Spinozist) and a deficient Enlightenment, which took the wrong turn (see sections 5.3 and the Conclusion).

It does make sense to evaluate the various currents and individual authors of the Enlightenment. Judgments and assessments of this kind are common and justified.[37] Yet these judgments should be nuanced, avoiding clichés, narratives, templates, and simplistic black-and-white thinking. Like the other assumptions, these patterns triumph here, but this time in the evaluation of currents *within* the Enlightenment.

Assumption 8
The European Enlightenment was racist and supported colonialism and slavery

Some postcolonial theories claim that the European Enlightenment was an accomplice of, or openly supported, colonialism, imperialism, slavery, and racism. Tenets of these ideologies, it is said, were a belief in European cultural and racial superiority, fantasies of possessions, an essentialist distinction between "colonizer" and "colonized," the portrayal of non-Europeans as passive, primitive, and unenlightened, and the creation of Western cultural knowledge and narratives to dominate non-European peoples. In their attempts to understand "the Other", they were inevitably Eurocentric, imperialist, "and contaminated by European fantasies of power."[38]

---

[36] Himmelfarb, *The Roads to Modernity*, 227. Volker Depkat, Angewandte Aufklärung? Die Weltwirkung der Aufklärung im kolonialen Britisch Nordamerika und den USA, in: Wolfgang Hardtwig, ed., *Die Aufklärung und ihre Weltwirkung*. Göttingen: Vandenhoeck & Ruprecht 2010, 205–41, at 206–9 discusses some problems of this questionable interpretation of the US-American Enlightenment.
[37] See for example Louden, *World We Want*.
[38] See among others Antony Anghie, *Imperialism, Sovereignty and the Making of International Law*, Cambridge: Cambridge University Press 2005. The quote is from Jürgen Osterhammel, *Un-*

There is plenty of evidence supporting the claim that many enlighteners held racist beliefs, defended slavery, were Eurocentric, or advocated colonialism. As noted above, David Hume held that "negroes, and in general all the other species of men [...] to be naturally inferior to the whites," and praised white civilization as the pinnacle of human evolution (see assumption 5).[39] John Locke (1632–1704) and his notorious labor theory of property was fully compatible with, and explicitly justified, European expansion and colonial empires at the expense of native nomadic populations.[40]

Again, sweeping generalizations should be avoided. There are numerous examples of authors who harshly criticized European colonialism, colonial practices, slavery, or the slave trade, among them the German philosopher, jurist and historian Samuel Freiherr von Pufendorf (1632–1694), the German philosopher Christian Wolff (1745–1679), the writer and journalist Abbé de Raynal (1713–1796), Denis Diderot, Immanuel Kant, and Jeremy Bentham (1748–1832). Others spoke up against European arrogance or racism.[41] To take just one example: Young German ethnologist and naturalist Georg Forster (1754–1794) became famous with his work *A Voyage Round the World* (1777). Chunjie Zhang argues that Forster's account did not simply reflect his "white, male and imperial ego in a self-congratulatory way." It also "discloses a form of relativism and moments in which Oceania challenges, changes and regenerates his [own] cultural identity during his encounters with indigenous people."[42] Forster endorsed a form of cultural relativism: "The ideas of happiness are infinitely various in different nations, according to their manners, principles, and degrees of civilization. As the productions and apparent good qualities of our globe are either profusely or sparingly distributed on

---

fabling the East. The Enlightenments Encounter with Asia, translated by Robert Savage, Princeton and Oxford: Princeton University Press 2018, x.

39 Hume, Of national characters [1748], in: *Political Essays*, edited by Knud Haakonssen, Cambridge: Cambridge University Press 1994, 86 note.

40 See my own *Imperfect cosmopolis: studies in the history of international legal theory and cosmopolitan ideas*, Cardiff: University of Wales Press 2011, 33–5 with more references.

41 See, among others, Sankar Muthu, *Enlightenment against Empire*, Princeton and Oxford: Princeton University Press 2003, Jonathan Israel, *The Enlightenment that Failed. Ideas, Revolution, and Democratic Defeat, 1748–1830*, Oxford: Oxford University Press 2019, 420–32, Robertson, *The Enlightenment. The Pursuit of Happiness*, 609–54, Devin J. Vartija, *The Color of Equality. Race and Common Humanity in Enlightenment Thought*, Philadelphia: University of Pennsylvania Press 2021 and my own Vitoria, Grotius, Pufendorf, Wolff and Vattel: Accomplices of European Colonialism and Exploitation or True Cosmopolitans? in: *Journal of the History of International Law*, 10 (2008), 181–209.

42 Chunjie Zhang, Georg Forster in Tahiti: Enlightenment, Sentiment and the Intrusion of the South Seas, in: *Journal for Eighteenth-Century Studies*, 36 (2013), 263–277, at 267.

its different parts, the diversity of human opinions is a convincing proof of that sublime wisdom and paternal love of the creator."[43] Forster bridges the gap, or even abyss, between allegedly superior European civilization and progress on the one hand, and the idealization of the island of Tahiti as an earthly paradise on the other, if perhaps only for a moment. The non-European "other" is valued despite—or because of—its differences. Some representatives of the European Enlightenment had novel ideas here as well (see 4. 4 on Enlightenment cosmopolitanism).

It can even be argued that philosophers like Diderot, the abbé Raynal, or Chevalier Louis de Jaucourt (1704–1779) created a new narrative, namely that of the greedy, cruel, deceitful, barbaric, and exploitative Europeans who have relished dominating innocent natives since the Renaissance. Without doubt, there is considerable diversity and disagreement in the *History of the Two Indies*, the *Histoire philosophique et politique des établissements et du commerce des Européens dans les deux Indes* (1770–1780), as various anonymous authors with divergent opinions contributed to the volumes.[44] Yet Diderot rewrote many articles, and Jean-Joseph de Pechméja (1741–1785) even argued that "whoever justifies [slavery] merits a contemptuous silence from the *philosophe* and a stab of the dagger from the Negro." Diderot himself hinted at the theory of collective guilt, claiming that not only slave traders and planters were responsible, but also average Europeans, because they looked the other way: "The insatiable thirst for gold has given birth to the most infamous and atrocious of all trades, that of slaves. People speak of crimes against nature, and they do not cite slavery as the most horrific. Most European nations are soiled by it, and a vile self-interest has stifled in human hearts all the feelings we owe to our fellow men."[45] By the end of the century, the *Histoire des deux Indes* had turned into the Bible of anticolonialism.

---

43 Georg Forster, *A Voyage Round the World*, edited by Nicholas Thomas and Oliver Berghof, Honolulu: University of Hawaii Press 2000, 381, translation altered. For a generic introduction to the issues of 18th century cross-cultural contact, Enlightenment attempts to classify humans, and its thinking on race, see Outram, *The Enlightenment*, 55–66.
44 Guillaume Thomas Raynal, ed., *Histoire philosophique et politique des établissements et du commerce des Européens dans les deux Indes*, 4 vols., Amsterdam 1770; 8 vols., The Hague 1774. 10 vols., Geneva 1780. The book is usually abbreviated as *Histoire des deux Indes*. See Kates, *The Books that Made the European Enlightenment*, 299–326 and Robertson, *The Enlightenment. The Pursuit of Happiness*, 631–37 for an introduction.
45 Raynal, ed., *Histoire des deux Indes*, vol. 4, 167–68 (1770 edition), quoted in Andrew S. Curran, *Diderot and the Art of Thinking Freely*, New York: Other Press 2019, 366, and Raynal, ed., *Histoire des deux Indes*, vol. 9, 309, in: Diderot, *Political Writings*, 212.

Assumption 9
The Enlightenment has failed

This assumption or narrative sums up the accusations of previous assumptions (the Enlightenment only undermined and destroyed, it deified reason, it was racist and an accomplice of colonialism, and so on) and concludes that it has ultimately failed. For many, the Enlightenment has become "a convenient scapegoat on which those who feel ill at ease in the modern world can vent their frustrations."[46] I shall consider this assumption in some of the following chapters and in the Conclusion.

There is also the opposite narrative, which may be called the triumphalist narrative of Enlightenment secularism, and which runs as follows: The Enlightenment ushered in a new era, namely modernity. Since the 18th century, a battle has been going on between two camps, namely the "Enlightenment party" and "the enemies of the Enlightenment." Representatives of the first camp fought against religious fanaticism and political despotism and for rationality, freedom, human rights, democracy, individualism, tolerance, peace, and cosmopolitanism. The dark forces of the Enlightenment's enemies have distorted history, stuck to absurd ideologies such as Roman Catholicism or postmodernism, and have linked a progressive and innocent Enlightenment to the French Revolution, the Reign of Terror, genocide, and totalitarianism. The typical heroes of the Enlightenment party might include Voltaire, Kant, or Diderot. The list of enemies varies. For the Italian historian Vincenzo Ferrone, for instance, they are a motley bunch, including, above all, Hegel, Marx, Nietzsche, Horkheimer, and Adorno, Martin Heidegger, Michel Foucault, Pope Benedict XVI, and the Catholic theologian Romano Guardini. Despite their differences, they all offered "misleading interpretations of an ideological and political nature that go far astray of the historical truth."[47] This narrative also needs to be viewed skeptically.

---

46 Schmidt, Inventing the Enlightenment, 442.
47 Vincenzo Ferrone, *The Enlightenment. History of an idea*, translated by Elisabetta Tarantino, Princeton and Oxford: Princeton University Press 2015, xv–vi, 12–54. Another triumphalist narrative has been offered by Steven Pinker, *Enlightenment Now. The Case for Reason, Science, Humanism, and Progress*, New York: Random House 2018 (see the Conclusion).

Chapter 1
What was, what is, and what might the Enlightenment be?

1.1 The Concept of enlightenment and Currents of the Enlightenment

What does enlightenment mean? This question has been asked since the end of the 18th century, often referred to as the "Age of Enlightenment." The question continues to be answered in different ways to this day. It makes sense to distinguish the various conceptions of the European Enlightenment.[1]

Firstly, however, I want to examine the distinction between concept and a conception.[2] A *concept* is the generic term, as in "the concept of justice", the "concept (or idea) of morality" or "the concept of enlightenment". It "offers only a general account of something," and "refers to both the general goal and the process of replacing darkness with light, taken metaphorically to refer to wisdom or insight (however defined) replacing ignorance or a lack of understanding."[3] In contrast, a *conception* is one specific interpretation or variation. An example is the European Enlightenment as a historical phenomenon.

Historiography refers to the "Greek Enlightenment," the "Islamic Enlightenment," "Buddhist Enlightenment", the "religious Enlightenment" of European medieval times, the "Jewish Enlightenment," and 15th century Humanism as the "first century of Enlightenment."[4] These are all various *conceptions* of enlightenment. Enlightenment as a process is theoretically possible in all cultures and epochs but can only take place under certain conditions. In all these cases, enlightenment

---

[1] See Manfred Geier, *Aufklärung. Das europäische Projekt*, 2nd ed., Reinbek bei Hamburg: Rowohlt 2012 and Schneiders, *Aufklärung*, 7–20.
[2] This follows John Rawls, *A Theory of Justice* [1971], Cambridge, Massachusetts: Harvard University Press, reprint 2005, 5–6, Graeme Garrard, Tilting at Counter-Enlightenment Windmills, in: *Eighteenth-Century Studies*, 49 (2015), 79–80 and Garrard, *Counter-Enlightenments*, 5–6.
[3] Garrard, Tilting at Counter-Enlightenment Windmills, 79.
[4] Albrecht Beutel, *Kirchengeschichte im Zeitalter der Aufklärung*, Göttingen: Vandenhoeck & Ruprecht 2009, 17–8; Geert Hendrich, *Islam und Aufklärung. Der Modernediskurs in der arabischen Philosophie*, Darmstadt: Wissenschaftliche Buchgesellschaft 2004, Kurt Flasch and Udo Reinhold Jeck, eds., *Das Licht der Vernunft. Die Anfänge der Aufklärung im Mittelalter*, München: Beck 1997, Norbert Waszek, Die jüdische Aufklärung (Haskala) um Moses Mendelssohn, in: Hofmann, *Aufklärung*, 107–124, Shmuel Feiner, *Haskala. Jüdische Aufklärung*, Hildesheim, Zürich und New York 2007.

is understood as an intercultural phenomenon "involving the replacement of ignorance or darkness with knowledge or insight of *some* kind."[5] This is the first and most basic definition of enlightenment.

Secondly, the Enlightenment as a historical period and conception refers to the cultural and intellectual history of Europe, North and Latin America in the 18th century, or the period from the 1650s to the 1800s, with currents that continued into the 1830s. In this book I use the term "the European Enlightenment" for this conception. Its characteristics include (in addition to the characteristics of the concept) rational criticism, especially of inherited traditions, and religious-dogmatic worldviews; a turn toward humanity, continuing older currents in this regard; an emphasis on the independence and self-activity of the individual in moral, religious, political, and economic matters; the idea of the improvement or perfectibility of individuals and societies, and thus an emphasis on education and formation (*Bildung*); and finally, a strong turn toward experience and a tendency toward methodical "restriction to immanent modes of explanation."[6] In this work I use the term "European Enlightenment" for this historical epoch or era.

Within the European Enlightenment, different currents can be distinguished. Although a clear classification is difficult, I propose the following distinctions: "enlightenment of the intellect" is concerned with the struggle against ignorance, lack of understanding, superstition, and prejudices, and the clarification of concepts. This third form of Enlightenment was probably the lowest common denominator that all representatives of the European Enlightenment could agree on.

Fourthly, "enlightenment through science" is the shorthand for the scientific model of the Enlightenment, promoted, among others, by the French Encyclopedists. Georg Wilhelm Friedrich Hegel (1770–1831), philosopher, and representative of German idealism, later criticized this understanding as "reasonable [*verständig*] Enlightenment," namely, as a type of Enlightenment that only ac-

---

5 Garrard, Tilting at Counter-Enlightenment Windmills, 80.
6 Beutel, *Kirchengeschichte*, 21–22, Louden, *The World We Want*, Ursula Reitemeyer, *Umbruch in Permanenz. Eine Theorie der Moderne zwischen Junghegelianismus und Frankfurter Schule*, Münster and München: Waxmann 2007, and Martus, *Aufklärung*, 763–834. See Carsten Zelle, Anthropologisches Wissen in der Aufklärung, in: Hofmann, Hrsg., *Aufklärung*, 191–207 for the "anthropological turn" and Tal Gilead, ed., *A History of Western Philosophy of Education in the Age of Enlightenment*, London, New York and Dublin: Bloomsbury Academic 2021 as well as Daniel Tröhler, ed., *A Cultural History of Education in the Age of Enlightenment*, London et al.: Bloomsbury Academic 2020 for an overview of Enlightenment educational philosophy. Robert B. Louden, *Johann Bernhard Basedow and the Transformation of Modern Education. Educational Reform in the German Enlightenment*, London et al.: Bloomsbury Academic 2021 covers the German teacher and educational reformer Basedow, whom Louden sees as the "the unacknowledged father of the progressive education movement."(3)

knowledges the dimension of the intellect related to experience. The world is examined, measured, categorized, and demystified using the intellect (*Verstand*). Amidst all the facts and figures, there may be no room left for anything beyond one's own intellect or understanding (*intellectus* or *Verstand*) and sensory perception, such as reason (*ratio* or *Vernunft*), emotions, beauty, morality, or faith. The could result in the dominance of "instrumental reason" (Horkheimer and Adorno), of utilitarianism (only utility matters), and a naive empiricism. I refer to naive empiricism as the conviction that knowledge is based solely on sensory experiences, with anything beyond sensory experiences dismissed as nonsense.

There is a certain tension between the conception of "enlightenment through science" and the formal understanding of the fifth conception. Here, enlightenment coincides with the effort to think for oneself. It can also be called the emancipatory understanding of the Enlightenment. It focuses primarily on liberation from various forms of guardianship, whether social, religious, political, or cultural, that are subject to scrutiny. The means of overcoming unfreedom are primarily the effort of independent thinking, of self-reflection, and of expanded modes of thinking. Kant expressed this conception in a famous essay in 1784:

> Enlightenment is the human being's emergence from his self-incurred minority (Unmündigkeit). Minority is the inability to make use of one's own understanding without direction from another. This minority is *self-incurred* when its cause lies not in lack of understanding but lack of resolution and courage to use it without direction from another. *Sapere Aude!* Have courage to use your *own* understanding! is thus the motto of enlightenment.[7]

This conception partially overlaps with the concept of enlightenment as an intercultural phenomenon of gaining crucial knowledge and insight. This emancipatory conception of the enlightenment (lower case) also justifies speaking of an "Enlightenment project", the goal of which was the liberation from unjustified forms of tutelage and unfreedom. However, it is more meaningful, in my opinion, to speak of "projects in the age of European Enlightenment," as there is a high degree of diversity and heterogeneity here.

The sixth conception is the religious Enlightenment. It encompassed religious as well as theological currents which aimed at an enlightened religiosity, namely a form of religious faith that was compatible with the Enlightenment, understood as

---

[7] Immanuel Kant, An answer to the question: What is enlightenment (1784), in: *Kants Werke. Akademie-Textausgabe*, ed. Akademie der Wissenschaften zu Berlin, Berlin: de Gruyter 1902 ff., vol. 8, 33–42, at 35. The English translations are from the *Cambridge Edition of the Works of Immanuel Kant*, New York: Cambridge University Press 1992 ff. Claudio La Rocca, Was Aufklärung sein wird. Zur Diskussion um die Aktualität eines Kantischen Konzepts, in: *Deutsche Zeitschrift für Philosophie*, 52 (2004), 347–60 offers a profound discussion of Kant's motto *sapere aude!*

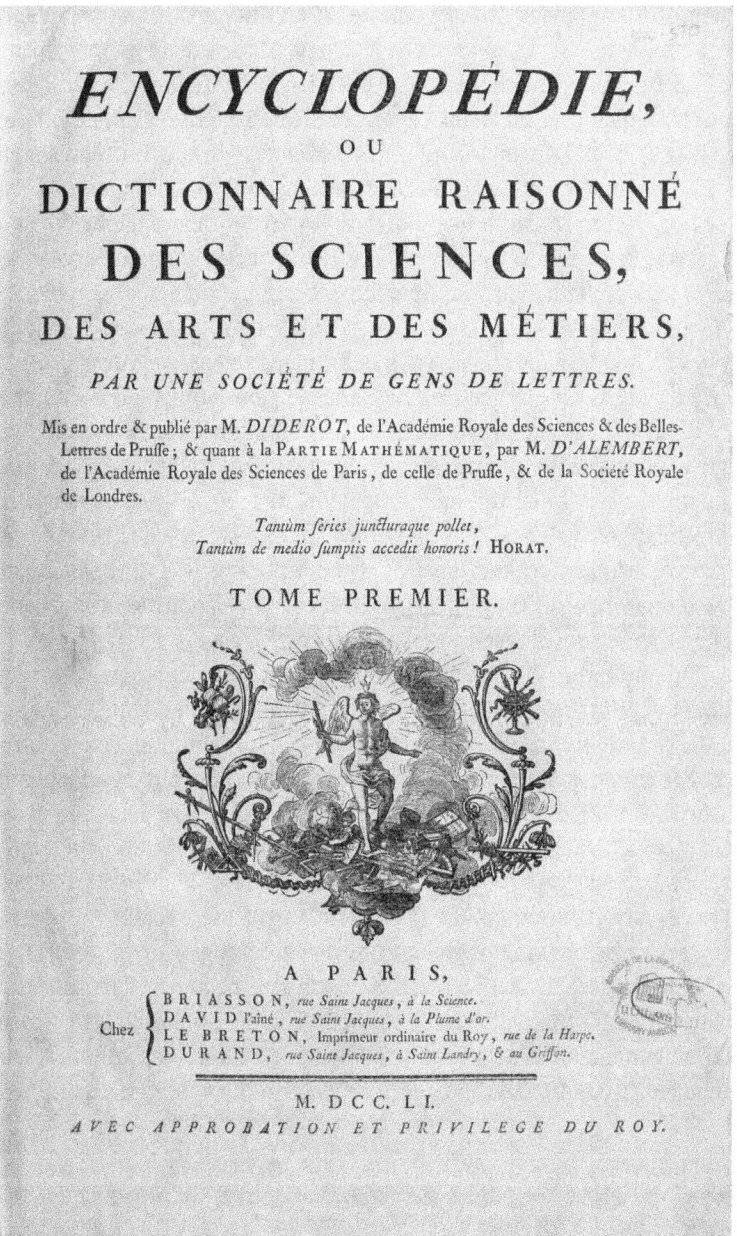

Figure 2: The *Encyclopédie ou Dictionnaire raisonné des sciences, des arts et des métiers*, published from 1751 to 1780, attempted to summarize humanity's knowledge in a systematic manner. It encompasses more than 70,000 articles. It frequently clashed with the censors. The *Encyclopédie* is one of the most important works of the Enlightenment and was heavily influenced by English empiricism.

"enlightenment of the intellect" (conception no. 3) and the emancipatory understanding (conception no. 5). Examples are Neology, a current of Lutheranism, the Catholic Enlightenment, the Haskalah, the Jewish Enlightenment with Moses Mendelssohn (1729–1786) as its main representative (see also Chapter 5), and deism. There was a Greek Enlightenment in the orthodox world, with representatives such as Nikephoros Theotokis (1731–1800) and the radical Christoduoulos Pablekis (1733–1793). Recent research has shown that parts of this religious Enlightenment were global in reach.[8] Typical texts are John Locke's *The Reasonableness of Christianity* (1695), Johann Joachim Spalding's bestseller *Die Bestimmung des Menschen* (*The Vocation of the Human Being*, 1748), Kant's *Religion innerhalb der Grenzen der bloßen Vernunft* (*Religion Within the Boundaries of Mere Reason*, 1793), and various works on physico-theology. The religious enlighteners attempted to combine faith and reason, promoted the academic study of the Bible, emphasized natural religion, usually rejected dogmatic orthodoxy, religious fanaticism, and superstition, but cherished the moral elements of their religious traditions, advocating practical benevolence. They were inclined to reject the doctrine of *peccatum originale* or original sin and favored a more optimistic anthropology, or conception of human nature. They spoke up in favor of religious toleration and usually justified divine providence in their search for a theodicy.[9]

The seventh conception can be termed the secular Enlightenment. It is not identical with, but closely related, to the current "enlightenment through science" (number 4). Margaret C. Jacobs has argued that the cultural and intellectual shifts during the Enlightenment did "not necessarily deny the meaning or emotional hold of religion, but it gradually shifted attention away from religious questions toward secular ones." The focus was on secular issues like society, economy, government, politics, education, or life in general "without constant reference to God."[10] There were moderate and radical versions of this secular Enlightenment, the radical ones showing open hostility toward religion in general and the Christian faith in particular. There was a continuum between moderate and radical versions. Jonathan Israel's "package logic" should be avoided, in which "true" secular enlighteners were inevitably followers of Dutch-Jewish philosopher Baruch de Spinoza (1632–1677), who advocated determinism, materialism, athe-

---

[8] See especially Ulrich Lehner, *The Catholic Enlightenment. The Forgotten History of a Global Movement*, Oxford: Oxford University Press 2016. Literature on the religious Enlightenment is listed in Chapter 5.

[9] This partly follows Robertson, *The Enlightenment. The Pursuit of Happiness*, 136–98.

[10] Margaret C. Jacob, *The Secular Enlightenment*, Princeton and Oxford: Princeton University Press 2019, 1. Robertson, *The Enlightenment. The Pursuit of Happiness*, 199–260 offers an excellent introduction to the debates surrounding narratives of secularization.

ism, freedom of thought, freedom of the individual, democracy, republicanism, human rights, cosmopolitanism, and world peace (see also 5.3).[11] The history of the Enlightenment is one of diversity, unlikely alliances, unintended consequences, nuances, and dynamic currents rather than clear-cut and static camps.

These distinctions between different conceptions of the European Enlightenment should be qualified. They refer to tendencies and should not present these Enlightenment models as fixed, ontological entities with no overlapping. These Enlightenment models should be understood as aids to orientation that leave room for differentiation. One case in point is Denis Diderot. He could be seen—or labeled—as a typical representative of the "enlightenment through science" model. However, with some justification, he can also be assigned to the emancipatory version or the "enlightenment through reason" model.[12] Conversely, it can also be argued that the representatives of the *Encyclopédie* or the "enlightenment through science" model were by no means naive believers in science, progress, and technology, with a clear-cut positivist, and utilitarian orientation.

1.2 Is there really such a thing as the Enlightenment?

In Enlightenment historiography, two opposing positions are held. The first claims that strictly speaking there was no such thing as "the European Enlightenment". Representatives claim that the various manifestations of the Enlightenment were entirely different and often incompatible, sharing no common foundational ideas. In short, there was a lack of unity amid the diversity. Historians J. G. A. Pocock and Sankar Muthu argue along these lines. James Schmidt, for example, claims "The very notion that there was a single thing called 'the Enlightenment' appears, more, and more, to be an illusion [...]."[13] The opposite position asserts the unity of the Enlightenment. Despite all its diversity, it is seen as a meaningful

---

11 Jennifer J. Davis, The Radical Enlightenment and Movements for Women's Equality, in: Steffen Ducheyne, ed., *Reassessing the Radical Enlightenment*, New York: Routledge 2017, 292–308, at 294. Most philosophers blended radical, moderate, and conservative ideologies in their texts (Ducheyne, *Reassessing the Radical Enlightenment*, 293).
12 See especially Curran, *Diderot and the Art of Thinking Freely*, passim.
13 James Schmidt, Inventing the Enlightenment: Anti-Jacobins, British Hegelians, and the *Oxford English Dictionary, Journal of the History of Ideas*, 64 (2003), 421–43, at 442. Pocock and Muthu are quoted in Garrard, *Counter-Enlightenments*, 7. The concept as well as the history of interpreting the European Enlightenment are the topic of the volume by Ryan Patrick Hanley and Darrin M. McMahon, eds., *The Enlightenment. Critical Concepts in Historical Studies*, vol. 1 Definitions, London and New York: Routledge 2010. Useful recent introductions are Fitzpatrick et al., eds., *The Enlightenment World*, London: Routledge 2004 and Meyer, *Die Epoche der Aufklärung*.

concept. Jonathan Israel, for instance, emphasizes that the Enlightenment was indeed a European phenomenon, encompassing all of Europe, so that a national, or regional approach is insufficient. "[C]ommon impulses and concerns shaped the Enlightenment as a whole."[14] Greek intellectual historian and philosopher Panagiotis or Panajotis Kondylis (1943–1998) argues that there is unity only in the questions asked during the Enlightenment, not in the attempted *answers*, which varied greatly and were characterized by polemics, "diversity, and multidimensionality."[15]

We should refrain from any form of essentialism, avoiding references to an alleged "nature" or essence of the European Enlightenment. Instead, the movement should be seen as encompassing unity alongside diversity. The Enlightenment had "thin coherence." Certain general characteristics of this Enlightenment can be identified without denying "the existence of numerous conflicts, tensions, and divisions between different variants of the Enlightenment."[16] This diversity, polyphony, and heterogeneity, along with the numerous tensions within the European Enlightenment, should always be considered. Recognizing the diversity and complexity of this Enlightenment can prevent the emergence of blanket judgments, of it being allegedly mistaken, failed, unenlightened or glorious, unparalleled, and indispensable.

I have noted some general characteristics of the European Enlightenment above, namely: A reflective awareness, a methodical increase in knowledge, popularization of scientific, or philosophical insights, rational criticism, a focus on the human species that continued older trends, the emphasis on the independence and self-activity of individuals in various aspects of life, the idea of the improvement or perfectibility of individuals and societies, and thus the emphasis on education and formation (*Bildung*), and finally, a tendency to limit explanations to immanence for methodological reasons. Other characteristics have emerged in the various forms of Enlightenment, such as the attempt at independent thinking. In the following paragraphs, I would like to provide some examples and evidence of the characteristics or aspects of the European Enlightenment that almost all representatives shared.[17]

---

14 Jonathan Israel, *Radical Enlightenment. Philosophy and the Making of Modernity 1650–1750*, Oxford: Oxford University Press 2001, v.
15 Panajotis Kondylis, *Die Aufklärung im Rahmen des neuzeitlichen Rationalismus*, Stuttgart: Ernst Klett 1981, 20–1.
16 Vartija, *The Color of Equality*, 194, Louden, *The World We Want*, 8. See also Schneiders, *Hoffnung auf Vernunft*, 18.
17 Carl Henrik Koch, Schools and Movements, in: Knud Haakonssen, ed., *The Cambridge History of Eighteenth-Century Philosophy*, Cambridge, UK: Cambridge University Press 2006, 45–68 is a

The turn to personal reason or intellect. It would be meaningless to claim that the European Enlightenment was the first to "invent" the turn to people's own reason. There were earlier approaches, such as in the late Middle Ages and the Renaissance. However, in the European Enlightenment, this turn was radicalized. Reason was no longer an all-encompassing *recta ratio* with metaphysical and/or theological elements with a capital "R", but turned into *ratiocinatio*, namely the faculty of reasoning and argumentation. An early and obvious example is John Locke. Along with friends, he discussed moral, metaphysical, and religious topics in the late 1660s. The discussions reached an impasse in the spring of 1671. Locke later wrote, "After we had awhile puzzled ourselves, without coming any nearer a resolution of those doubts which perplexed us, it came into my thoughts that we took a wrong course; and that before we set ourselves upon inquiries of that nature, it was necessary to examine our own abilities, and see what objects our understandings were, or were not, fitted to deal with. This I proposed to the company, who all readily assented; and thereupon it was agreed that this should be our first inquiry."[18] The examination of one's own faculty of knowledge thus took center stage. How do we know anything? This was still one of the central questions for Kant at the end of the next century. Where are the sources and limits of our knowledge? These questions are also the focus of the next chapter. The European Enlightenment not only posed perhaps the most important question in philosophy but also provided fascinating and often very convincing answers. These answers are still being discussed today—and deservedly so.

Enlightenment as an attempt to think for oneself. I have already quoted Kant's famous passage from his essay on Enlightenment ("*the human being's emergence from his self-incurred minority (Unmündigkeit)*"). Now one could argue that this was the retrospective self-definition of a single Enlightener when this movement had almost ended. However, the motive behind thinking for oneself is quite common during that period. Here are some examples. Dutch-Jewish philosopher Spinoza ended a letter to Albert Burgh, a young man who had just converted to Roman Catholicism, with the advice that he should examine religions and denominations different from his own with the help of his own understanding. Spinoza concluded: "Do you ascribe it to arrogance and pride that I use reason, and that I

---

recent attempt to establish general features of the European Enlightenment, contrasting it with seventeenth century philosophy.

18 John Locke, *An Essay Concerning Human Understanding* [1690], Oxford: Oxford University Press 1999, 14. For an introduction to the issue of reason and understanding in European Enlightenment philosophy, see Michel Malherbe, Reason, in Knud Haakonssen, ed., *The Cambridge History of Eighteenth-Century Philosophy* (Cambridge, UK: Cambridge University Press, 2006), 319–42, especially 320–1.

trust in this true Word of God, which is in the mind, and can never be distorted or corrupted? Away with this pernicious superstition! Recognize the reason God has given you, and cultivate it, unless you want to be considered one of the brute animals."[19] John Locke argued in *Some Thoughts Concerning Education* (1693) that children should be taught to internalize the "habit" of thinking on their own. He therefore rejected "slavish discipline" based on punishments and rewards.[20] In his *Essay Concerning Human Understanding* (1690), Locke humbly called himself "an under-laborer in clearing the ground a little, and removing some of the rubbish that lies in the way to knowledge," as opposed to "master-builders" like Huygens or Newton.[21] The helper enabled others, as self-thinking, and hard working individuals, to follow the arduous path to knowledge themselves. Thus, very early on Locke had formulated "a central program idea of Enlightenment which would shape the entire 18th century."[22] Anthony Collins (1676–1729) believed that a principle of reason was the duty to think freely. The alternative to independent thinking was simply repeating other opinions without questioning them. "For if they will not think for themselves, it remains only for them to take the opinions they have imbibed from their grandmothers, mothers or priests, or owe to such like accident, for granted." Only in this way can the search for truth based on the "evidence of things" replace random opinions. Independent thought is legitimate if there is reasonable or meaningful disagreement among experts (or alleged experts).[23]

The program of thinking for oneself was not uncontested. Moses Mendelssohn, the most important representative of the Jewish Enlightenment, had a fic-

---

[19] Benedictus de Spinoza, *The Collected Works of Spinoza*, Volume II, ed. Edwin Curley, Princeton: Princeton University Press 2016, 477 (Spinoza to Albert Burgh, late 1675 or early 1676). See also Edwin Curley, Spinoza's Exchange with Albert Burgh, in *Spinoza's Theological Political Treatise: A Critical Guide*, ed. Yitzhak Melamed and Michael Rosenthal, Cambridge: Cambridge University Press, 2010, 11–28.

[20] John Locke, Some Thoughts Concerning Education, in *The Works of John Locke in ten Volumes*, reprint Aalen: Scientia Verlag 1963, vol. IX, 1–205, at § 50, p. 38. More examples are listed in Marie-Luisa Frick, *Mutig denken. Aufklärung als offener Prozess*, Ditzingen: Reclam 2020, 25–48.

[21] Locke, *Essay Concerning Human Understanding*, 13.

[22] Geier, *Aufklärung*, 57, with more evidence in Geier, *Aufklärung*, 98–117.

[23] Anthony Collins, *A Discourse of Free-Thinking* [1713], ed. Günter Gawlick, Stuttgart, Bad Cannstatt: Frommann 1965, 32 and 33. See also Manuel Fasko, Questioning Authority: Anthony Collins' Challenge to Orthodox Anglican Authority Figures and George Berkeley's Reply, *Archiv für Geschichte der Philosophie*, 106 (2022), 1–26 and Ute Horstmann, *Die Geschichte der Gedankenfreiheit in England. Am Beispiel von Anthony Collins: A Discourse of Free-Thinking*, Meisenheim: Anton Hain 1980, especially 172–7.

tional Englishman say in *On Sentiments* that he valued *"accurate* thinking" more than *"free* thinking" and had therefore gone to Germany, the land of thoroughness. Mendelssohn's criticism was directed at some French Enlightenment thinkers who were accused of lacking depth, having a frivolous attitude, a "seductive imagination" and were engaged in superficial criticism of religion.[24] Mendelssohn clearly saw that independent thought challenged authorities.

The process of enlightenment is at least as important as its results. John Locke described how he and friends discussed philosophical topics together, often over several bottles of wine.[25] The *Berlin Wednesday Society*, which met from 1783 onwards, is perhaps one of the finest examples of where the process of mutual enlightenment took center stage. Academics from various scientific disciplines met every two weeks to "mutually enlighten their minds through friendly exchange of thoughts and thereby make various concepts clear to themselves and subject them to impartial examination." Writer and bookseller Christoph Friedrich Nicolai (1733–1811) praised the attitude or mindset of the participants, who were not concerned with "power plays," manipulations, or appealing to an inner voice. They all endeavored to justify what they considered the truth "through reasons" (*durch Gründe geltend machen*).[26] Members of the society included Moses Mendelssohn, the publicist, and philosopher Johann Erich Biester, the educator and politician Friedrich Gedike (1754–1803), and Friedrich Nicolai. Biester and Gedike jointly published the *Berlin Monthly* (*Berlinische Monatsschrift*), which became the most important journal of late Enlightenment in Prussia. Perhaps with an eye on this Wednesday Society and other 18th century Enlightenment processes, Kant claimed that it was difficult for individuals to enlighten themselves on their own. "But that a public should enlighten itself is more possible; indeed, this is almost inevitable, if only it is left its freedom. For there will always be a few independent thinkers […]."[27] However, it should be conceded that enlighteners were not immune to constructing a worldview or even "a system of thought detached from reality."[28] In that case, a fixed component of "enlightened knowledge" triumphed over the process. In any case, for many thinkers,

---

24 Moses Mendelssohn, *Philosophical Writings*, ed. Daniel O. Dahlstrom, Cambridge: Cambridge University Press 1997, 7.
25 Locke, *Essay Concerning Human Understanding*, 14.
26 Friedrich Nicolai, Ueber meine gelehrte Bildung, über meine Kenntniß der kritischen Philosophie [1799], in: *Gesammelte Werke*, ed. Bernhard Fabian and Marie-Louise Spieckermann, Hildesheim, Zürich und New York: Georg Olms 1997, vol. 1, 2, 65–6. See Geier, *Aufklärung*, 212–20 on the Wednesday Society.
27 Kant, What is enlightenment, vol. 8, 36.
28 Schneiders, *Aufklärung*, 12.

enlightenment was an ongoing, never-ending process. Along these lines, Kant only considered the "emergence" from self-imposed immaturity as possible.[29] Considering oneself fully enlightened would be a case of hubris.

The turn toward experience. This turn was about the gradual methodological restriction to explanations that eschew transcendence—that is, everything beyond the realm of experience. In the sciences, but also in philosophy, phenomena were interpreted less and less with recourse to concepts like "God," "divine providence," or "grace." However, references to God were still frequent, especially in natural philosophy. Despite this qualification, there was a profound change: In the German-speaking world, philosophy distinguished itself as "world wisdom" (*Weltweisheit*) from "theology" (*Gottesgelehrtheit*). In the European Enlightenment, "sensibility and experience were philosophically dignified."[30] Numerous examples support this claim. Many enlighteners were enthusiastic about the results of natural sciences, of experiments, and statistics.

There is the symptomatic and fascinating case of a fifteen-year-old girl and alleged child murderer that Christian Thomasius (1655–1728) took on as a lawyer in Leipzig in the early 1680s.[31] The accused claimed to have given birth to a dead child, but many pieces of evidence pointed against her. In this situation, the defense turned to scientific, empirically supported research. The medical faculty of the University of Wittenberg conducted an examination focusing on the lungs of animals related to various causes of deaths. The accused was acquitted due to lack of evidence (although she was sentenced to eight weeks in prison for fornication and concealing the pregnancy). The case can serve as an example of the shift toward experience and the "enlightenment of the intellect."

In most cases, this did not mean that these philosophers or scientists abandoned their personal (Christian) faith. However, there was now a much clearer distinction among scientific disciplines and concepts. In *The Reasonableness of Christianity, as delivered in the Scriptures* (1695), John Locke, for example, differentiated between revelation, reason, and experiential knowledge. Locke did not give up his Christian faith, but he subjected it to a critical examination, as independent from prejudice as possible. Here, the outlines of a systematic distinction

---

29 Kant, What is enlightenment, vol. 8, 35.
30 Martus, *Aufklärung*, 14. See his examples Martus, *Aufklärung*, 342–53 and more evidence in Kondylis, *Die Aufklärung*, 42–59 and 210–86, and Robertson, *The Enlightenment. The Pursuit of Happiness*, 42–84.
31 Martus, *Aufklärung*, 344. Thomasius founded his own philosophical school, sometimes subsumed under the term "the Thomasian Enlightenment." His main opponents in the Holy Roman Empire were Christian Wolff, his followers and so-called Wolffianism; see Koch, Schools and Movements, 61.

Figure 3: Joseph Wright of Derby, *An Experiment on a Bird in the Air Pump* (1767/68). The focal point of the painting is the reaction of the two girls who are being taught by their father and are horrified by the outcome of the experiment, as the bird dies in the vacuum. The experimenter has control over life and death. This, too, was enlightenment of the intellect and "Enlightenment through science."

between the philosophy of religion and theology are recognizable (see also Chapter 5). In most cases, the study of nature did not imply that nature stopped being seen as designed by God. A conflict between religion and science was alien to the eighteenth century. "For the Enlightenment, scientific knowledge was the enemy of superstition, but not of religion: only of the false beliefs that often flourished under the aegis of religion."[32] The turn toward experience also did not mean that reason became less important. It is important to avoid binary oppositions in this context. When it came to the question of the causes of phenomena, reason still played a crucial role. Many Enlightenment thinkers would perhaps have agreed with Christian Freiherr von Wolff (1679–1754) and Johann Christoph Gottsched (1700–1766) and his statement the sage "believes what he sees or

---

[32] Robertson, *The Enlightenment. The Pursuit of Happiness*, 83.

feels, not because he senses it but because it corresponds with reason." Thus, the motto was rather reason *and* experience.[33]

Enlightenment of the intellect (*Verstand*) and the Age of Reason (Thomas Paine). The Age of Reason is a misleading concept. It suggests a questionable opposition between reason and religion (see Chapter 5); it ignores the fact that many if not most Enlighteners also focused on emotions, sensibility and sympathy (see 2.2); and it supports the cliché that Enlighteners deified reason (Assumption 3). Perhaps it is fair to generalize that most Enlighteners spelled "reason" with a small "r" (as opposed to prior metaphysical rationalists), emphasizing personal reason and the mode of thinking (rather than what to think).[34] Philosophical tradition often distinguished between reason (*ratio*) and intellect or understanding (*intellectus*). These terms were defined differently, and the same holds true for the Enlightenment. For systematic reasons, I am following a distinction proposed by Kant. According to Kant, the intellect or understanding (*Verstand*) pertains to sensory impressions processed with the help of categories. Reason (*Vernunft*), on the other hand, is the faculty of ideas. An example of this enlightenment of the intellect (conception no. 3) would be that proposed by Christian Thomasius. He introduced a new understanding of graceful erudition, focusing on sagacity, worldly knowledge, and proximity to experience while distinguishing himself from the imitation and abstract erudition that emphasized Latin.[35] This understanding of academic enlightenment placed the intellect at its core.

The enlightenment of reason, by contrast, involved reflection on this enlightenment of the mind. It was an "enlightenment about the Enlightenment" on a meta-level. Concepts like self-reflection and autonomy of thought were central. Attempts were made to transcend the level of the intellect restricted to the realm of experience (see 2.3 and 5.3). Secondly, this version of the Enlightenment drew on ideas of reason, such as truth, human dignity, and human rights, tolerance, and the rule of law (see 4.3 and 4.4). It thus went beyond the scientific Enlightenment model of some encyclopedists.

With the enlightenment of the intellect and their hope for and commitment to reason, most enlighteners adhered to the standard of truth of the philosophical tradition. Criticizing dogmatism, narrow-mindedness, and prejudices drew from, and appealed to truth and the perpetual quest for it. In the words of Enlighten-

---

33 Martus, *Aufklärung*, 349.
34 Robertson, *The Enlightenment. The Pursuit of Happiness*, xvii–xviii.
35 Robertson, *The Enlightenment*, 98–9.

ment historian Werner Schneiders, the Enlightenment aimed to "get to the heart of the matter", in contrast to some postmodern or constructivist currents.[36]

The Age of Criticism. In 1696, at the end of one of his works, Christian Thomasius stated: "[A]ll my teachings go no further than to convince the learned and the students how everything is full of dung and filth in the prevailing scholarship and how this *should be cleared away.*"[37] These were sharp words and radical language. The academic establishment reacted with indignation to this provocation ("dung and filth"), a factor Thomasius had probably judged to be a clever marketing strategy. Be that as it may, familiar elements of the European Enlightenment are recognizable here: criticism of traditions, authorities, and the establishment; the claim to be able to persuade others in the sense of having the better arguments on one's side. In a famous passage from the *Encyclopédie*, Denis Diderot asserted that it was the task of the critical and independent philosopher to tread "underfoot prejudice, tradition, age, universal agreement, authority, in short everything that subjugates the mass of minds." He "dares to think for himself [...] and admit nothing except on the testimony of his experience and his reason."[38] In the *Critique of Pure Reason* (1781), Kant described the European Enlightenment in retrospect as "the genuine age of *criticism*, to which everything must submit."[39] This Enlightenment was radical when it went "back to its roots," fundamentally disregarding any form of authority, including religious, or state authority. It examined the foundations of our knowledge, our moral judgments, worldviews, theories, religions, and philosophical systems. According to Kant, the European Enlightenment differed from earlier forms of critical thinking in asking these fundamental questions. "Our age is the age of criticism, that is, a (sharp) judgment of the foundation of all claims [...], of which the ancients knew nothing and were so accustomed to uncertain opinions."[40] The radical chal-

---

36 Schneiders, *Hoffnung auf Vernunft*, 21. See also Schneiders, *Hoffnung auf Vernunft*, 172, 173, 176 and 185, and Susan Wilson, Postmodernism and the Enlightenmenn, in: Fitzpatrick et al., eds., *The Enlightenment World*, 648–59.
37 Christian Thomasius, Ausübung der Sittenlehre [1696], in: *Ausgewählte Werke*, ed. Werner Schneiders, 2nd reprint of the edition Halle, Hildesheim, Zürich, New York: Olms 1999, vol. 11, 527.
38 Denis Diderot, Eclecticism, in: *Encyclopédie*, ed. by Diderot and d'Alembert, vol. 5, (1755), 270, translated in: *The Encyclopedia of Diderot & d'Alembert. Collaborative Translation Project* (umich.edu), 10.3.2024.
39 Immanuel Kant, *Critique of Pure Reason*, Preface, A XI note (in: *Werke*, vols. 3 und 4). As is customary, the first *Critique* is cited according to the original pagination.
40 Immanuel Kant, reflection 5645, in: *Werke*, vol. 18, 287–8. See also Winfried Schröder, Radikalaufklärung in philosophiehistorischer Perspektive, in: Jonathan Israel and Martin Mulsow, eds., *Radikalaufklärung*, Berlin: Suhrkamp 2014, 187–202, at 187–8.

lenging of foundations reached its peak at the end of the European Enlightenment, roughly after the 1750s (see also 5.3).

The attempt to transcend thinking within the framework of a metaphysical system and to engage in systematic philosophizing. Many enlighteners had a skeptical attitude toward comprehensive metaphysical systems. In particular, the philosophical systems of the 17th and early 18th centuries, such as those of Descartes, Spinoza, or Leibniz, were often rejected. One of the reasons for this was the turn toward experience and sensibility previously noted. German philosopher Ernst Cassirer (1874–1945) considered this criticism of *Systemdenken* to be one of the central "modes of thought" of the Enlightenment era. Most enlighteners rejected the *esprit de système*, that is, the "spirit of systems" or thinking within the framework of a metaphysical system. In its place, they advocated the *esprit systématique*, namely systematic thinking. The focus was no longer on an elaborate metaphysical system based on axioms independent of experience, but on empirical phenomena, and provisional assumptions. They could in turn be challenged by further research or investigation. The distinction goes back to Jean Le Rond d'Alembert (1717–1783), one of the editors of the *Encyclopédie*. The *esprit systématique* gave rise to a new understanding of philosophy. "Philosophy, according to this interpretation, is no special field of knowledge situated beside or above the principles of natural science, of law, and government, etc., but rather the all-comprehensive medium in which such principles are formulated, developed, and founded."[41]

Most enlighteners did not hold a naive belief in reason. They were usually aware of the finitude and limitations of human reasoning. In contrast to 17th century rationalists, as a rule they did not investigate the essence or nature of things beyond empirical phenomena. For Voltaire, for instance, human fallibility was a fact. "Let not these errors become our misery!" he prayed to the God of all beings, all worlds and all ages [...].

> Grant that we may help each other to bear the burden of a short and painful life; that the slight differences in the clothes that cover our fragile bodies, the differences between our inadequate languages, variations in all our ridiculous customs, imperfect laws, and foolish opinions, differences between all the social conditions that are so important to us and so trivial to You; that all the little nuances that distinguish the atoms known as human beings may not become occasions for hatred and persecution![42]

---

[41] Ernst Cassirer, *The Philosophy of the Enlightenment* [1932], updated edition, Princeton: Princeton University Press 2009, xiii. See also Robertson, *The Enlightenment. The Pursuit of Happiness*, 26–31.

[42] Voltaire, *Treatise on Toleration* [1763–5], translated by Desmond M. Clarke, London: Penguin Books 2016, ch. 23.

In his *Philosophical Thoughts* (1746), Denis Diderot did not offer a straightforward attack on theism, Christianity, or Roman Catholicism. Instead, his underlying attitude was skeptical, even in terms of his own convictions. He found "difficulties" everywhere, and "remained wary of the emptiness of atheism."[43] However, against Cassirer, it must be emphasized that even in the European Enlightenment, there were recurring cases of the "spirit of systems" or the *esprit de système*. The identity of these enlighteners is a matter of debate and judgment. A possible candidate is the French mathematician and political economist Marie Jean Antoine Nicolas de Caritat, Marquis of Condorcet (1743–1794) and his *Sketch for a Historical Picture of the Progress of the Human Mind* (1793).[44]

"**A sea change in sensibility" (Ritchie Robertson).** There was a tendency among enlighteners to emphasize intellect, reason, and experience. Yet they "increasingly sought a more rounded conception of humanity, in which emotions, and sensibility could coexist harmoniously with reason."[45] They stressed sympathy, namely relating to others emotionally, and empathy, namely assuming another person's point of view. The cognitive capacity of empathy is the focus of a later section (see 2.2 and 3.2).[46] This new anthropology, psychology, and moral theory can be found in representatives of British moral sense theory, as seen in the works of the English politician and philosopher Anthony Ashley Cooper, the third Earl of Shaftesbury (1671–1713), the Irish philosopher Francis Hutcheson (1694–1746), David Hume, and the Scottish moral philosopher and pioneer of political economy Adam Smith (1723–1790). The new concepts of German literature, especially from around 1750 onwards, were *Empfindsamkeit* (sensibility) and an appeal to sensuality (aesthetics). A case in point are the works of the poet Christian Fürchtegott Gellert (1715–1769) or the epistolary novels of the late Enlightenment, among them Rousseau's *Julie ou la nouvelle Héloise* (1761). Another aspect of changing attitudes toward emotions and sensibility were sexual desire and sexual behavior. Some enlighteners saw sexual morality as a matter of private judgment,

---

43 Andrew S. Curran, *Diderot and the Art of Thinking Freely*, New York: Other Press 2019, 72–3 and Charles Devellennes, *Positive Atheism. Bayle, Meslier, d'Holbach, Diderot*, Edinburgh: Edinburgh University Press 2021, 156–8.
44 In his *Sketch*, Condorcet offers a triumphalist narrative of the Enlightenment. History is presented as a deadly fight between two forces, namely the evil powers of superstition, religions, despotism, and priesthood and the bright forces of Reason (spelled with a capital "R"), Enlightenment, science, and progress. The triumph of Enlightenment Reason is the ultimate meaning and end of history. Condorcet's *Sketch* is binary, Manichaean and simplistic. For an introduction see David Williams, *Condorcet and Modernity*, Cambridge: Cambridge University Press 2004.
45 Robertson, *The Enlightenment. The Pursuit of Happiness*, xviii and 261.
46 See Robertson, *The Enlightenment*, 324 on the distinction between sympathy and empathy, and Robertson, *The Enlightenment*, 261–305 for the following.

just like matters of religious belief. In the "Supplement to Bougainville's Voyage" (around 1772), Diderot openly attacked the Christian ideal of chastity as contrary to nature as well as reason. Works of pornography could also circulate more freely than before, among them Diderot's *Les bijoux indiscrets* (*The Indiscreet Jewels*, 1748). However, resulting sexual freedom in some quarters, especially upper-class society, usually benefited men rather than women, whose sexual freedom was still associated with indecency and depravity.[47]

The reinforced turn toward the human species and the individual. This shift is evident in various domains. The Swedish botanist and zoologist Carl von Linné (1707–1778) and the French Georges-Louis Leclerc, Comte de Buffon (1707–1788) initiated the advent of scientific natural history. For Linné, humans were no longer considered outside the animal kingdom but, like other natural beings, became subjects of scientific exploration. Buffon conceptualized humans as part of a dynamic natural history in his 36-volume work *Histoire naturelle Générale et particulière* (1749–1788).[48] The earliest reconstructions of human history distanced themselves from the Genesis narrative and the biblical creation story. An example is the *Philosophical Speculations on the History of Mankind* (1764) by the Swiss writer Isaak Iselin (1728–1782). The reinforced turn toward humanity is also evident in anthropology. The German physician Ernst Platner (1744–1818) replaced theological-philosophical anthropology, which primarily focused on the relationship between body and soul, with a more empirically oriented anthropology. This trend aligned with the increased emphasis on experience. Modern scientific anthropology was founded, largely sidelining classical metaphysical questions for methodological reasons and turning to physiological, historical, and cognitive aspects of the human species.[49]

The "discovery of the human" (Annette Meyer) manifested itself in various areas, such as a flood of travel reports. One example is the young ethnologist and naturalist Georg Forster, who became famous with his work *A Voyage Round*

---

[47] Robertson, *The Enlightenment*, 303–4 and Faramerz Dabhoiwala, *The Origins of Sex: A History of the First Sexual Revolution*, Oxford: Oxford University Press 2012, p. 85–7 and 232–3.

[48] Meyer, *Die Epoche der Aufklärung*, 45 and Peter Hanns Reill, *Vitalizing Nature in the Enlightenment*, Berkeley, Los Angeles, London: University of California Press 2005.

[49] Meyer, *Die Epoche der Aufklärung*, 47, Manfred Beetz, Jörn Garber and Heinz Thoma, eds., *Physis und Norm. Neue Perspektiven der Anthropologie im 18. Jahrhundert*, Göttingen: Wallstein 2007, Larry Wolff and Marco Cipolloni, eds., *The Anthropology of the Enlightenment*, Stanford: Stanford University Press 2007, Robertson, *The Enlightenment. The Pursuit of Happiness*, 42–84 and Christa Knellwolf, The Science of Man, in: Martin Fitzpatrick et al., eds., *The Enlightenment World*, London: Routledge 2004, 194–206.

the World (1777).⁵⁰ Symptoms of a changed conception of the human species included popular insurance policies and the emphasis on individual responsibility, particularly in areas related to illness and poverty. Numerous novels, biographies and autobiographies documented the new interest in the individual, in specific living conditions, self-observation, one's own emotional life, and the cultivation of personal, especially moral qualities such as empathy and sympathy.⁵¹ This "reassessment" of humans enabled, at least in part, a fresh perspective on inequality, on women, Jews, Africans, Asians, cruelty to animals, and slavery (see also 3.2 and 4.3).

The "pursuit of happiness" and the idea of perfection. The quote is taken from the US-American Declaration of Independence (1776) and describes one of the three natural and unalienable rights endowed by God to humans, the other two being life and liberty. "Happiness" (*bonheur, Glückseligkeit*) was a central term of the Enlightenment. Enlighteners could build upon a rich tradition going back to Greek and Roman philosophies, where *eudaimonía* was the goal or *telos* of almost all ethical theories. This *eudaimonía* was understood in comprehensive terms, encompassing not only pleasure, but above all a good and fulfilling life.⁵² Enlighteners also endorsed a broad understanding. They emphasized public happiness, a fine balance between cognitive, emotional and moral capacities, and usually "a glimpse of the eternal happiness of heaven."⁵³ For them, "it meant attaining the preconditions for personal happiness, including domestic affection, material sufficiency, and a suitable degree of freedom."⁵⁴ Some were skeptical, but others believed that this happiness could be achieved in the here and now. Another central Enlightenment concept was the idea of the perfection or *perfectibilité* of individuals as well as societies. A related concept was that of the vocation (*Bestimmung*), developed, among others, by writers like Johann Joachim Spalding, Mendelssohn, and Kant. Sometimes the concepts of perfection and vocation were combined with nascent cosmopolitan theories (see 4.4).⁵⁵

---

50 Meyer, *Die Epoche der Aufklärung*, 49; see also Meyer, *Die Epoche der Aufklärung*, 47–8 and Chunjie Zhang, Georg Forster in Tahiti: Enlightenment, Sentiment and the Intrusion of the South Seas, in: *Journal for Eighteenth-Century Studies*, 36 (2013), 263–277.
51 Meyer, *Die Epoche der Aufklärung*, 105, 130–3 and Robertson, *The Enlightenment. The Pursuit of Happiness*, 323–50.
52 Michaela Masek, *Antike Glücksethik*, Wien: Facultas 2023.
53 Caroline Winterer, *American Enlightenments: Pursuing Happiness in the Age of Reason*, New Haven: Yale University Press 2016, 3.
54 Robertson, *The Enlightenment. The Pursuit of Happiness*, 3.
55 See Tricoire, *Die Aufklärung*, 124 and 129–46 and Georg Cavallar, *Theories of Dynamic Cosmopolitanism in Modern European History*. Oxford: Peter Lang, 2017, 1–30 and same, Dynamic cosmopolis: The 'Westphalian World Order' and Beyond, in: Howard Williams et al., eds., *The*

The turn toward history. Experts still disagree whether enlighteners, and specifically the "philosophical historians" such as Montesquieu, Voltaire, Vico, Rousseau, Adam Ferguson (1723–1816), Hume, Herder, and Edward Gibbon (1737–1794) laid the foundations for modern historical science or were ultimately "unhistorical" and superficial dilettantes. What is unmistakable, however, is a strong orientation of the historical works of that time toward philosophy.[56] Using the example of the American Revolution, I will later argue that the European Enlightenment established a new temporal semantics (see 4.3). Its origins can be traced back to the 16th century when the awareness of living in a new epoch emerged. It would be an oversimplification to claim that during the 18th century, "the Enlightenment thinkers introduced a completely new, philosophically grounded view of history in opposition to a millennia-old, theologically understood concept of history."[57] The transformation process was much more complex and had a stronger theological influence than is commonly assumed. In general, however, the European Enlightenment tended to implement a more precise methodological separation between various academic disciplines—in this case, between theology, and history. Gradually, sacred history, as in the works of the French theologian and bishop Jacques-Bénigne Bossuet (1627–1704), was replaced by secular history. Göttingen and Edinburgh developed into centers of historical research. The modern concept of history as a singular collective noun emerged at the end of the 18th century, and earlier authors had already distinguished be-

---

Palgrave Handbook of International Political Theory, Volume I (Basingstoke: Palgrave Macmillan 2023), 167–84.

56 For introductions see Johnson Kent Wright, Historical Writing in the Enlightenment World, in: Fitzpatrick et al., eds., *The Enlightenment World*, 207–216, Robertson, *The Enlightenment. The Pursuit of Happiness*, 555–99, Karen O'Brien, *Narratives of Enlightenment. Cosmopolitan History from Voltaire to Gibbon*, Cambridge: Cambridge University Press 2009, and Andreas Urs Sommer, *Sinnstiftung durch Geschichte? Zur Entstehung spekulativ-universalistischer Geschichtsphilosophie zwischen Bayle und Kant*, Basel: Schwabe 2006. The seminal study on Edward Gibbon is John Greville Agard Pocock, *Barbarism and Religion*, 6 vols., Cambridge: Cambridge University Press (1999–2015).

57 Vincenzo Ferrone, *Die Aufklärung – Philosophischer Anspruch und kulturgeschichtliche Wirkung*, Göttingen: Vandenhoeck und Ruprecht 2013, 24. See also same, *The Enlightenment. History of an idea*, translated by Elisabetta Tarantino, Princeton and Oxford: Princeton University Press 2015, 5. See for the following Reinhart Koselleck, Erfahrungsraum und Erwartungshorizont. Zwei historische Kategorien, in: *Vergangene Zukunft. Zur Semantik geschichtlicher Zeiten*, 8. Aufl., Frankfurt am Main: Suhrkamp 2013, 349–75, same, Neuzeit. Zur Semantik moderner Bewegungsbegriffe, in: Koselleck, *Vergangene Zukunft*, 300–48, same, Die Verzeitlichung der Utopie, in: *Zeitschichten. Studien zur Historik*, Frankfurt am Main: Suhrkamp 2000, 131–49, Andreas Urs Sommer, *Sinnstiftung durch Geschichte? Zur Entstehung spekulativ-universalistischer Geschichtsphilosophie zwischen Bayle und Kant*, Basel: Schwabe 2006, Edelstein, *The Enlightenment*.

tween multiple histories, the theology of history included in the Bible, the philosophy of history, and historical research. Like the representatives of Enlightenment philosophy of history or the US revolutionaries, some Enlightenment theologians also repositioned the temporal dimensions of past, present, and future in relation to each other. They abandoned the traditional focus on the past and placed an open future at the center (see 5.2).

These are some key characteristics of the European Enlightenment, including a focus on individual reason, self-thinking, and the process of Enlightenment through dialogue and discussion. However, it is important to remember that the Enlightenment was not a monolithic movement, and there were variations in thought and emphasis among its proponents. The Enlightenment was a complex and multifaceted movement that evolved over time and in different cultural and national contexts.

Chapter 2
The limits of reason: Experience, intellect, reason

2.1 How rational was the Enlightenment?

According to a popular cliché, the enlighteners believed in the superiority of reason, and their emotions were "sicklied o'er with the pale cast of thought" (see Introduction). This description arose quite early, and was turned into an accusation, notably by the Romantic movement. Nowadays, the claim is often repeated. It is asserted, for example, that the Enlightenment declared "freedom from sensual desires in favor of pure freedom of reason [...] as the goal of world history."[1]

It is, indeed, not difficult to find examples where Enlightenment thinkers clearly exhibited a naive faith in reason. Prussian statesman and educational reformer Wilhelm von Humboldt (1767–1835), for instance, traveled to Paris in the summer of 1789 as a kind of "revolutionary tourist." He wrote with enthusiasm in his diary about ordinary people speaking of equality and freedom. "So the revolution has already elevated and enlightened people; what is it going do in the future?"[2] In September 1791, the French playwright and early feminist Olympe de Gouges (1748–1793) used these emphatic words: "The tocsin of reason sounds throughout the universe: Recognize your rights. The powerful empire of nature is no longer surrounded by prejudice, fanaticism, superstition, and lies. The torch of truth has dispersed all the clouds of folly and usurpation."[3] In defense of Humboldt, it should be noted that he was only 22 years old at the time. He also witnessed the violence, misery, and coercion imposed on citizens. Soon, he engaged in critical and systematic reflections and distanced himself from the radicalization of the Revolution. Olympe de Gouges condemned the execution of the king and correctly predicted the dangers posed by the radical Jacobins and Maximilien Robespierre. She paid for her public criticism with her life in November 1793, when she was guillotined. Overall, it is problematic to generally assert a naive belief in reason among enlighteners based on selected examples.

---

1 Stefan Greif, Georg Forster, 132.
2 Wilhelm von Humboldt, *Gesammelte Schriften*, ed. Albert Leitzmann et al., Preussische Akademie der Wissenschaften, Berlin: Behr 1922, vol. 14, 124.
3 Olympe de Gouges, The Rights of Woman, in : John R. Cole, *Between the Queen and the Cabby. Olympe de Gouges's Rights of Woman*, Montreal, Kingston, London and Ithaca: McGill-Queen's University Press 2011, 30–40, at 34. See also Paul Noack, *Olympe de Gouges, 1748–1793. Kurtisane und Kämpferin für die Rechte der Frau*, München: Deutscher Taschenbuch-Verlag 1992 and Carol L. Sherman, *Reading Olympe de Gouges*, New York: Palgrave Macmillan 2013.

The typical criticism of any position that relies on reason is this: even those who rely on reason presuppose a belief, namely belief in the competence of reason. I suspect that plenty of enlighteners were aware of this problem. Hence their constant search for the sources of knowledge and the limits of our understanding. Self-reflective philosophizing involves critically examining the authority one relies upon. The examination of our own capacity for reasoning and knowledge came to the forefront during the Enlightenment, with the works of John Locke at the latest. What can I know? Is knowledge based on reason, experience, intuition, or all three? How do we properly use our intellect or reason? Where are the boundaries of our knowledge? A first argument against the accusation that the Enlightenment endorsed a naive belief in reason is therefore a very simple one. Each act of reflection relies on what is commonly referred to as understanding or reason in the very process of reflection. For example, if I argue that my feelings are superior to reason "because reason can err, but feelings never do," I am once again invoking an aspect of reason. I appeal to the rational insights of my fellow human beings and assume they can follow my argument. In other words, I presuppose the very authority of the rationality I have called into question. I can only argue with the help of reason that there is no reason, that it should be ignored, or that it is unreliable. If I am not aware of this, I commit a "performative self-contradiction."[4]

The characterization of the Enlightenment as "believing in reason" is therefore overly simplistic and misleading. Epochs before or after the Enlightenment have also implicitly or explicitly relied on reason. This applies, for example, to theological positions: Although they usually presuppose faith in revelation or a sacred text, the elaboration of the theological system itself usually claims to be rationally comprehensible. The Islamic theologian and reformer Muhammad Abduh (1849–1905) even went so far as to claim that Islam had "freed hearts from the slavish adherence to the ways of the forefathers. [...] It released reason from its shackles, liberated it from blind imitation that had enslaved it, and placed it back where it rightfully belongs, making wise decisions—in humility toward God alone."[5] Islam, according to Abduh, is rational, or rationally comprehensible; reason itself is only required to show humility toward Allah. Once again, there is a reliance on reason. Its authority is not challenged in the name of faith. It is assert-

---

4 According to Habermas, a performative self contradiction occurs "when a constative speech act $k(p)$ rests on noncontingent presuppositions whose propositional content contradicts the asserted proposition p"; see Jürgen Habermas, *Moral Consciousness and Communicative Action* [1983], introduction by Thomas McCarthy, Cambridge: Polity Press 1992, 80. See also Lasse Thomassen, Performative Self-Contradiction, in: Amy Allen and Eduardo Mendieta, eds., *The Cambridge Habermas Lexicon*, Cambridge: Cambridge University Press 2019, 291.
5 Quoted in Alexander Flores, *Islam. Zivilisation oder Barbarei?* Berlin: Suhrkamp 2015, 123.

ed that this brand of Islamic theology is rationally comprehensible. Anyone who wishes to argue against this theology must also rely on reason.

I therefore propose that, when considering the European Enlightenment, we assume or posit gradual differences (this statement, dear reader, appeals to your intellect and reason). Compared to earlier epochs in European cultural history, there was a stronger emphasis on intellect and reason, and a greater willingness to subject all aspects of life to rational, reasonable, and critical examination. In the words of historian Steffen Martus, the enlighteners "expanded the competent jurisdiction of reason without forgetting the bodies of sensory beings with failings."[6] Werner Schneiders claimed: "Reason (*ratio*) and understanding (*intellectus*) have always been key concepts in the self-reflection of human thought. In the Age of Enlightenment, they acquired a new, all-dominating significance, and they even served to characterize and self-characterize the era."[7] Schneiders also qualified this description. German Enlightenment was characterized more by a "hope for reason" than by a clear supremacy of the rational. Some Enlightenment historians like Ritchie Robertson or Daniel Fulda even suggest that the emphasis on emotions and on sensibility should be seen as a characteristic of the European Enlightenment (see 1.2, "A sea change in sensibility"). It is important to distinguish between two types of emotions: Passions and affects, and proper emotions. Most enlighteners were skeptical of the former and advocated sensible, moderate control. One's own emotions and their exploration largely belonged to the process of self-discovery and emancipation, especially among members of the urban middle class or the *bourgeoisie* who differentiated themselves from the nobility in this way. "All of this suggests that the Enlightenment should be seen less for its belief in reason and more for its ever-expanding emphasis on emotions, setting it apart from tradition."[8]

However, the matter is not yet settled. Even among enlighteners, there was by no means a consensus on what exactly was meant by understanding (*Verstand*) and reason (*Vernunft*), and some did not even differentiate between the two. Dur-

---

6 Martus, *Aufklärung*, 686.
7 Werner Schneiders, ed., *Lexikon der Aufklärung. Deutschland und Europa*, München: Beck 1995, 429.
8 Daniel Fulda, Die Aufklärung als Epoche einer fundamentalen Emotionalisierung – reflektiert durch Schillers romantische Tragödie, Die Jungfrau von Orleans, in: same, Sandra Kerschbaumer and Stefan Matuschek, eds., *Aufklärung und Romantik. Epochenschnittstellen*, Paderborn: Fink 2015, 101–117, at 107. See also the other contributions in this volume. Katja Battenfeld et al., eds., *Gefühllose Aufklärung. Anaisthesis oder die Unempfindlichkeit im Zeitalter der Aufklärung*, Bielefeld: Aisthesis-Verlag 2012 examines the complex interplay between insensitivity or lack of feeling on the one hand and emotion and sensitivity (*Empfindsamkeit*) on the other hand in the culture of the German Enlightenment.

ing the Enlightenment, the interest in the "Other" or opposite of reason did not wane. There are at least three factors supporting this claim. The first relates to the role of emotions, sympathy and sensitivity (see section 2.2). This phenomenon aligns with the general turn toward the individual, which, in the prevalent view, naturally encompasses both reason, and emotions, often in a state of tension. For example, the goal of Christian Fürchtegott Gellert's ethics was the connection of reason and emotion, understanding, and heart. "Morality, or the knowledge of human duty, should shape our *understanding* into *wisdom* and our *heart* into *virtue*, and through *both* lead us to happiness." Gellert wanted to present his audience with "moral teaching primarily from the perspective [...] where it touches, forms, and improves the heart."[9] This approach sought to reconcile the head and the heart and bring them into balance. Passions and enthusiasm were not supposed to rule over human beings unchecked, although feelings like tenderness, and even carefully measured emotional exuberance were entirely acceptable. This tension between reason and emotion was a theme and motif in numerous novels of the 18th century, from Samuel Richardson to Rousseau, Mary Wollstonecraft, Jane Austen, and Olympe de Gouges.

The second symptom is the interest of many intellectuals in "higher reason," "higher world wisdom," "higher knowledge," "higher enlightenment," rational metempsychosis, belief in spirits, ancient mysteries, hermetic natural mysticism, and esotericism in general. These movements are not always reactions to, but often part of, the Enlightenment, or intersect with it. Mozart's opera *The Magic Flute* (1791) may serve as an example. German historian Monika Neugebauer-Wölk has shown that it is really challenging to draw clear boundaries, "distinguish relevant thought patterns, and define precise camps" because very often an "overlap of opposites" can be observed.[10]

The third symptom is the repeated criticism by some enlighteners of one-dimensional or simplistic conceptions of intellect or reason. The naturalist and ethnologist Georg Forster is a case in point. As a 17-year-old, he participated in the second circumnavigation of the world led by Captain James Cook, alongside his

---

9 Christian Fürchtegott Gellert, Moralische Vorlesungen. Moralische Charaktere, in: *Gesammelte Schriften*, ed. Bernd Witte, Berlin and New York: de Gruyter, 1988–2008, vol. 6, 13 and 7. See also Martus, *Aufklärung*, 554–79 and Sikander Singh, Christian Fürchtegott Gellert und die Empfindsamkeit, in: Hofmann, ed., *Aufklärung*, 27–43.
10 Monika Neugebauer-Wölk, Esoterik im 18. Jahrhundert – Aufklärung und Esoterik. Eine Einleitung, in: same and Holger Zaunstöck, eds., *Aufklärung und Esoterik*, Hamburg: Felix Meiner 1999, 1–37, at 34. See also Monika Neugebauer-Wölk, Renko Geffarth and Markus Meumann, *Aufklärung und Esoterik: Wege in die Moderne*, Berlin, Boston: de Gruyter; 2013, Schneiders, *Hoffnung auf Vernunft*, 165–70.

Figures 4.1 and 4.2: Daniel Nikolaus Chodowiecki (1726–1801), Series of Natural, and Affected Actions of Life, etching depicting "Sensation" (1779). On the left, a couple admirably observes the beauty of a sunrise with moderation. On the right, "sentimentalism" and the uncontrolled emotional excess of the *Sturm-und-Drang* movement are satirized. The couple on the right appears artificial and ridiculous.

father. Forster sharply criticized the European "tyranny of reason." According to Forster, universalistic ways of thinking tend to distort, categorize and idealize. This in turn hampers any attempt to properly understand real African Bedouins, for instance. He believed that universalist thinking would impose an "ideal" on established cultures and, for example, stereotypically declare "a conflicting ideal of equality and unboundedness as the fundamental constitution of a people."[11] A related criticism of a universalist conception of rationality can be

---

11 Greif, Georg Forster, 125 and 126; Georg Forster, Vorrede zur Geschichte des Schiffbruchs des Herrn von Brisson [1790], in: *Werke*, ed. Akademie der Wissenschaften der DDR, Berlin: Akademie Verlag 1985, vol. 5, 373–4, at 373.

found in the works of the Italian historian, philosopher, and jurist Giambattista Vico or in Herder's philosophy.

The label "rationalist" for Enlightenment philosophy is therefore an oversimplification. A more accurate description would focus on two aspects: firstly, the "Enlightenment of the intellect" as the struggle against ignorance, lack of understanding, superstition, and prejudices, and the clarification of concepts (see 1.1, third conception). Secondly, it would stress that emancipation took place in multiple areas, not just in the realm of rationality (intellect/understanding and reason). Enlightenment can then be described as the "striving for emancipation from the structures of inherited authority, not only as the emancipation of reason but also of sensibility, imagination, and feeling, with each forming changing combinations, coalitions, and oppositions."[12]

Are all humans endowed with reason? For some time, it was widely accepted that the enlighteners not only glorified reason but also attributed this capacity to all humans. Since the late 18th century, arguments were made from a historical perspective about how non-European cultures had developed different forms of rationality—or were simply incapable of European-style rational thinking and science. Often, this led to the formulation of racist theories with a strong Eurocentric bias. The claim that enlighteners attributed reason, or at least the potential and capacity for rational activity, to every individual must also be challenged. In recent decades, feminist authors have pointed out that male enlighteners frequently denied women any capacity for reason. Rousseau is a pertinent and famous example. Regarding the relationship between the sexes, he writes: "One ought to be active and strong, the other passive, and weak. One [side] must necessarily want and be able, it suffices that the other put up little resistance."[13] While Rousseau acknowledges that nature intended women to "think, to judge, to love, to know to cultivate their minds as well as their looks,"[14] he still opposes women who "arrogate to themselves the rights of men" (or rather, their privileges). According to Rousseau, women should follow their "inner sentiment" and show "obedience and fidelity" to their husbands. If modern society were not so corrupt, it would suffice "to a woman's being limited to the labors of her sex alone and left in com-

---

12 Ulrich Gaier, Gegenaufklärung im Namen des Logos. Hamann und Herder, in: Jochen Schmidt, ed., *Aufklärung und Gegenaufklärung in der europäischen Literatur, Philosophie und Politik von der Antike bis zur Gegenwart*, Darmstadt: Wissenschaftliche Buchgesellschaft 1989, 261–76, at 265.
13 Jean-Jacques Rousseau, *Emile or On Education* [1762], ed. Allan Bloom, New York, Basic Books 1979, 358. See also Rousseau, *Emile*, 357–93 and Barbara Schneider, *Jean-Jacques Rousseaus Konzeption der Sophie. Ein hermeneutisches Projekt*, Bonn, Universitätsdruckerei 2005.
14 Rousseau, *Emile*, 364.

plete ignorance of all the rest."[15] Rousseau was not alone in this view. Perhaps it can be asserted that several enlighteners were willing to challenge gender stereotypes. However, philosophical programs and practices often diverged. In addition, there were often ambiguities, inconsistencies, and contradictions. For instance, it was asserted that as human beings, women were entitled to have rights. Yet this universalist claim was often undermined by seeing them as basically irrational.[16] Intellectuals like Rousseau were influenced by civic republicanism or civic humanism, a brand of republicanism that emphasized civic virtue, male dedication to the common good and the republic, and the exclusion of women from politics. Some feared that virtue might decline in a commercial society if women got too influential in politics and the public sphere. The majority believed that there was a natural order and hierarchy which also applied to the relationship between the sexes. Eighteenth-century European societies were still estate-based societies. There were no broad debates challenging patriarchy or the dominance of the male sex.[17]

Yet some female as well as male enlighteners asked critical questions about concepts of gender, women's education, female rationality, and moral agency, women's roles in society, and societal discrimination. Objections to Rousseau and anthropological approaches that emphasized women's alleged deficiencies came from female writers, including Judith Sargent Murray (1751–1820) and Amalia Holst (1758–1829). In the process, some women became active participants in Enlightenment discourses.[18] Others contributed to the various fields of science, like the astronomer Nicole-Reine Lepaute (1723–1788) or the botanist and painter Madeleine Françoise Basseporte (1701–1780). It has been argued that by the end of the century, French women who turned to writing saw themselves as creative,

---

15 Rousseau, *Emile*, 382.
16 See Martus, *Aufklärung*, 399, Christa Kersting, Ambivalenzen der Aufklärung am Beispiel weiblicher Bildung, in: Faber and Wehinger, eds., *Aufklärung in Geschichte und Gegenwart*, 101–21, Outram, *The Enlightenment*, 84–98, Israel, *Enlightenment that Failed*, 318–45, and Claudia Opitz, *Aufklärung der Geschlechter, Revolution der Geschlechterordnung. Studien zur Politik- und Kulturgeschichte des 18. Jahrhunderts*, Münster et al.: Waxmann 2002.
17 See Tricoire, *Die Aufklärung*, 205–29.
18 Mary Seidman Trouille, *Sexual Politics in the Enlightenment: Women Writers Read Rousseau*, Albany, NY: State University of New York Press 1997. See also Karen O'Brien, *Women and Enlightenment in Eighteenth-Century Britain*, Cambridge: Cambridge University Press 2009, Joanna Wharton, *Material Enlightenment. Women Writers and the Science of Mind, 1770–1830*, Woodbridge: Boydell Press 2018, and Frick, *Mutig denken*, 38–48.

self-determining individuals.[19] Early British feminist philosopher Mary Wollstonecraft (1759–1797) attacked Rousseau's position in her work *A Vindication of the Rights of Woman* (1792): "[t]he nature of reason must be the same in all, if it be an emanation of divinity, the tie that connects the creature with the Creator; [and] the inquiry is whether she have reason or not. If she has, which, for a moment, I will take for granted, she was not created merely to be the solace of man, and the sexual should not destroy the human character."[20] Wollstonecraft forcefully argued for a universal standard of morality not based on gender differences. Olympe de Gouges advocated women's rights as well as the rights of African slaves. Catharine Macaulay (1731–1791) became a celebrated historian; she was in fact the first female English historian. German writer Marie Sophie von La Roche (1730–1807) published the first German-language women's magazine called *Pomona: Für Teutschlands Töchter*. Another German intellectual, Luise Adelgunde Victorie Gottsched Kulmus (1713–1762), married to Johann Christoph Gottsched, was likely one of the most educated women of the time and, according to Steffen Martus, "did more for the deepening and dissemination of the Enlightenment than many men."[21] Typical Enlightenment arguments can be found. Writers questioned the justifications for discriminating against and disadvantaging women, especially in view of their lack of educational opportunities. Some male intellectuals occasionally also protested discrimination, such as Theodor Gottlieb von Hippel the Elder (see 3.2). Supporters of women's equality were a motley bunch in terms of their philosophies, religious affiliations, and social backgrounds.[22]

---

19 See Nina Rattner Gelbart, *Minerva's French Sisters. Women of Science in Enlightenment France*, New Haven and London: Yale University Press 2021 and Carla Hesse, *The Other Enlightenment. How French Women Became Modern*, Princeton and Oxford: Princeton University Press 2003.
20 Mary Wollstonecraft, *A Vindication of the Rights of Woman* (1792), in: *The Vindications*, ed. D. L. Macdonald and Kathleen Scherf, Orchard Park, NY.: Broadview Press 1997, 99–344, at 167.
21 Geier, *Aufklärung*, 307–332, Meyer, *Die Epoche der Aufklärung*, 188–90, Helga Meise, Sophie von La Roche und der Genderdiskurs, in: Hofmann, ed., *Aufklärung*, 61–74, Martus, *Aufklärung*, 395–9, with the quotation ibdi., 395. See also Robertson, *The Enlightenment. The Pursuit of Happiness*, 572–82 on Catharine Macaulay.
22 Jennifer J. Davis, The Radical Enlightenment and Movements for Women's Equality, in: Ducheyne, *Reassessing the Radical Enlightenment*, 292–308. The history of women's movements is one of diversity and unlikely alliances, in which the Radical Enlightenment played a significant but not always a positive role (Ducheyne, *Reassessing the Radical Enlightenment*, 294).

Figure 5: Mary Wollstonecraft (1759–1797) was an early advocate of women's rights, and an early feminist philosopher. Her major work is *A Vindication of the Rights of Woman* (1792). She died at the age of 38 after giving birth to Mary Shelley, her second daughter, who became famous as the author of the novel *Frankenstein; or, The Modern Prometheus* (1818).

2.2 Emotions and feelings against understanding and reason

I have already argued that sympathy and empathy played important roles (see 1.2). The representatives of British moral sense theory, among them Shaftesbury, Hutcheson, and Smith, formulated moral theories that emphasized cultivated and reflective feelings between individuals based on sympathy.[23] German studies specialist Michael Hofmann has proposed that German literature in the 18th century be described as a dynamic process of development. In the first phase, literature sought legitimacy by aligning itself with enlightened reason. Johann Christoph Gottsched, in the context of his theory of art, advocated a synergy between passion and reason. This turned out to be a tricky and intricate procedure: the artist needed personal experience of passion, yet detached reason was necessary to describe these experiences. The content of poetry, in essence, originated from the artist's imagination and passions, while the artwork itself was—in formal terms—a product of intellectual activity. Thus, it was essential that "the poet needed measure and law to avoid being consumed by passion."[24] Gradually, in a second phase resistance to the orientation toward reason, seen as one-sided, began to take shape. The new concepts, especially from around 1750, were *Empfindsamkeit* (sensibility) and an appeal to sensuality (aesthetics). *Empfindsam* was a translation of the English term "sentimental." The elevation of sensibility can be observed in the works of Christian Fürchtegott Gellert, among others.[25]

The most prominent representative of this second phase, however, was Jean-Jacques Rousseau. One day in October 1749, Rousseau visited his friend Denis Diderot who was imprisoned in Vincennes. The Academy of Dijon's essay competition stirred in him an "excitement bordering on madness." This visit sparked fundamental theses about society, culture, and civilization. Rousseau believed that modern sciences and the arts had not refined morals but, on the contrary, corrupted them. His agitation continued as he walked along the street: "A violent palpitation oppressed me; unable to walk for difficulty of breathing, I sank under one of the trees of the avenue, and passed half an hour there in such a condition of

---

[23] See Michael L. Frazer, *The Enlightenment of Sympathy. Justice and Moral Sentiments in the Eighteenth Century and Today*, Oxford: Oxford University Press 2010. Rationalistic elements can also be identified in these theories, such as principles of fairness and reciprocity, or the ability to see things from a different perspective.
[24] Marie- Hélène Quéval, Johann Christoph Gottsched – Maß und Gesetz, in: Hofmann, ed., *Aufklärung*, 11–25, at 20.
[25] Michael Hofmann, Einleitung, in: Hofmann, ed., *Aufklärung*, 7–10, at 8; Singh, Gellert, in: Hofmann, *Aufklärung*, 27–43.

excitement that when I arose, I saw that the front of my waistcoat was all wet with my tears, though I was wholly unconscious of shedding them."[26]

Rousseau's own account of this episode is probably highly fictionalized. Be that as it may, in the following years, Rousseau turned many of the prevailing beliefs of his era upside down, including some of the Enlightenment. Authentic feeling triumphed over refinement and artificiality of manners, sympathy over science, the intellect, and calculation, authenticity over pretense, an idealized countryside over the decadent and corrupt Paris, individuality over social conventions, even if they were considered "enlightened." Rousseau's epistolary novel *Julie, or the New Héloise* (1761) became a bestseller, with at least 70 editions being published by the end of the century. The love story between the young aristocratic lady Julie and her tutor Saint-Preux contains a simple moral message: there is a difference between sentiments and passions; an authentic morality of the heart or soul should triumph over social conventions, unless these coincide with the ethics of authenticity. Saint-Preux writes: "I am fully capable of distinguishing the empire the heart has been able to establish from the frenzy of an overheated imagination."[27] What really matters is one's soul, that "divine model" of virtue, "that timeless effigy of the truly beautiful, the sight of which inspires us with a holy enthusiasm, and which our passions constantly sully but can never destroy." Who are the persons who do not help in these matters? They are the "sad reasoners" and the "vain moralists"![28] In one scene, the tutor kneels in tears after parting from his noble lover Julie. As Ernst Cassirer has written, "as St. Preux covers the cold stone with his kisses, his tears flowing, one immediately senses the spirit of a new era. A new form of poetry emerges here: here, Goethe's Werther arises before us."[29] *The Sorrows of Young Werther* (1774), an epistolary novel by German polymath Johann Wolfgang von Goethe (1749–1832), strongly influenced the Romantic movement. Samuel Richardson (1689–1761) had prepared the ground with his epistolary novels, among them *Pamela; or Virtue Rewarded*

---

26 Jean-Jacques Rousseau, *The Confessions* [1782], translated by Edmund Wilson, New York: Knopf 1923, vol. 1, ix. Jeremy L. Caradonna, *The Enlightenment in Practice. Academic Prize Contests and Intellectual Culture in France, 1670–1794*, Ithaca and London: Cornell University Press 2012 covers the history of academic prize competitions in France. Rousseau was just one prominent winner among many others.
27 Jean-Jacques Rousseau, *Julie, or the New Heloise. Letters of two Lovers who live in a small Town at the foot of the Alps* [1761], translated an annotated by Philip Stewart und Jean Vaché, Hanover and London: University Press of New England 1997, 44. See also Rousseau, *Julie*, 10 and 183–4.
28 Rousseau, *Julie*, 184 and 183.
29 Ernst Cassirer, Das Problem Jean Jacques Rousseau, *Archiv für Geschichte der Philosophie*, 41, 3 (1933), 479–513, at 484. See also Robertson, *The Enlightenment. The Pursuit of Happiness*, 325–40.

(1740) and *Clarissa: Or the History of a Young Lady* (1748). These novels were also psychological studies; they explored the complex emotions and mentalities of their protagonists. Readers reacted with enthusiasm. Reading *Clarissa*, a lady declared that she had shed "a Pint of Tears", and an army general stated that he had finished *La Nouvelle Héloise* "no longer weeping, but shouting, howling like an animal."[30] Enlightenment historian Ritchie Robertson concludes that evidence such as personal letters "suggests a much higher emotional temperature in the later 1700s than earlier in the century."[31] Sympathetic emotions and sensibility eventually also extended to social ills like poverty, slavery, and the slave trade. Others attacked wanton cruelty toward animals.[32]

By the end of the 18th century, the emphasis on sensibility underwent critical examination once again. Adam Smith preferred a Stoic attitude and the "spirit of manhood" to "the desponding, plaintive, and whining tone of some modern systems."[33] It is striking how frequently the early feminists wrote against what seemed to be a widespread elevation of the personal emotional life—in line with the elevation of one's own individuality at the time. Mary Wollstonecraft argued that women who succumbed primarily to their own "sensibility," often due to cultural reasons, were "blown about by every momentary gust of feeling." Rational thinking would be difficult for them because they would become "the prey of their senses."[34] Wollstonecraft wrote in the 1790s and shared many Enlightenment concepts: she criticized aristocratic privileges and advocated a qualified equality between men and women, grounded in equality before God. Wollstonecraft did not pit reason or common sense against emotions; they were not meant to act independently of each other. The ideal lay in a balanced relationship where both faculties would mutually instruct and enrich each other.[35]

What is the significance of these reflections for the present day? While the outright condemnation of "reason", "Enlightenment" or "Western rationality" is prevalent in some circles, this is not very convincing. It can be argued that some enlighteners advocated a one-sided "hegemony" of reason. However, criti-

---

30 Quoted in Robertson, *The Enlightenment. The Pursuit of Happiness*, 335.
31 Robertson, *The Enlightenment*, 342.
32 Robertson, *The Enlightenment*, 342–50.
33 Adam Smith, *The Theory of Moral Sentiments* [1759], ed. Knud Haakonssen, Cambridge: Cambridge University Press 2002, VII.1.29., 334.
34 Wollstonecraft, *A Vindication of the Rights of Woman*, 177. See also David J. Denby, Sensibility, in: Kors, ed., *Encyclopedia*, vol. 4, 59–64.
35 Chris Jones, Mary Wollstonecraft's *Vindications* and their political tradition, in: *The Cambridge Companion to Mary Wollstonecraft*, ed. Claudia L. Johnson, Cambridge: Cambridge University Press 2002, 42–58, at 46.

 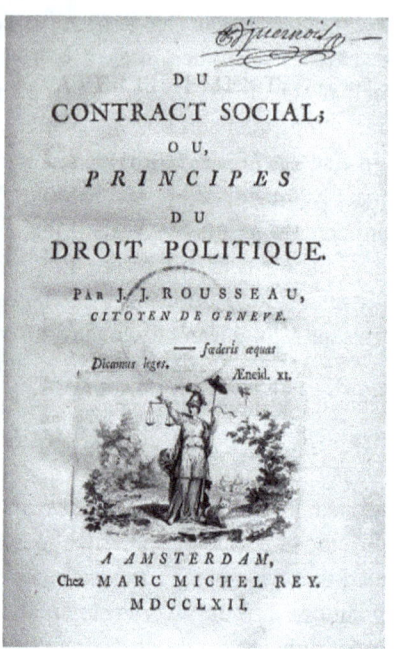

Figures 6.1 and 6.2: The Genevan Jean-Jacques Rousseau (1712–1778) was both an Enlightenment thinker and one of its sharpest critics. As an educator, philosopher, composer, and novelist, he influenced the theorists of the French Revolution and shaped Romanticism, modern reform pedagogy, and, with his work *The Social Contract* (1762), the political philosophy of the subsequent two centuries. As an early critic of commercial society, he also became a pioneer of modern social and cultural criticism.

cism of this form of Enlightenment always risks falling into irrationalism, performative self-contractions (see above) and dogmatic attitudes. It is also true that an endless reflection on the reflection of reflection can become tedious. On the other hand, we may want to join Werner Schneiders in asking: "What is the alternative? There is no need to argue about the dull feeling that our faculty of understanding (*Verstand*) is not everything. However, urgent reflection is needed if it were claimed that reason (*Vernunft*) must sacrifice itself in the name of something."[36] The key lies in a clear distinction between understanding and reason (see 1.2). Put simply, we should not throw out the baby with the bathwater. Extreme nationalism and National Socialism, especially in Central Europe, can serve as cautionary examples of the dangers of irrationalism and irrational ideologies. In this sense, Ger-

---

36 Schneiders, *Aufklärung*, 133. See also *Hoffnung auf Vernunft*, 172, 175 and 179–82.

man intellectual Carolin Emcke warns against a "naive upgrading of affects" in public discourses "as if emotions are inherently appropriate, as if emotions inherently possess unassailable legitimacy. [...] But every child learns that not all emotions are equally meaningful or opportune. This should be remembered when certain political positions are currently rhetorically trivialized with the help of emotions."[37] The questions asked should be: Are these emotions appropriate? Do they harm other people? These and other questions, however, require reason and judgment. Therefore, a qualified commitment to these two faculties is indispensable.

2.3 In search of the limits of reason

The Enlightenment began with a series of significant developments. In 1670, Baruch de Spinoza published his *Theological-Political Treatise*. In 1686, French philosopher Pierre Bayle (1647–1706) followed with the first two volumes of his *Philosophical Commentary*, advocating toleration in religious matters. Three years later came John Locke's *Letter on Toleration*. Bayle engaged in his work with the arguments of those who, since Augustine, had justified forced conversions, and the persecution of other religious communities. Bayle argued that the arguments of all sides could be traced back to a common "noble principle": "*I have the Truth on my side, therefore my Violences are good Works: Such a one is in Error, therefore his Violences are criminal.*"[38] Against this mindset of violence and intolerance, Bayle put forward a skeptical attitude and the corresponding thesis of the limits of human reason. Reason is finite and, due to inherent boundaries, cannot answer metaphysical questions about the "true religion" or a "higher truth." Because we are finite beings, we often fall into errors and may only in later life come to recognize "the falsehood of a thousand things" of which we were previously convinced. Sometimes, we decide to believe something based only on "probabilities" even though other rational individuals are not convinced by them.[39] Humans can only recognize truths "incompletely." This is particularly true for *a priori* proofs, derived solely from reason, where we quickly become entangled in absurdities and contradictions—these are the realms of metaphysics

---

[37] Bert Rebhandl, Carolin Emcke: Nicht kleinkriegen lassen vom Hass, *Der Standard*, October 22, 2016, Album A 4.
[38] Pierre Bayle, *A Philosophical Commentary on These Words of the Gospel, Luke 14.23, Compel Them to Come In, That My House May Be Full*, ed. John Kilcullen and Chandran Kukathas, Indianapolis: Liberty Fund 2005, part I, ch. 10, 134.
[39] Bayle, *A Philosophical Commentary*, I, 5, 93–4.

and religion. As a result, under human conditions, it is "inevitable that Men in different Ages and Countries should have very different Sentiments in Religion, and interpret some one way some another, whatever is capable of various Interpretations."[40] This actual pluralism is the outcome of our object ignorance in metaphysics and religious matters.

Acknowledging human lack of knowledge is a common theme of the European Enlightenment. Locke early on employs the traditional assumption of a candle to symbolize our understanding. The realm of what we can know is quite limited. Nevertheless, we can say "The candle that is set up in us shines bright enough for all our purposes. The discoveries we can make with this ought to satisfy us." Much, namely the entire domain of metaphysics, plunges us into impenetrable darkness. In a domain inaccessible to reason, it would be presumptuous to demand "certainty" where only probability can be obtained, "which is sufficient to govern all our concernments."[41]

For many enlighteners, including Locke, Hume, Voltaire, Condillac, and Diderot, it becomes a kind of commonplace: our knowledge ends where our sensory perception ends. All knowledge begins with and originates in sensory impressions. This empirical approach was also embraced by most authors of the French *Encyclopédie* (1751–1772). D'Alembert formulated this fundamental idea—much like Diderot—in this way: all knowledge ultimately relies on sensory perceptions; the intellect only processes and combines these impressions. "All our direct knowledge can be reduced to what we receive through our senses; whence it follows that we owe all our ideas to our sensations."[42] This amounted to a significant critique of rationalist currents and theologically inspired theories of cognition.[43] Classical rationalism, as exemplified by Descartes, Leibniz, Wolff, or Baumgarten, had asserted that human reason possessed innate ideas that did not derive from experience. Little wonder the editors of the *Encyclopédie* constantly had to strug-

---

40 Bayle, *A Philosophical Commentary*, II, 6, 207–8. John Christian Laursen, Pierre Bayle, in: Diego E. Machuca and Baron Reed, eds. *Skepticism. From Antiquity to the Present*, London et al.: Bloomsbury 2018, 355–68 characterizes Bayle as an original representative of skepticism, since he refused "to take any philosophical issue as settled" (Machuca and Reed, *Skepticism*, 366). See also Richard H. Popkin, Scepticism, in: Haakonssen, *The Cambridge History of Eighteenth-Century Philosophy*, 426–50 on the fate of skepticism in the 18th century and the numerous attempts to refute it.
41 Locke, *Essay Concerning Human Understanding*, vol. 1, Introduction, 4.
42 Jean Le Rond d'Alembert, Preliminary Discourse to the Encyclopedia, part I, 10, in: Denis Diderot, Jean Le Rond d'Alembert, eds., *Encyclopédie*, vol. 1 (1751), i–xIv, in: The Encyclopedia of Diderot & d'Alembert Collaborative Translation Project (umich.edu), 19.9.2023.
43 See Curran, *Diderot*, 110.

gle with censorship, saw whole articles truncated, their volumes declared illegal, and placed on the Index of the Catholic Church.

I have previously argued that the European Enlightenment brought about a much clearer methodological separation between different academic disciplines. In the natural sciences, but also in philosophy, phenomena were increasingly explained without recourse to concepts like "God," "predestination," or "grace." In the German-speaking world, philosophy thus distanced itself from theology by positioning itself as "world wisdom." In most cases, enlighteners retained their religious beliefs, albeit in a much more individual and personal form than before. There were significant differences between countries. In England, the German-speaking world, and North America, the mainstream of Enlightenment thinking was moderate, particularly in religious matters, but sometimes in political matters as well (see also Chapter 5).[44]

France followed a completely different trajectory. It was heavily influenced by French absolutism under Louis XIV and his principle of "one faith, one law, one king." In the centralized state, the monarchy, and the Catholic Church formed an alliance that led, for instance, to the persecution, and forced conversion of the Huguenots. Their right to practice their religion was eventually revoked in the *Edict of Fontainebleau* in 1685. For the writers and intellectuals who had referred to themselves as *les philosophes* since the early 18th century, emigration was initially the only option.[45] Pierre Bayle is a good example. From the mid-18th century onward, the French Enlighteners became more radical in political and religious issues and gained wider influence. The struggle against the "religious party" (*parti dévot*) intensified. The monumental work of the *Encyclopédie* (1751–1780), consisting of a total of 35 volumes, edited by Jean Le Rond d'Alembert and Denis Diderot, marked a turning point. Voltaire and others had brought the English-style empiricism to France. Although individual volumes were repeatedly censored, the *Encyclopedia* represented "the breakthrough of the Enlightenment in France." The philosophical endeavors of Diderot, Claude-Adrien Helvétius (1715–1771) or Baron d'Holbach (1723–1789) increasingly moved toward sensualism, materialism, determinism, deism, or atheism. To this day, Voltaire and some *philosophes* of the *Encyclopedia* have shaped the assumption of the French

---

[44] See Schneiders, *Aufklärung*, 21–51 (on England) and 83–115 (on the Holy Roman Empire), Volker Depkat, Angewandte Aufklärung? Die Weltwirkung der Aufklärung im kolonialen Britisch Nordamerika und den USA, in: Hardtwig, eds., *Die Aufklärung und ihre Weltwirkung*, 205–41 and Schneiders, *Hoffnung auf Vernunft*, 28–48 and 146–70.

[45] Sometimes, authors use the term *les philosophes* exclusively for the group of atheists and materialists in France, not generically for any public intellectual with a philosophical bent; see Koch, Schools and Movements, p. 59.

Enlightenment and sometimes even of the European Enlightenment as a whole—as materialistic, anti-clerical, anti-Christian, and atheist. As noted earlier, this development had much to do with the historical situation in France since the time of Louis XIV. The "rigid unity of the church and monarchy" provoked radical criticism that saw a break with "the established system of politics and morality as a whole" as the only option.[46] It has also been argued that France had a unique system of patronage, which facilitated the—often limited—publication of radical or heterodox ideas. Aristocrats, ministers, but also princes and princesses outside France helped writers like Voltaire, Diderot, Raynal or Rousseau. These authors would in turn advertise the policies and interest of their patrons. Censorship was also laxer than in Great Britain.[47] The "imported" empiricism from England meant that knowledge was traced back to sensory impressions. Therefore, there was little room for theology and faith in the *Encyclopédie*, also for systematic reasons. This was made clear in d'Alembert's *Preliminary Discourse*. Philosophy was no longer subservient to theology but stood above it. Similarly, scientific research triumphed over religious faith and the Bible.

From the very beginning, the French Enlighteners had opponents in the camp of the Catholic "religious party." However, a much more formidable adversary emerged from within their own ranks. That adversary was Jean-Jacques Rousseau. He turned the weapons of the Enlightenment against itself.[48] In terms of taking articles of Christian faith as his starting point, Rousseau's standpoint, or perspective was not positioned outside the French Enlightenment. His critique was immanent, as he pointed out contradictions within the Enlightenment conception of the *philosophes*. He rejected the "enlightenment through science" model of the *encyclopédistes*. His alternative approach argued for a more profound enlightenment that cultivated the faculty of judgment and reasoned argument. The emphasis was on the enlightenment of individuals, not on prefabricated knowledge (or alleged knowledge) contained in the erudite volumes of the Enlightenment literati, an in-

---

46 Schneiders, *Aufklärung*, 55–56. See also Schneiders, *Aufklärung*, 52–82 and Geier, *Projekt*, 93–165. The encyclopedia with the widest impact in the 18th century was probably the Zedler (and not the *Encyclopédie*): *Grosse vollständige Universal-Lexicon Aller Wissenschafften und Künste* of Leipzig publisher Johann Heinrich Zedler (1706–1751), which appeared between 1732 and 1754 in 65 volumes and 4 supplementary volumes. See Schneider, *Die Erfindung des allgemeinen Wissens. Enzyklopädisches Schreiben im Zeitalter der Aufklärung*, especially 73–128.
47 Tricoire, *Die Aufklärung*, 78–90. He argues that the power of the Catholic Church was not the crucial factor.
48 See especially Mark Hulliung, *The Autocritique of Enlightenment. Rousseau and the Philosophes*, Cambridge: Harvard University Press 1994 and Rainer Enskat, *Bedingungen der Aufklärung. Philosophische Untersuchungen zu einer Aufgabe der Urteilskraft*. Weilerswist: Velbrück Wissenschaft 2008.

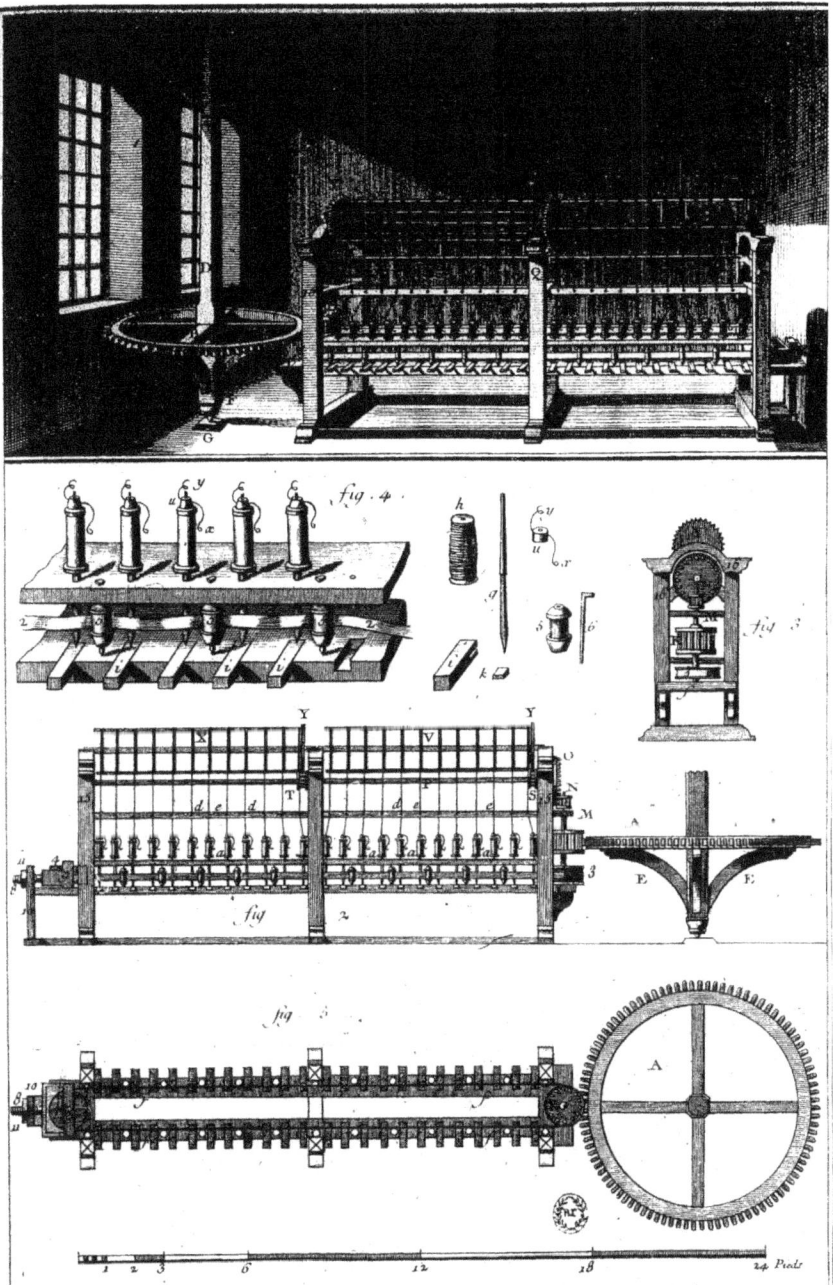

Figure 7: *The Encyclopédie ou Dictionnaire raisonné des sciences, des arts et des métiers* attempted to systematically summarize humanity's knowledge in over 70,000 articles. Numerous illustrations accompanied the written text.

tellectual elite. This also amounted to a skeptical attitude toward empiricism and scientific knowledge (see Chapter 1, fifth conception).

In his so-called *First Discourse*, Rousseau already noted a decline in judgment caused by the mere transmission of information from second or third hand within the scientific community of his time. This, he argued, had led to "obscurity" and "blindness" rather than independent thinking. According to Rousseau, true enlightenment was only possible "through the constant public cultivation of the cognitive virtues of practical judgment," which should reach as many people as possible, not just a "functional elite."[49] Rousseau placed the moral and political question of the *significance* of scientific information at the center of his investigations. In Rousseau's educational novel *Émile* (1762), education, and learning took a completely new direction. The focus was on learning to judge independently, using one's own reason, and acquiring a universal mindset or *esprit universel*, which Kant later referred to as the enlarged way of thinking.[50]

In contrast to Rousseau's approach, the French *philosophes*, in the words of the Savoyard Vicar, were "proud, assertive, dogmatic (even in their pretended skepticism), ignorant of nothing, proving nothing, mocking one another." Émile differed from them with his modest knowledge, the withholding of judgments, his "learned ignorance," and his "universal spirit."[51]

Rousseau's criticism offered rational arguments against the model of "enlightenment through science," and he also attacked the secular Enlightenment. His criticism was rational because empiricist, materialistic, sensualistic, and deterministic positions are not free of philosophical difficulties. Firstly, these difficulties revolve around the fact that they rely on metaphysical and/or rational assumptions that lack scientific verification. For example, the proposition "Only sentences that relate to sensory input are justified, rational and meaningful" is neither obvious nor any of these three—it is an assertion waiting for a justification. Yet this justification cannot be based on sensory input or experience in general. It must appeal to some conception of rationality, for instance. This appeal can, in turn, be challenged. Secondly, empiricist or sensualistic approaches are often accused of reductionism, as they simplify a complex reality into simplistic and supposedly self-evident theories, such as natural mechanics.[52] Thirdly, empiricist, materialis-

---

49 Enskat, *Bedingungen*, 644.
50 Rousseau, *Emile*, 203–7 and the excellent interpretation in Lutz Koch, *Lehren und Lernen. Wege zum Wissen*, Paderborn: Schöningh 2015, 269–74.
51 Rousseau, *Emil*, 268.
52 Hans Schelkshorn, Hobbes und die Folgen. Zur Genese und Transformation des naturalistischen Projekts der Moderne, in: Wilfried Grießler, ed., *Reduktionismen – und Antworten der*

tic, sensualistic, or deterministic positions also face challenges revolving around the tensions between descriptions and normative claims. For example, if materialism is true, what is the status of the criterion of truth itself, which is a non-material, cognitive concept? If humans are determined, is this assertion about human determinism itself determined? Is materialism true or merely another illusion, much like the belief in human free will? How can an empiricist distinguish between true statements and deceptions? How can the catastrophic moral consequences of materialism be avoided, which denies free will, and thus the distinction between good and evil, virtue, and vice? Does this not imply that anything is permissible, including genocide, the extermination of heretics, or any form of oppression and deceit? Materialism runs into contradictions and aporias when it attempts to distance itself from ethical nihilism on one hand, but polemically engages with the moral discourse of theologians on the other.

The result, as ironically noted by Panajotis Kondylis, was a dilution of materialism toward a normative concept of nature or a logical contradiction, or sometimes both in the works of Helvétius, d'Holbach, and Diderot. Consequently, adherents of materialistic, sensualistic, and deterministic positions need to ask themselves whether they tend—like d'Holbach—to idealize "Nature" as a moral or metaphysical entity, almost deifying it. In this view, nature becomes a force that "punishes all crimes committed on Earth" and is seen as the embodiment of "eternal justice," knowing how to punish "without distinction of persons", inflicting punishment "commensurate with the crime".[53] Holbach transfers the attributes of the Christian God to Nature (capital "N"). His atheism comes with a scholastic background theory. Nature as a quasi-deity capable of administering just punishment: Where do science and enlightenment end here, and where do superstition and dogmatic metaphysics begin?

Some French materialists were more self-reflective. French physician and philosopher Julien Offray de La Mettrie (1709–1751) questioned his own materialism, tempered his famous machine metaphor in *L'Homme plus que machine* (1748), and added a skeptical question mark to his own "spirit of systems."[54] Diderot was

---

Philosophie, Würzburg: Königshausen & Neumann 2012, 209–241 and Kondylis, *Die Aufklärung*, 503–536.
53 Paul Thiry d'Holbach, *The System of Nature, or, the Laws of the Moral and Physical World*, volume 2, ch. 14, Project Gutenberg, https://gutenberg.org/ebooks/8910 (last accessed October 2, 2025). See also Tricoire, *Die Aufklärung*, 242–3 and Michael Allen Gillespie, *The Theological Origins of Modernity*, Chicago and London: University of Chicago Press 2008, 275–6.
54 See the interpretation of Philipp Blom, *A Wicked Company. The Forgotten Radicalism of the European Enlightenment*, New York: Basic Books 2012, ch. 3 compared to Schelkshorn, Hobbes und die Folgen, 231–235.

evidently aware of the contradictions and tensions within his own theory.[55] These two thinkers embody that reflective element of enlightenment which is characteristic of the third and fifth conceptions (see 1.1).

Rousseau's criticism also pointed to a problem that can be described with the terms "external enlightenment" and "coercive enlightenment." Enlightenment, he implies, can only be self-enlightenment, and a benevolent invitation to others to do the same. Enlightenment has nothing to do with an attitude that regards others as fundamentally ignorant, mentally retarded, backward, or unenlightened, and seeks to indoctrinate them with one's own philosophy or sets of beliefs. Rousseau clearly recognized the danger of sliding into dogmatic and perhaps coercive Enlightenment (capital letter only). Enlightenment, "if it does not always genuinely respect the reason and freedom of others, is already on the path to the same incapacitation (*Entmündigung*) that it combats with its demand to think for oneself."[56] In theory, Enlightenment is also a program for maturity and becoming mature, but in practice, it can quickly turn into its opposite. There is thus a risk of a "performative self-contradiction."

Rousseau's criticism did not just offer rational arguments against the model of "enlightenment through science" and against the French materialists. It was also a hurtful polemic. With the *Encyclopedia* and Rousseau's critique, the differences within the Enlightenment had become apparent. Several factions emerged. On one side were the "godless materialists," who were allegedly intent on destroying religion and accelerating the decline of morality, as stated by the royal prosecutor Omer Joly de Fleury in 1759. On the other side were the supporters of the mostly Catholic and conservative "religious party." They were in turn often divided, for instance in Jansenists, and their opponents, among them the Jesuits. Rousseau formed his own one-man party. Representatives from all factions often employed similar patterns of thought. They saw themselves as champions of reason and truth, while viewing others as prejudiced and unenlightened.

The debate on the sources and limits of our knowledge took on a new quality with Kant. This can be illustrated using the example of the empiricist and materialist Claude-Adrien Helvétius. He was convinced that perception or sensibility alone gives rise to ideas. "I say that physical sensibility and memory, or rather, to be more exact, that sensibility alone produces all our thoughts. In fact, memory is merely an organ of physical sensibility."[57] Kant argued that the proposition it-

---

55 Schelkshorn, Hobbes und die Folgen, 237 as well as Kondylis, *Die Aufklärung*, 535–6.
56 Schneiders, *Hoffnung auf Vernunft*, 178.
57 Claude-Adrien Helvétius, *On the Mind (1758)*, in: Margaret L. King, ed., *Enlightenment Thought. An Anthology of Sources*, Indianapolis and Cambridge: Hackett Publishing Company, Inc. 2019, 101–3, at 102.

self cannot be derived from perception. All that perception reveals is a succession of sensory impressions and ideas. Sensibility apparently came first, followed by ideas. However, perception alone can never justify or explain sensibility as the *cause* of ideas. This assertion is made by our faculty of judgment. This, in turn, relies on a principle of understanding, namely that each phenomenon must have a cause.

With great acumen, Kant uncovered other internal contradictions in the empirical approach. Kant agreed with Locke when he emphasized that enthusiasts ignore the limits of knowledge and, in their excess, believe in personal revelations that surpass all experience and reason. But Locke overlooked that he himself did not consistently adhere to the limits of knowledge. This is the case, for example, when Locke begins to speculate about the causes of religious enthusiasm, attributing it to melancholy, and self-satisfaction.

> Hence we see that, in all ages, men in whom melancholy has mixed with devotion, or whose conceit of themselves has raised them into an opinion of a greater familiarity with God, and a nearer admittance to his favor than is afforded to others, have often flattered themselves with a persuasion of an immediate intercourse with the Deity, and frequent communications from the Divine Spirit.[58]

Kant agreed with Locke that it is problematic to assume an immediate experience of God as if it were a fact. It is also dubious to assume that a "divine spirit" is the necessary cause of personal inspirations or so-called "religious experiences." But Kant hit upon the Achilles' heel of Locke's own argumentation. If we are indeed convinced that knowledge is impossible without sensory impressions, then knowledge about the religious enthusiasts and the cause of their enthusiasm is also impossible. In principle, we cannot with absolute certainty know why certain individuals tend toward enthusiasm. This inclination might have many causes that we can *think of* but cannot *know about*.

In some cases, the argument about the limits of our reason was strategic. This means that in discussions or polemics, this argument was used to gain the upper hand and attack an opponent's position. However, in a different context or when it came to one's own philosophy, these imposed limits were no longer considered. Another strategy was to downplay reason and experience to emphasize the central importance of divine revelation. Theologian William Leechman (1706–1785), a representative of the *Moderate Party* in the Presbyterian Church of Scotland, can serve as an example. According to Leechman, "We cannot with certainty conclude from what the philosophers have actually taught that the light of reason by

---

[58] Locke, *Essay Concerning Human Understanding*, vol. 2, ch. 19, section 5.

its own power extended so far, for we see that some of the oldest and best philosophers admitted that they had not themselves explored some of their most important doctrines but had drawn them from ancient traditions, which likely had their origin in divine revelation."[59]

This partiality and selective application cannot be attributed to all Enlightenment thinkers. This is evident in the case of Kant, who acknowledged the limits of reason even when his own convictions were concerned. One of the main theses of the *Critique of Pure Reason* (1781) is: All cognition of things out of mere pure understanding or pure reason is nothing but sheer illusion, and there is truth only in experience.[60] Here, Kant fully agreed with empiricism. Beyond experience, in the realm of metaphysics and religion, there is no knowledge, only thought, or thinking without corresponding *Anschauung* or intuition. He adopted the legal judgment *non liquet* from Roman jurisprudence: "It is not clear" means that a claim or a fact is not clarified by proof or counterproof. This means, for example, that the free will of humans cannot be proven, but neither can the opposite assumption. The epistemological impossibility of a positive proof of God does not imply that there is no God. Propositions like "there is a God, and there is a future life" cannot be demonstrated. From this follows the certainty "that no human being will ever step forward who could assert the *opposite* with even the least plausibility, let alone assert it dogmatically."[61] The freedom of the will, God's existence and the immortality of the soul are not objects of experience but matters of belief (see 5.2 and 5.3).

Kant also challenged empiricism. While knowledge does indeed start with perceptions, it does not solely *originate* from them. For "perceptions without concepts are blind." Concepts here refer to categories, such as possibility, reality, and necessity, and synthetic principles, such as the principle of causality. When a philosopher like Locke wishes to explain why certain individuals tend toward fanaticism, they employ the principle of causality. This principle evidently does not stem from perception or sensory impressions but is a prerequisite for organizing these sensory impressions and transforming them into knowledge. When, like Locke, I assert that melancholy and self-conceit are the causes of religious fanaticism, I am using this causal principle inherent in reason (which Kant therefore calls *a priori*). Sensory perception merely provides me with examples of individ-

---

59 Quoted in Thomas Ahnert, Fortschrittsgeschichte und Religiöse Aufklärung. William Robertson und die Deutung außereuropäischer Kulturen, in: Hardtwig, ed., *Die Aufklärung und ihre Weltwirkung*, 101–22, at 112, with more examples in Hardtwig, *Die Aufklärung*, 109–113.
60 Kant, Prolegomena to any future metaphysics that will be able to come forward as science [1783], in: *Werke*, vol. 4, 253–383, at 374.
61 Kant, *Critique of Pure Reason*, A 742.

uals who are melancholic, self-conceited, and simultaneously fanatical. It offers me a succession of specific phenomena, never a cause-and-effect relationship. The inclination toward fanaticism can indeed have many causes; Locke may have erred in his causal interpretation. However, the error lies not in perception but in thought. Whenever we contemplate, we necessarily employ categories, as is the case in these sentences. It makes a difference whether I assert, "The inclination toward fanaticism *might* have many causes" (category of possibility) or "The inclination toward fanaticism must *necessarily* have many causes" (category of necessity). A sentence containing the category of possibility ("Locke may have erred with his causal theory") conveys something different than a sentence which employs the category of reality ("Locke has erred. Period!").

What were the results of Kant's critique of reason? In line with his criticism, we can only make conjectures here. Moses Mendelssohn referred to Kant as a "destroyer of everything" (*Alleszermalmer*). This was perhaps an accurate description of Kant's critique of dogmatic metaphysics, which posited that "thoughts without content are empty." Kant's first "victims" were the systems of rationalist philosophy (Spinoza, Descartes, Leibniz, Wolff) and the proponents of traditional rational theology who adhered to proofs of God and the immortality of the soul (such as Mendelssohn himself). Kant evidently saw himself as a defender of autonomous morality (see 4.2) and of monotheism with strong sympathies for Christianity (see below 5.2 and 5.3). In the preface to the second edition of the *Critique of Pure Reason*, Kant refers to one key advantage of the critique of reason, namely that "it puts an end for all future time to objections against morality and religion in a *Socratic* way, namely by the clearest proof of the ignorance of the opponent."[62] Kant later specifies whom he has in mind. They are those who advocate "*materialism, fatalism, atheism,* [...] freethinking *unbelief,* [...] *enthusiasm* and *superstition*," and finally "*idealism* and *skepticism*."[63] This is not exclusively, but also (and perhaps primarily) directed against the French materialists, "freethinkers," and atheists. In line with the European Enlightenment, Kant opposes "enthusiasm" and "superstition" as deformations of religion (see 3.3). However, this stance is supplemented by a new opposition to currents within the Enlightenment. In other words, Kant not only confronted religious orthodoxy but also fought against the proponents of radical atheist Enlightenment and against Human skepticism.

All those who, like Bayle, had distinguished between knowledge and belief and were convinced that "the mysteries of the Gospel are above reason" [*dessus de la Raison*] could find confirmation in Kant. Like Kant, Bayle had also invoked

---

62 Kant, *Critique of Pure Reason*, B XXXI.
63 Kant, *Critique of Pure Reason*, B XXXIV.

Figure 8: Immanuel Kant, born in Königsberg in 1724, is the most significant German-language philosopher of the Enlightenment. His magnum opus, the *Critique of Pure Reason* (1781), presented an epistemology that can be understood as a synthesis of empiricism and rationalism.

an awareness of the limits of reason, which "can never attain to what is above itself."[64] Representatives of various forms of agnosticism or of fideism could find

---

[64] Pierre Bayle, *Historical and Critical Dictionary, Selections* [1697], translated by Richard H.

support in Kant's philosophy, just like adherents of orthodoxy who understood their faith as belief—and not as metaphysical knowledge. Early German Romanticism and the emerging German Idealism appreciated Kant's critique of empiricism and those approaches which reduced enlightenment to science, understanding (*Verstand*), and prudence. Kant himself developed a conception of rational religion in the years following 1781 (see Chapter 5).

2.4 Contemporary relevance: Discussions about Islam

The search for the limits of reason, and an often-corresponding skepticism, or even blunt rejection, links currents of the Enlightenment with the present. Carl Henrik Koch even asserts that, "Belief in reason was shaken in the eighteenth century in the same way as belief in science has been shaken in the twentieth. In both cases, this has resulted in an increased interest in aesthetics."[65] We might also add that it has led to an increased interest in esotericism, do-it-yourself religion, and ideologies.

In this section, I will briefly illustrate with examples that contemporary discourses on Islam, Islamic culture and religion often do not maintain the level of argumentation that might be expected from an enlightened society. Keywords are the limits of reason, essentialism, and the problem of causality.[66]

In her autobiography, the feminist, ex-Muslim, and critic of Islam, Ayaan Hirsi Ali, refers to the Enlightenment and its "great thinkers", including Spinoza, Voltaire, Locke, and Kant. She describes the Enlightenment as follows: "It employs facts instead of faith, evidence instead of tradition. Morality in this worldview is determined by human beings, not by an outside force. It is a worldview that came into being mainly in reaction to a particular religion, Christianity, and a par-

---

Popkin and Craig Brush, Indianapolis: Bobbs-Merrill Company 1965, Second Clarification, 409–20, at 410–11. See also Rainer Forst, Toleranz, Glaube und Vernunft. Bayle und Kant im Vergleich, in: Heiner Klemme, ed., *Kant und die Zukunft der europäischen Aufklärung*, Berlin/New York: de Gruyter 2009, 183–209, especially 197–8 and Manfred Kuehn, Knowledge and Belief, in: Haakonssen, *The Cambridge History of Eighteenth-Century Philosophy*, 389–425 on Enlightenment debates in general.
65 Koch, Schools and Movements, 50.
66 For an extended analysis, see my own *Islam, Aufklärung und Moderne*. See also Heiner F. Klemme, Causality, Knud Haakonssen, ed., *The Cambridge History of Eighteenth-Century Philosophy*, Cambridge, UK: Cambridge University Press 2006, 368–88 on the Enlightenment debates concerning the principle of causality.

ticular institution of Christianity, the Roman Catholic Church."[67] Hirsi Ali's knowledge of the enlighteners is superficial, and she follows familiar clichés and narratives (see the Introduction). For instance, she misses the religious, and skeptical elements in the philosophies of Locke, Voltaire, and Kant. She ignores Kant's distinction between knowledge and mere thinking and belief. She describes her turning away from Allah as a move from "irrational" faith to the certainty of knowledge. Relying on the scientific model of the Enlightenment (conception no. 4), she explains how she waited for evidence of the existence of Allah, of angels, heaven, and hell, did not find any, and eventually concluded that these entities could not exist. Through her own reflection and reading, such as the *The Atheist Manifesto*, she eventually believed she knew: "God, Satan, angels: these were all figments of human imagination." Her tour of several museums in the Netherlands led her to the "realization that, when I die, I will become just a bunch of bones."[68]

What is missing here is the "enlightenment about the Enlightenment," a critical self-reflection on one's own presumed knowledge, and a reflection on the limits of reason. The "true" or "authentic" Islam is described as a totalitarian, cruel, and tyrannical system that enslaves Muslims. It stands in stark contrast to humanism, tolerance, nonviolence, and other "Western values." Two typical patterns of thought emerge. First, there is essentialism, namely the belief that there are entities such as "Islam," "the Enlightenment," and "the West." Second, Hirsi Ali thinks in binary oppositions: here is the good West with its Enlightenment and science, and there is evil Islam. This kind of thinking may be psychologically understandable for biographical reasons (her early life was an ordeal), but it is not appropriate in terms of philosophic or scientific merit. In a discussion with Hirsi Ali, the English historian Timothy Garton Ash criticized this binary thinking and her polemical attempt to turn the heterogeneous European Enlightenment into a weapon against a monolithic "Islam." Enlightenment should not simply be equated with a secular and anti-religious modernity. Ash criticized Hirsi Ali of having replaced religious fundamentalism by "Enlightenment fundamentalism" (see Introduction, Assumptions 1, 4, and 6).[69]

Symptoms of a new dogmatism in metaphysics have troubling consequences for discourses related to Islamic religion and culture. For instance, some representatives of *New Atheism* refer to themselves as "brights." This could be interpreted as intellectual arrogance, where religious people, theists, agnostics, or Muslims are labeled as unenlightened and intellectually inferior. The atheist Christopher

---

[67] Ayaan Hirsi Ali, *Nomad. From Islam to America: A Personal Journey through the Clash of Civilizations*, New York: Knopf 2010, 206.
[68] Ayaan Hirsi Ali, *Infidel: My Life*, New York: Free Press 2007, 281.
[69] See *Islam, Aufklärung und Moderne*, 22–33 with quotations.

Hitchens deplored the "cringe-making proposal that atheists should conceitedly nominate themselves to be called 'brights.'"[70] One result is the denigration and condemnation of Islamic religion and culture. Richard Dawkins, for example, has made statements such as "to hell with their culture"[71] and "I'm pessimistic about the Islamic world. I regard Islam as one of the great evils in the world."[72]

Particularly problematic is the assertion by many *new atheists* that religions in general and Islam in particular lead to violence and terrorism. However, there is evidence both for and against the causal connection between Islam and terrorism. Religion can have both pacifying and incendiary effects. Anthropologist Scott Atran, drawing from his own field studies, has examined the various arguments and evidence and concluded that the factor "religion" cannot be isolated as the sole or most important cause of Islamist violence. Atran has little patience for the unscientific, ignorant, and dogmatic attitudes of many new atheists regarding religion and history: "The scientific ignorance and foolishness of many of the new atheists with respect to religion and history make me almost embarrassed to be an atheist."[73]

Uncritical Islam bashing is by no means limited to the representatives of *New Atheism*. In recent years, peculiar alliances have formed between left-wing and right-wing radicals, liberals, and conservatives, fundamentalist Christians, and right-wing populists. I mention just two examples here. Political scientist Michael Ley, who had previously gained recognition for his studies on National Socialism and the Holocaust, provided an almost apocalyptic depiction of Europe's future with *The Suicide of the West: The Islamization of Europe* (2015). Islam and enlightenment are seen as irreconcilable opposites. "Islam" is purportedly in the process of conquering and colonizing Europe. European elites, like the "enlightened" figures of the past, are described as "Islamophilic" and supportive of "Islamization."[74]

---

70 https://en.wikipedia.org/wiki/Brights_movement (last accessed October 2, 2025).
71 http://www.express.co.uk/news/uk/611231/Richard-Dawkins-in-extraordinary-blast-at-Muslims-To-hell-with-their-culture (last accessed October 2, 2025).
72 http://freethoughtnation.com/richard-dawkins-islam-is-one-of-the-great-evils-of-the-world/ (last accessed October 2, 2025).
73 Scott Atran, *Talking to the Enemy. Faith, Brotherhood, and the (Un)Making of Terrorists*, e-book version, New York: Harper Collins 2010, 474. Atran refers to Sam Harris, *The End of Faith: Religion, Terrorism and the Future of Reason*, New York: Norton 2004, but also to Dan Dennett, Christopher Hitchens und Richard Dawkins. He summarizes his criticism of new atheists in *Talking to the Enemy*, 450–74: Bad faith: The new Atheist salvation.
74 See my extensive analysis in *Islam, Aufklärung und Moderne*, 22–7.

These are sweeping and undifferentiated statements. The underlying philosophy of history is apparently uncritical and indulges in wild speculations about the future. The general attack on Islam does not even spare its early history. The early Quranic texts are claimed to be nothing more than the writings of Syrian-Aramaic and Arab Christians. "Mohammed and his successors cannot be historically verified and can confidently be relegated to the realm of myths. Consequently, the Quran and the assumed prophet have no historical connection but were retroactively merged into a foundational myth like the biblical tradition, shaping Arabic Christianity into Islam."[75] Everywhere you look, nothing but myths, and fictions! Ley's adherence to the European Enlightenment and to an enlightened attitude seems to remain on the surface. Ley does not appear to be interested in alternative interpretations offered in Islamic studies, which are mostly characterized by an attitude of respect. The claim that the Prophet Mohammed never existed sounds more like a conspiracy theory. It seems odd that Ley is described as an "unconditional advocate of the Enlightenment."[76]

The fundamental problem with the thesis that Islam leads to violence is the uncritical use of the principle of causality. In their book on the Israeli settler movement since 1967, Israeli historians Idith Zertal and journalist Akiva Eldar argue that the "very reasons" for Palestinian terrorism within the Green Line after the failure of the Oslo process can be attributed to the "constant harassment of the extremists among the settlers—and especially the massacre of Muslim worshippers in Hebron, which loosened the demons of violence."[77] The opposite viewpoint is more frequently expressed in Europe. The true cause of terrorism is seen as Islamic religion, and the Islamic societies, and cultures shaped—or rather deformed—by Islam. For example, a Palestinian who converted to Christianity stated in an interview: "You Jews should be aware: You will never, but never have peace with Hamas. Islam, as the ideology that guides them, will not allow them to achieve a peace agreement with the Jews. They believe that tradition says that the Prophet Mohammed fought against the Jews and that therefore they must continue to fight them to the death. [...] An entire society sanctifies death and the suicide

---

75 Michael Ley, *Der Selbstmord des Abendlandes. Die Islamisierung Europas*, Osnabrück: Hintergrund Verlag 2015, 70 and *Islam, Aufklärung und Moderne*, 51 with the counterarguments of some Islamic scholars.
76 https://de.wikipedia.org/wiki/Michael_Ley (last accessed October 2, 2025).
77 Idith Zertal and Akiva Eldar, *Lords of the Land. The War for Israel's Settlements in the Occupied Territories, 1967–2007*, New York: Nation Books 2007, 178.

terrorists. In Palestinian culture, a suicide terrorist becomes a hero, a martyr. Sheikhs tell their students about the 'heroism of the shaheeds.'"[78]

A third explanation is provided by Mohammed Bin Ali. The central factor, he argues, is the doctrine of *Al-Walā' wa-l-barā'*, which is widespread in Wahhabism and Salafist Islam and calls for unconditional loyalty to one's "true" believers and the avoidance of non-believers.[79]

Some analyses by former Muslim Hirsi Ali are also uncritical. She appears to be convinced of a homogeneous Islam, a "core of Islam," which she describes as a "rigid belief system" that breeds cruelty and violence. After the attacks on the World Trade Center, she articulated this causal theory in simple terms: "This was not just Islam, this was the core of Islam."[80] Sometimes, authors tend to emphasize factors that relate to their area of research or mirror their philosophical, political, or ideological agendas, or convictions. For instance, Slovenian left-wing philosopher Slavoj Žižek argues that the "true" reason or the "ultimate cause" of the mass migration to Europe in 2015, as well as for Islamic terrorism, are the "dynamics of global capitalism, as well as the process of Western military intervention."[81] "It needs to be said that the true threat to our common way of life does not come in the shape of refugees but lies in the dynamic of global capitalism."[82] This, too, is binary, and monocausal thinking. It further complicates matters because distant causes are particularly challenging to assess, especially when dealing with a complex phenomenon like "global capitalism."

Islamic scholar and publisher Hans-Peter Raddatz, by contrast, does not see capitalism as the problem, unlike the politically left-leaning Žižek. As a conservative thinker, he identifies the decadence of the Western world as the key factor, which, in his view, leaves it vulnerable to Islam. In a section on the "Intellectual Decline in Progress," he discusses the alleged intellectual deterioration in modern industrial societies, which has ultimately turned toward an "intercultural mass ideology." "Under the dominant influence of modern secular societal dynamics and significant intellectual narrowing, the orientation toward fetishes of material, electronic, and foreign cultural origin began to assume compulsive characteristics,

---

[78] Avi Issacharoff, Hamas' Christian convert. I've left a society that sanctifies terror, in: Haaretz, July 31, 2008, http://www.haaretz.com/hamas-christian-convert-i-ve-left-a-society-that-sanctifies-terror-1.250831 (last accessed October 2, 2025).
[79] Mohammed Bin Ali, *The Roots of Religious Extremism. Understanding the Salafi Doctrine Al-Wala' wal Bara'*, London: Imperial College Press 2016.
[80] Hirsi Ali, *Infidel: My Life*, 269.
[81] Slavoj Žižek, *Against the Double Blackmail. Refugees, Terror and Other Troubles with the Neighbours*, London: Penguin 2016, 43.
[82] Žižek, *Against the Double Blackmail*, 19–20.

as the loss of intellectual-political emancipation gave rise to a new form of moral-dogmatic disenfranchisement."[83] I find it challenging to fully comprehend what is meant by "moral-dogmatic disenfranchisement" or "fetishes," and do not know if Raddatz's sweeping generalizations are accurate. It is noteworthy, however, that the principle of causality is invoked twice when mentioning "influence" and, at the end, "gave rise to." Here, causal connections are asserted, but no attempt is made to verify them.

German theologian and philosopher Jürgen Manemann has distinguished five possible patterns of interpretation of jihadist violence.[84] According to the pattern of demonization, the jihadist is seen as pure evil and inhuman, perhaps even excluded from the circle of humanity. The pattern of religionizing attributes the decisive, essential, or sole cause to Islam. The sociological approach highlights sociological factors like social class, gender, or peer groups, while ethnicization focuses on the false, distorted, or nonsensical moral arguments that jihadists put forth, apparently motivating their actions. Manemann himself advocates a fifth pattern of interpretation, which I would call psychologizing. According to this view, jihadists practice pathological narcissism, and active nihilism, defined as "the deliberate neutralization of inhibitions to deny the Other the right to life." Violence becomes a habit and way of life, eventually even a kind of religion.[85]

What can be concluded from a critical analysis of our causal thinking? In my opinion, we are invited to adopt a skeptical or critical stance. The actions of jihadists can be attributed to a variety of possible causes, all of which claim a certain plausibility, such as individual, or psychological predispositions, their perceived experiences of discrimination, or social, psychosocial, economic, or cultural factors. Monocausal explanations are usually too simplistic and do not do justice to the complexity of reality. It makes sense to assume "a bundle of mutually reinforcing causes." The potency of religious beliefs should not be downplayed. However, these beliefs are always embedded in individual, social, political,

---

[83] Hans-Peter Raddatz, *Von Gott zu Allah? Christentum und Islam in der liberalen Fortschrittsgesellschaft*, München: Herbig 2001, 443.

[84] Jürgen Manemann, *Der Dschihad und der Nihilismus des Westens: Warum ziehen junge Europäer in den Krieg?*, Bielefeld: Transcript 2015, 17–31.

[85] Manemann, *Dschihad*, 38, 56 and 60. Manemann also mentions additional factors, which are once again situated within the realm of psychology, such as identity disorders, emotional emptiness, or "process melancholy;" see Manemann, *Dschihad*, 89–99.

and cultural contexts, which, in turn, have consequences for these religious beliefs.[86]

How did the enlighteners assess Islam and the Quran? Again, a complex picture emerges. The *Traité des trois imposteurs* (1719), with an unclear origin, ran to eight editions and clandestine circulation in the 18th century. As the title indicates, the anti-religious essay claims that the three founders of the Abrahamic religions, namely Judaism, Christianity, and Islam, were scoundrels, establishing sects characterized by fanaticism, superstition, and violence. It treated the followers of Mohammed as "at best fearful, superstitious, and credulous followers [...] and at worst as ignorant imbeciles undeserving of respect."[87] This disrespectful attitude can also be found in Voltaire, who described Mohammed in the play *Fanaticism, or Mahomet the Prophet* (1736) as a deceitful impostor, fanatic, and hypocrite. Voltaire's assessment of the prophet became more positive in later writings. According to Alexander Bevilacqua, the Protestant, and Catholic Oriental scholars of the 17th and early 18th centuries were more open-minded, more charitable, and less prejudiced than enlighteners like Montesquieu, Voltaire, Diderot, or Gibbon. Islamic scholars like the French Barthélemy d'Herbelot de Molainville (1625–1695), Dutch Adriaan Reland (1676–1718) or the British George Sale (1697–1736) were committed to "a long tradition of humanistic scholarship." Bevilacqua concludes: "The reconsideration of a foreign religion and its history, including its cultural attainments, did not have to await the development of a secular intellectual culture."[88]

Despite their shortcomings, the considerations of enlighteners can help avoid mistakes in contemporary debates about Islam, and similar discussions. In the first place, skeptical, and critical attitudes are essential, which also applies to one's own thinking. Our own thinking and judgment should be exposed to continuous examination. In concrete terms, the following principles or maxims

---

86 Petra Bahr, Von der Befreiung der Bilder – ein etwas anderer Blick auf den reformierten Bildersturm, in: Emidio Campi, Peter Opitz, Konrad Schmid, eds., *Johannes Calvin und die kulturelle Prägekraft des Protestantismus*, Zürich: Theologischer Verlag 2009, 45–56, at 49.
87 John Marshall, The Treatise of the Three Impostors, Islam, the Enlightenment, and Toleration, in: Gianni Paganini, Margaret C. Jacob, and John Christian Laursen, eds., *Clandestine Philosophy. New Studies on Subversive Manuscripts in Early Modern Europe, 1620–1823*, Toronto: University of Toronto Press 2020, 307–27, at 324.
88 Alexander Bevilacqua, *The Republic of Arabic Letters. Islam and the European Enlightenment*, Cambridge, Mass. and London: Harvard University Press 2018, especially 167–99, the quotation at 198–9. See also John Tolan, *Faces of Muhammad: Western Perceptions of the Prophet of Islam from the Middle Ages to Today*, Princeton and Oxford: Princeton University Press 2019 and Robertson, *The Enlightenment. The Pursuit of Happiness*, 637–8.

emerge:[89] Polemical terms, battle cries and catchphrases like "Islam" and "modernity" should be avoided or carefully defined and used. We should stay clear of binary thinking and blanket statements. Monocausal explanations are usually inadequate and should be replaced by an awareness that recognizes how phenomena can have multiple causes and may be intertwined. Essentialist assumptions about the nature of entities such as the Enlightenment, modernity, or Islam should be questioned. Finally, assuming different perspectives, and practicing the enlarged way of thinking—that can be found among many enlighteners—should be practiced, as discussed in the next chapter.

---

89 See Cavallar, *Islam, Aufklärung und Moderne*, 173–5.

Chapter 3
Humor, cynicism, and the enlarged way of thinking

Winter 1706 in London. French Camisards from the Cevennes have fled to the English capital, escaping from the soldiers of King Louis XIV.[1] In the Edict of Fontainebleau (1685), the King had revoked the Edict of Nantes granting Calvinist Protestants the freedom of worship and full citizenship rights. These Huguenots in the southern French Cevennes called themselves Camisards. Following the Edict of Fontainebleau, a partisan war began which escalated into the brutal Cevennes War (1702–1705). The uprising was brutally suppressed, and many Camisards fled to England. In the eyes of English enlighteners, they became victims of royal oppression and of Catholic fanaticism. However, the matter was not quite that simple. In London, the victims also became perpetrators. Camisard leader Élie Marion (1678–1713) founded the community of the *Enfants de Dieu* or the "French Prophets", who began to greatly annoy many English Protestants: the prophets proclaimed a Millennial Kingdom, preached the end of the world and the destruction of London, and often fell into trances. How should one deal with these fanatical enthusiasts? Was it permissible to ridicule these brethren in faith? Or should they be respected, considering that they were, after all, persecuted because of their denomination or faith?

3.1 Humor, satire, parody, and cynicism

English enlighteners such as John Locke and Anthony Ashley Cooper, the third Earl of Shaftesbury (1671–1713), pondered questions like these. Shaftesbury proposed a test, the "Test of Ridicule," inspired by the comedians at the fair who depicted the fervent Camisards as puppets manipulated from the outside. This test was not directed against religion in general but rather against enthusiastic reli-

---

[1] See Chrystel Bernat, ed., *Die Kamisarden. Eine Aufsatzsammlung zur Geschichte des Krieges in den Cevennen (1702–1710)*, Mit einem Vorwort von Philippe Joutard, aus dem Französischen übertragen von Eckart Birnstiel, Bad Karlshafen: Verlag der Deutschen Hugenotten-Gesellschaft 2003 for the historical background. My text follows Geier, *Aufklärung*, 78–92 and Robertson, *The Enlightenment. The Pursuit of Happiness*, 209–10. A related case was that of the Parisian convulsionaries, followers of Jansenism.

gious zeal and blind fanaticism. The mocking laughter was intended to expose the hypocrites who were insincere and talked about divine inspirations they apparently did not possess. "For that imposture should dare sustain the encounter of a grave enemy is no wonder. A solemn attack, she knows, is not of such danger to her. There is nothing she abhors or dreads like pleasantness and good humor."[2] True religiosity, according to Shaftesbury, was marked by a cheerful disposition, by "good humor." Fanatical enthusiasm, on the other hand, stemmed from "ill humor," the inability to keep occasional discontents and religious fervor in check. The Test of Ridicule relies on other people. Everyone should have the courage to subject their own convictions to a humorous examination by others. This examination should not be hurtful but, in Shaftesbury's view, was constrained by the "Culture of Politeness" that a "Gentleman Philosopher" should exhibit. "Let but the search go freely on, and the right measure of every thing will soon be found. Whatever humor has got the start, if it be unnatural, it cannot hold, and the ridicule, if ill-placed at first, will certainly fall at last where it deserves."[3] Shaftesbury's "freedom of wit and humor" avoided the hurtful cynicism that ridiculed the weaker. The freedom that enabled "refinement" was based on common sense, the ancient *sensus communis*. This common sense firstly encompasses the capacity to distinguish and discern, for instance between genuine religiosity and religious delusion. However, common sense also represents a moral attitude oriented toward the common good and the natural rights of all humans. It is a character trait that signifies "a sense of public weal and of the common interest, love of the community, or society, natural affection, humanity, obligingness, or that sort of civility which rises from a just sense of the common rights of mankind, and the natural equality there is among those of the same species."[4]

German theologian and educational reformer Friedrich Gedicke (1754–1803) followed Shaftesbury's approach in a speech given at the Wednesday Society in 1784, roughly 80 years later. "Cold, reasonable refutation" would not help against the "cancerous disease" of fanaticism, only "the biting means of *mockery* and satire."[5] Around the time of Shaftesbury, Christian Thomasius in Leipzig provoked

---

2 Anthony Ashley Cooper, Third Earl of Shaftesbury, A Letter Concerning Enthusiasm, in: *Characteristics of Men, Manners, Opinions, Times*, ed. Lawrence Klein, Cambridge: Cambridge University Press 2000, 4–28, at 17.
3 Shaftesbury, *Characteristics of Men*, 7–8. See also Shaftesbury, *Characteristics of Men*, 13 and Shaftesbury, An Inquiry Concerning Virtue or Merit, in: Shaftesbury, *Characteristics of Men*, 163–230, at 194.
4 Shaftesbury, Sensus Communis, an Essay on the Freedom of Wit and Humour in a Letter to a Friend, in: Shaftesbury, *Characteristics of Men*, 29–69, at 48.
5 Quoted in Geier, *Aufklärung*, 218.

his contemporaries with a "mixture of information and invective, satire, and sophisticated criticism." He made fun of Aristotle and defended Epicurus, who was regarded as a prototype of a freethinker, libertine, and atheist.[6]

Humor, ridicule, taunt, witticisms, mockery, satire, or cynicism became an indispensable part of the European Enlightenment after Shaftesbury.[7] German physicist and satirist Georg Christoph Lichtenberg (1742–1799) is an excellent example. Here are a few samples from his notebooks, published posthumously. He called them *Sudelbücher* ("waste books" or "scrapbooks"):

"Like a great philosophical chatterer, he is concerned not so much with the truth as with the sound of his prose."

"Just because sermons are preached in churches does not mean they do not need lightning conductors."

"Our theologians wish with force to make of the Bible a book in which there is no *human* understanding or common sense."

"When a book and a head collide and it sounds hollow, is it always the fault of the book?"

"The man was such an intellectual he was of hardly any use in this world."

"A clever child raised with a foolish one can itself become foolish. Man is so perfectible and corruptible that he can become a fool through reason."

"The foolish man argues coldly from the first impression, while the sensible man occasionally turns around to hear what instinct has to say."

"Every mistake appears unbelievably foolish when others make it."[8]

Lichtenberg also played masterfully with the Enlightenment's metaphor of light. Regarding the Enlightenment, the European Enlightenment, and the French Revolution, he noted:

> What is said of the benefits and harms of the Enlightenment can certainly be well represented in a fable of fire. It is the soul of inorganic nature; its use in moderation makes life enjoyable for us, and it warms our winters and illuminates our nights. But this must be done with candles and torches—to illuminate the streets with burning houses is a quite wicked form of illumination. Children must also not be allowed to play with it.[9]

Voltaire skillfully used irony and satire under the motto *écrasez l'infâme* to write against the churches, especially the Catholic Church, against religious intolerance,

---

6 Martus, *Aufklärung*, 105.
7 For an excellent introduction see Ross Carroll, *Uncivil Mirth. Ridicule in Enlightenment Britain*, Princeton and Oxford: Princeton University Press 2021.
8 Georg Christoph Lichtenberg, *Philosophical Writings*, translated, edited and with an Introduction by Steven Tester, Albany: State University of New York Press 2012, 54, 164, 111, 60, 81, 72.
9 Lichtenberg, *Philosophical Writings*, 158.

Figure 9: Francisco Rizi (1614–1685), *Auto de Fe en la plaza Mayor de Madrid*, 1683.

fanaticism, and partly against religions in general—and to promote his own deistic "religion of reason." In this journalistic, polemical, and political battle, Voltaire ridiculed theologians, and philosophers like Leibniz, as seen in his famous novel *Candide* (1759). For example, he ironically described theologians from the University of Coimbra who decided "that the spectacle of a few people being ceremonially burned over a low flame is the infallible secret of preventing earthquakes." The public executions during the *auto-da-fés*, of course, did not have the desired effect, because on the same day, the earth trembled again.[10] *Auto-da-fés* were the pronouncements of judgment by the Spanish or Portuguese Inquisition against heretics, non-Catholics, and those who deviated from the "true faith." In some cases, the condemned were publicly burned at the stake. Many *auto-da-fés*, as described in the novel, had the character of public festivals. However, other aspects are clichéd and polemically exaggerated.[11] Voltaire used these and other episodes

---

[10] Voltaire, *Candide and Other Stories*, translated with an Introduction and Notes by Roger Pearson, Oxford: Oxford University Press 2006, chapter 6, 14.

[11] See for instance Gerd Schwerhoff, *Die Inquisition. Ketzerverfolgung in Mittelalter und Neuzeit*, 3rd ed., München: Beck 2009, 79–95. Despite all the cruelty and legitimate fear of the Spanish Inquisition, Schwerhoff emphasizes: "In hindsight, the procedures of the Spanish Inquisition, judged by the standards of the time, do not appear to be particularly cruel and inhumane, nor

of his narrative as a stick with which to beat Christianity, and particularly the Catholic Church. This did not diminish the effectiveness of Voltaire's novel.

Voltaire's criticism targeted, among others, dogmatic metaphysical system thinkers who assumed a necessary connection between human behavior and the occurrence of earthquakes. Like many enlighteners, Voltaire was convinced of the limits of our reason, especially in the spheres of metaphysics and religion. "In metaphysics, we scarcely reason on anything but probabilities. We are all swimming in a sea of which we have never seen the shore. Woe to those who fight while they swim! Land who can: but he that cries out to me, 'You swim in vain, there is no land' disheartens me, and deprives me of all my strength."[12] This is entertaining, witty, and vividly expressed. In this context, land symbolizes the realm of experience and practice, to be shaped by universal moral principles.

Friedrich Nicolai humorously mocked the somewhat extreme Werther cult of his time in *The Joys of Young Werther* and *The Sorrows and Joys of Werther the Man* (1775), one year after the young Johann Wolfgang Goethe had published his famous epistolary novel *The Sorrows of Young Werther*. Fans had dressed up as Werther or Lotte, there was an "Eau de Werther," and even coffee sets with the likenesses of the two main characters. The most passionately unhappy lovers even tried to faithfully recreate Werther's suicide. Nicolai made a "single small change" in the story and continued it differently: Lotte's fiancé showed understanding, and the lovers could marry and face the realities of daily life. However, their daily lives were utterly miserable. Although the couple lost their first child, Werther had to earn a living and therefore had no time for melancholy, pessimism, and self-pity. He realized how much "strength" and "courage" were needed—not to take his own life, but to endure "inevitable bourgeois circumstances." The first troubles and disagreements in their marriage arose because Lotte missed Werther's undivided affection. When the couple moved to the countryside, they had issues with a wealthy neighbor who, following the fashions, preferred a blend of English and Chinese landscape design. The neighbor wrecked Werther's garden. At the end of the satire, Werther, "tempered by experience," recognized that the neighbor might indeed be a genius, "but I can see, a genius is a poor neighbor. While it may be beneficial to oneself to speak as a genius, it often

---

less legally formal than those of other courts. By contrast, certain elements even stand out positively" (Schwerhoff, *Die Inquisition*, 92–3).
[12] Voltaire, *A Philosophical Dictionary*, 2 vols., London: Dugdale 1843, Article God, Gods, vol. 1, 567.

makes others quite uncomfortable when one acts like a genius."[13] Goethe was reportedly outraged by the satire.

In general, satire, parody, humor, and sometimes mockery provided many enlighteners with the opportunity to effectively disseminate their own philosophical positions and to partially evade censorship. Humor allowed enlighteners to distance themselves from a situation, address contradictions and paradoxes, or attempt to expose an apparent contradiction. Humor addresses human limitations and absurdities, allowing for a change in perspective and a fresh look at the familiar. Humor tends to be subversive. It questions thought processes that have become habitual, it liberates, and it can contain condensed thought experiments. Humor is inclusive, whereas mockery hurts, and excludes.[14] Classics of Enlightenment satire in Europe include not only Voltaire's *Candide* and Lichtenberg's aphorisms, but also Jonathan Swift's *Gulliver's Travels* (1726), Montesquieu's *Persian Letters* (1721), Diderot's novels, and many English novels. Notable figures in this regard include Henry Fielding and Laurence Sterne. Authors attacked, among others, religious intolerance, fanaticism, inhumanity like slavery or the slave trade, or plain stupidity.[15]

A famous and fine example of satire is *A Modest Proposal* (1729) by the Anglo-Irish author and cleric Jonathan Swift. Its full title is *A Modest Proposal for Preventing the Children of Poor People from Being a Burthen to Their Parents or Country, and for Making Them Beneficial to the Publick*. Poor people in Ireland, the text suggests, might improve their economic situation and contribute to the "public good" by selling their newborn to the rich—as food. In the words of Swift, these children should "be offered in sale to the persons of quality and fortune, through the kingdom, always advising the mother to let them suck plentifully in the last month, so as to render them plump, and fat for a good table."[16] Too many children are born into poor families each year, Swift contended, and they are simply useless mouths that have to be fed till the age of twelve, when they might turn into "salable" commodities for merchants. "I have been assured by a

---

13 Friedrich Nicolai, *Freuden des jungen Werthers* und den *Leiden und Freuden Werthers des Mannes* (1775), http://gutenberg.spiegel.de/buch/freuden-des-jungen-werthers-leiden-und-freuden-werthers-des-mannes-3820/1 (accessed August 9, 2017). See also Karl Robert Mandelkow, ed., *Goethe im Urteil seiner Kritiker. Dokumente zur Wirkungsgeschichte Goethes in Deutschland, Teil I: 1773–1832*, München: Beck 1975 and Martus, *Aufklärung*, 789–799 on the historical background.
14 For an introduction, see Geert Brône, Kurt Feyaerts and Tony Veale, eds., *Cognitive Linguistcs and Humor Research*, Berlin, Boston: de Gruyter 2017.
15 See Carroll, *Uncivil Mirth* for an overview.
16 Jonathan Swift, *A Modest Proposal*, Webster's German Thesaurus Edition, San Diego: ICON Classics 2005, 4. For an introduction, see Robert Phiddian, Have You Eaten Yet? The Reader in *A Modest Proposal*, Studies in English Literature 1500–1900, 36 (1996), 603–621.

very knowing American of my acquaintance in London, that a young healthy child well nursed, is, at a year old, a most delicious nourishing, and wholesome food, whether stewed, roasted, baked, or boiled; and I make no doubt that it will equally serve in a fricasie, or a ragout."[17] *A Modest Proposal* mocks English rule in Ireland, social engineering proposed by followers of Francis Bacon, and contempt for the poor and for Irish Catholicism. It ridicules utilitarianism *avant la lettre*, a pragmatic or "scientific" approach to social problems, the use of statistics, and the prioritization of public happiness over basic humanist principles. Swift's own underlying moral principles are obvious: Humans must not be seen and used as commodities because they are ends in themselves (see 4.4). The serious tone of Swift's proposal underlines the utter absurdity and immorality of the scheme.

German literary historian Annette Hilker refers to "carnivalization as a medium of the Enlightenment."[18] Drawing on the Russian cultural semiotician Mikhail Bakhtin, she defines carnival as an experience of ambivalence. "It celebrates the joyful relativity of everything. [...] Absolute denial is as foreign to the carnival as absolute assertion."[19] During carnival, existing hierarchies and certainties are playfully questioned by turning the world "upside down." According to Hilker, the "carnivalization" of philosophical writers like Voltaire or Diderot problematized philosophical discourses and metaphysical worldviews, while being self-reflective, and deconstructive. Pangloss in *Candide* is ironically mocked as a metaphysical and dogmatic thinker who ignores reality. However, the criticism is not solely destructive but rather emphasizes that philosophical debates are inherently inconclusive. In this context, the limits of one's own reason and intellect—and perhaps of some currents of the Enlightenment are often highlighted (see 2. 3.). Furthermore, the anti-metaphysical, and deconstructive elements are often not the final word. For example, Voltaire concludes his novel *Candide* with an appeal to practice and hope for the future. When Voltaire compares the realm of metaphysics to a sea in which we all swim and whose shores we have never seen, there is also a constructive aspect here. Because "whoever calls out to me, 'You swim in vain, there is no harbor!' takes away my courage and robs me of all my strength."[20]

---

17 Swift, *A Modest Proposal*, 4.
18 Annette Hilker, *Karnevalisierung als Medium der Aufklärung. Fontenelle, Fénelon, Voltaire, Diderot*, Hannover: Wehrhahn 2006.
19 Michail Bachtin, *Probleme der Poetik Dostoevskijs*, München: Hanser 1971, 140, quoted in Hilker, *Karnevalisierung*, 13.
20 Voltaire, *A Philosophical Dictionary*, 2 vols., London: Dugdale 1843, Article God, Gods, vol. 1, 567.

In the end, there is a cacophony of voices, conceptions, and ideas, often full of ambivalence, often published in fiction such as novels, often with twisted, unclear, or hidden messages. Diderot's novel *Jacques le fataliste et son maître* (written between 1765–1780) is probably a case in point. The servant Jacques professes to be a fatalist—everything that happens has been preordained, he asserts. Yet the events demonstrate that Jacques is not a passive victim of circumstances, fate, or divine intervention, but instead shapes his own life by determined action. Despite the novel's title, his master is not really the boss—it is the courageous, swashbuckling, cunning, and sometimes aggressive Jacques who carries the day. Jacques' master actually depends on him, so he is in a way the real servant. And the insolent Jacques is not reluctant to let him know this.[21] French philosophers also needed a thick skin, because they sometimes became the targets of *anti-philosophe* satires. The most prominent example is the comedy *Les philosophes* (1760) by the French playwright Charles Pallisot de Montenoy (1730–1814). It was staged by the *Comédie-Française*, became the event of the season, and caused a scandal.[22]

Since we are dealing with the European Enlightenment, Shaftesbury's "Examination of the Ridiculous" also underwent a critical and systematic examination. The Anglo-Dutch satirist and philosopher Bernard de Mandeville (1670–1733), Francis Hutcheson, and David Hume are prominent examples.[23] Moses Mendelssohn had a very reasonable and quite timely objection. There was, in fact, the danger that jest and humor might lead to pretense rather than to more enlightenment:

> However, true enlightenment surely does not occur when people try to hide their superstitions for fear of being ridiculed. At most they prefer the mask of sound reason, may even jest along where this fashion prevails, and are nonetheless in their innermost being enthusiasts, seduced, and seducing enthusiasts. The only means to promote enlightenment is *enlightenment* itself. [...] The source of evil can only be stopped up by enlightenment. Shed light on the subject, and the ghosts disappear.[24]

The line between ridicule and exposure on the one hand and benevolent humor on the other is difficult to draw. Since, according to Shaftesbury, the Examination of the Ridiculous also occurs in community, there is a risk that external conformity, but no personal insight, may result due to group dynamics. Mendelssohn sug-

---

21 Cf. Curran, *Diderot*, 402, 383 and 381.
22 See Curran, *Diderot*, 183–6.
23 See Carroll, *Uncivil Mirth*, 70–116.
24 Quoted in Geier, *Aufklärung*, 219.

gests that especially those who have fallen prey to the seduction of other enthusiasts should be approached "with leniency and without the scourge of satire." These people deserve "compassion rather than ridicule."[25]

"The only means to promote enlightenment is *enlightenment*." Kant clearly took this insight to heart. Enlightenment processes take place in community and in the public sphere; they allow for the mutual examination of all judgments before the forum of critical reason (see 1.1, conception no. 5 and below). The young, so-called pre-critical Kant (referring to his works before the publication of the *Critique of Pure Reason* in 1781) was more aligned with Shaftesbury than with the thoughtful Mendelssohn. The most important writing in this regard is *Dreams of a Spirit-Seer, Illustrated by Dreams of Metaphysics* (1766).[26] On the surface, it is an ironic confrontation with the Swedish spirit-seer, scientist, and mystic Emanuel Swedenborg (1688–1772), who claimed to be able to see and hear spirits. However, at least equally important is another dimension, namely Kant's *self-ironic* criticism of his own "love" for metaphysics, which he does not simply condemn. This self-reflective activity is a form of catharsis, a purification of exaggerated metaphysical claims and assertions. Irony serves two functions here. Firstly, it blurs the boundaries between serious philosophical reflection and playful literary activity. Secondly, it undermines clear meanings. Metaphysics as a science that goes beyond the limits of reason (see 2.3) seems impossible, yet also indispensable. Kant describes his dilemma in a letter to Mendelssohn about *Dreams of a Spirit-Seer* with the following words: "It was in fact difficult for me to devise the right style with which to clothe my thoughts, so as not to expose myself to derision. It seemed to me wisest to forestall other people's mockery by first of all mocking myself; and this procedure was actually quite honest, since my mind is really in a state of conflict on this matter."[27] Swedenborg is a dreamer of the senses, while the metaphysician is a dreamer of reason. Both claim to see something "which no other normal person sees."[28] Against this presumption, only the means of irony and self-irony help: *"If a hypochondriacal wind should rage in the guts, what matters is the direction it takes: if downwards, then the result is a f –; if up-*

---

25 Geier, *Aufklärung*.
26 For the following see Stelios Gadris, Two Cases of Irony: Kant and Wittgenstein, *Kant-Studien*, 107 (2016), 343–68 and Constantin Rauer, *Wahn und Wahrheit. Kants Auseinandersetzung mit dem Irrationalen*, Berlin: de Gruyter 2007.
27 Kant, Letter to Moses Mendelssohn, April 8. 1766, *Werke*, vol. 10, 70.
28 Immanuel Kant, *Dreams of a Spirit-Seer elucidated by Dreams of Metaphysics* [1766], in: *Werke*, vol. 2, 315–73, at 342.

wards, an apparition, or a heavenly inspiration."[29] Irony here is not an end in itself but serves to emphasize the illusory nature of dogmatic metaphysics.

3.2 Change of perspective, the enlarged way of thinking, and a skeptical attitude

Jean Le Rond d'Alembert contrasted the *esprit systématique* of many enlighteners like himself with the *esprit de système* that was typical of many parts of rationalist metaphysics in the 17th and early 18th centuries (see 2.3). German philosopher and dramatist Gotthold Ephraim Lessing (1729–1781) can serve as a prominent example of a self-reflective critique of metaphysical thinking. He distanced himself from his own work, *The Education of the Human Race* (1777–80), by immediately questioning the theses he had put forth, albeit with a certain degree of irony. In a letter written in 1778, he stated that the work was "by a good friend who enjoys making all sorts of hypotheses and systems, just to have the pleasure of tearing them down again." Apparent certainties are deliberately called into question, beginning with the paradoxical motto of Augustine: "All this is true in a certain sense for the same reasons it is false in a certain sense." For Lessing, as one interpreter suggests, it was typical to have "a lot of unfinished business" in his personal and literary life.[30]

Georg Christoph Lichtenberg had a similar mindset. He strongly distrusted any form of dogmatism and metaphysical systems based on axioms independent of experience. One of his aphorisms is as follows: "Even if my philosophy is not sufficient to discover anything new, it nevertheless possesses courage enough to regard as questionable what has long been believed true."[31] An interpreter has described this attitude with the following words: "Caution, doubt, and skepticism, which mistrust the appropriation of diverse phenomena by a logical 'system' […], encouragement of self-reflection, and self-experience."[32] Once again, we find skepticism toward uncritical *Systemdenken* that, while starting from experi-

---

29 Kant, *Dreams of a Spirit-Seer*, vol. 2, 348.
30 Gotthold Ephraim Lessing, Letter to Johann Albert Heinrich Reimarus, April 6, 1778, in: *Werke und Briefe*, ed. Wilfried Barner et al., Frankfurt am Main: Deutscher Klassiker-Verlag 1985–2003, vol. 12, 142–4, at 143, as well as vol. 10, 73; Hugh Barr Nisbet, Gotthold Ephraim Lessing, in: Hofmann, ed., *Aufklärung*, 75–90, at 76.
31 Lichtenberg, *Philosophical Writings*, 148.
32 Beiser, *Lichtenberg*, 164.

ence, leaves it behind, and begins to speculate. It should be kept in mind that this skeptical attitude did not necessarily imply complete relativism.[33]

Kant called the willingness to adopt the perspectives of others the "enlarged mode of thinking" at the end of the Enlightenment era. There are some examples of enlighteners who attempted to do just that. They challenged prejudices by assuming the perspective of others, such as Persians, Tahitians, the blind, or even extra-terrestrials. Among the most famous texts of the early Enlightenment is the *Persian Letters* (1721) by Charles-Louis de Secondat, commonly known as Montesquieu. In the preface, he ironically noted that he had always been surprised that nations had often understood more about other nations than their own. The Persians had even noticed things "which, I am certain, have escaped many Germans who have traveled in France."[34] Those who adhere to this principle of shifting perspectives quickly understand that it is senseless to try to persuade adherents of other denominations or religions to change their faith. Montesquieu has the Persian Usbek write in a letter: "He who tries to make me change my religion only does so, presumably, because he would never change his own, even were someone to try to force him to do so; so how can he find it strange that I should refuse to do something that he himself would not do, even perhaps were he offered the world as his empire?"[35] The Muslim and non-European becomes a representative of the Enlightenment, accusing Europeans of self-contradictions, and suggesting they should adopt the enlarged mode of thinking.

Around the same time, in the year 1721, Christian Wolff publicly praised "the practical philosophy of the Chinese." With a great deal of openness, Wolff noted the principle of meritocracy in governance, cases of state tolerance, virtues such as politeness, and self-control—much to the dismay of his theological colleagues, most of them Pietists. This episode can also be seen as an example of a successful shift of perspective and the enlarged mode of thinking. However, it might be ar-

---

[33] See Andreas Urs Sommer, Skepsis und Aufklärung: Der Fall des historischen Pyrrhonismus, in: Faber and Wehinger, eds., *Aufklärung in Geschichte und Gegenwart*, 85–98, John Christian Laursen und Gianni Paganini, eds., *Skepticism and political thought in the seventeenth and eighteenth centuries*, Toronto: University of Toronto Press 2015, and Sébastien Charles and Plínio J. Smith, eds., *Scepticism in the Eighteenth Century: Enlightenment, Lumiéres, Aufklärung*. Dordrecht: Springer 2013 on the skepticism of the European Enlightenment.
[34] Montesquieu, *Persian Letters* [1721], ed. Andrew Kahn, Oxford: Oxford University Press 2008, 4. For introductions to the *Lettres persanes*, see Genevieve Lloyd, *Enlightenment Shadows*, Oxford: Oxford University Press 2013, 21–44 and Gary Kates, *The Books that Made the European Enlightenment. A History in 12 Case Studies*, London et al.: Bloomsbury Academic 2022, 77–95. Sharpe, *The Other Enlightenment* is an excellent introduction to this Enlightenment practice some associate with postmodernism.
[35] Montesquieu, *Persian Letters*, 117.

gued that Wolff may have been interested more in provocation and successful marketing. In any case, he was expelled from the country by King Frederick William I of Prussia "under penalty of the gallows." This exile turned Wolff into a martyr of the Enlightenment.[36]

In the first half of the 18th century, the Principal of the University of Edinburgh liked to open meetings with a prayer: "Lord, repel, and suppress the spirit of coercion and persecution, not only among Papists but among Christians of all denominations."[37] This wording by a moderate was polemically directed against the *High Flyers* or Evangelicals in the Scottish church. However, it can also be seen as an example of an enlarged mode of thinking, as it acknowledged that the "spirit of coercion and persecution" could, in principle, occur in all denominations, not just in that of the traditional adversary, namely the Catholics. Some practiced the enlarged way of thinking in gender relations. The Prussian official and satirical writer Theodor Gottlieb von Hippel the Elder (1741–1796) criticized binary gender relations in his work *On Improving the Status of Women* (1792). He argued that women's intellectual abilities were neither different nor inferior but comparable to those of men. Hippel advocated coeducation in schools until puberty, equal education for women equivalent to that of men, and an opening of the professional world to women.[38]

Friedrich Nicolai described the meetings of the Berlin *Wednesday Society* as discussions among "true lovers of truth" to think more clearly about specific topics by contrasting different opinions and examining them from all angles.[39] The Prussian orientalist and diplomat Heinrich Friedrich von Diez (1751–1817) criticized the legal and social discrimination of Jews. In his work *On Jews* (1783), his most significant contribution to the discussion of the "civil improvement of Jews," he condemned the "extermination" of Jews in medieval Europe. He understood that due to their persecution, Jews needed their religion as a unifying bond: "Jews were born to suffer, just as others were born to persecute them. Grown up amidst contempt, mockery, misery, flight, and persecution, they were accustomed

---

36 See Martus, *Aufklärung*, 257–68. See Daniel Purdy, Chinese Ethics within the Radical Enlightenment: Christian Wolff, in: Carl Niekerk, ed., *The Radical Enlightenment in Germany. A Cultural Perspective*, Leiden and Boston: Brill Rodopi 2018, 112–30 for the wider context. Purdy argues that "Wolff's speech must be evaluated in relation to Catholic and Protestant missionary work in Asia" (Purdy, Chinese Ethics, 112).
37 Quoted in Karl Graf Ballestrem, *Adam Smith*, München: Beck 2001, 19.
38 Theodor Gottlieb von Hippel, *On Improving the Status of Women* [1792], translated by Timothy F. Sellner, Detroit: Wayne State University Press 1979. See also Kersting, Ambivalenzen der Aufklärung, 117 und Meyer, *Die Epoche der Aufklärung*, 188–90.
39 Friedrich Nicolai, Ueber meine gelehrte Bildung, vol. 1, 2, 65.

to fear everything and endure everything. [...] I am convinced that the Jew saved what was left of him by humans only through his religion."[40] The civil emancipation of Jews was a reasonable demand, regardless of their conversion to Christianity. In the process of enlightenment, Jews would reform their religion to be compatible with the "new civil conditions." Diez even speculated: "Perhaps the Jews will also become confessors of the pure religion of reason, to which the transition from Judaism is much easier than from any other positive religion."[41]

In many cases, turning points in an individual's biography may indicate an enlarged mode of thinking. Some enlighteners recount in their letters a lasting "transformation" or "change" in their way of thinking. In the 1750s, German poet Christoph Martin Wieland (1733–1813) read Rousseau with a female Swiss friend. She served as a counterpart to the French materialists and helped him to gradually overcome his own otherworldly enthusiasm. "I had to either reform my Platonism or seek a desert in Tyrol to live in. Experience took one delusion after another from me, and I finally found my balance."[42] In this case, it was the emphasis on experience, by way of Rousseau's writings, that questioned the speculative philosophy of Plato. Another biographical example is Lessing, who wrote in 1779:

> The better part of my life has—happily or unhappily?—fallen into a time when writings in defense of the truth of the Christian religion were, so to speak, fashionable. [...] Not for long; and I eagerly sought out each new writing *against* religion with just as much eagerness and gave it the patient and impartial hearing that I believed was due only to writings in favor of religion. So it remained for quite some time. I was torn from one side to the other; none satisfied me entirely. [...] The more one tried to prove Christianity to me, the more doubtful I became. The more someone else tried to completely trample it down and triumph over it, the more inclined I felt to at least uphold it in my heart.[43]

---

40 Heinrich Friedrich Diez, Ueber Juden [1783], in: *Frühe Schriften (1772–1784)*, ed. Manfred Voigts, Würzburg: Königshausen & Neumann 2010, 305–20, at 306. For an introduction, see Christoph Rauch and Gideon Stiening, eds., *Heinrich Friedrich von Diez (1751–1817). Freidenker – Diplomat – Orientkenner*, Berlin: de Gruyter 2020 and Manfred Voigts, Heinrich Friedrich Diez (1751–1817). Kanzleydirektor, Freygeist und Freund der Juden, in: Faber and Wehinger, eds., *Aufklärung in Geschichte und Gegenwart*, 175–96.
41 Diez, Ueber die bürgerliche Verbesserung der Juden [1783], in: *Frühe Schriften (1772–1784)*, 393–405, at 398.
42 Christoph Martin Wieland, letter to Julie Bondeli, in: *Sämmtliche Werke*, ed. Johann Gottfried Gruber, Leipzig: Göschen 1827, vol. 51, 403–423. See also Jutta Heinz, Christoph Martin Wieland, in: Hofmann, ed., *Aufklärung*, 91–105, at 94.
43 Gotthold Ephraim Lessing, *Werke. Vollständige Ausgabe in 25 Teilen*, ed. Julius Petersen and Waldemar von Olshausen, reprint Hildesheim und New York 1970, 312, quoted in Gotthold Ephraim Lessing, *Nathan der Weise. Ein dramatisches Gedicht in fünf Aufzügen*, ed. Thorsten Krause, Stuttgart: Reclam 2015, 187.

Lessing mentions elements of an enlarged mode of thinking here: openness to granting "impartial hearing" to all positions, a healthy skeptical attitude, and a willingness to postpone one's judgment for a long time. In the end, there is a hint of a solution: the religion of the heart (as also advocated by Rousseau), distinct from positive religions, and natural religion, but also distinct from skepticism, agnosticism, or atheism.[44]

Systematic reflections on a change of perspective and the enlarged way of thinking can be found in the works of various authors, including Adam Smith. In his *The Theory of Moral Sentiments* (1759), he wrote, "We endeavor to examine our own conduct as we imagine any other fair and impartial spectator would examine it."[45] Smith identifies two factors crucial to the ability to put oneself in another's position. First, it is based on imagination, and second, it relies on reflexive sympathy, which already involves cognitive normative evaluation.[46] As empathic and rational beings, we possess the ability to judge others. Consequently, we can also judge ourselves, understanding that our fellow human beings do the same. "We suppose ourselves the spectators of our own behavior and endeavor to imagine what effect it would produce upon us in this light. This is the only looking glass by which we can, in some measure, with the eyes of other people, scrutinize the propriety of our own conduct."[47] We can distance ourselves from our own perspective, even seeing our own biases and prejudices "as in a mirror." Paradoxically, it is often others, in whom we frequently observe these biases and prejudices, who assist us in this process. By doing so, we take on the role of the spectator. General reflective ability and the capacity for self-distancing ensure that we learn not only to relativize our own perspective but also that of others. Now, the perspectives of others can be diverse and contradictory, necessitating a standard by which to assess them. For Smith, this standard is one's conscience, serving as an instance of impartiality and reciprocity.[48] The impartial observer is thus capable of forming generalized maxims or principles. This overcomes relativism and

---

44 Gotthold Ephraim Lessing, *Werke und Briefe*, vol. 10, 626 and Robertson, *The Enlightenment. The Pursuit of Happiness*, 213.
45 Smith, *The Theory of Moral Sentiments*, III.1.2., 129. See also the analyses of David Daiches Raphael, *The Impartial Spectator. Adam Smith's Moral Philosophy*, Oxford: Oxford University Press 2007, Ballestrem, *Adam Smith* and Lloyd, *Enlightenment Shadows*, 81–110. The following passages are based on my article Die Denkungsart des Friedens. Ein vergessenes Erbe der Aufklärung, in: Clemens Sedmak, ed., *Frieden: Vom Wert der Koexistenz*, Darmstadt: Wissenschaftliche Buchgesellschaft 2016, 63–78, at 69–70.
46 See Ballestrem, *Adam Smith*, 66.
47 Smith, *Moral Sentiments*, III.1.5, 131.
48 Smith, *Moral Sentiments*, I.3.3.26, 170, I.3.3.28, 171, I.3.4.4, 183.

3.2 Change of perspective, the enlarged way of thinking, and a skeptical attitude — 87

perspectivism, resulting in moral judgments that can at least lay claim to intersubjectivity or general agreement.

Kant elaborated on these reflections, using the concepts of "common sense (*Gemeinsinn*)" or *sensus communis* and "the enlarged way of thinking." Central to these concepts is the ability to transcend the "subjective private conditions" of one's own judgment and to "think in the place of others" (see also section 5.3 below).[49] In a previous section, I cited Kant's famous definition of enlightenment: "Have courage to make use of your *own* understanding! is thus the motto of enlightenment" (1.1, conception no. 5). In another brief essay, Kant clarified what he meant by "thinking for oneself." It differs from the mere accumulation of knowledge, which may not be self-critical and not be reflected upon in debates with others. Making use of one's own reason, on the other hand, "means no more than to ask oneself, whenever one is supposed to assume something, whether one could find it feasible to make the ground or the rule on which one assumes it into a universal principle for the use of reason."[50] Enlightenment is education for self-reflection. This can take place individually or in exchange with others. As in ethics, it revolves around the principle of generalization.

In his systematic writings Kant analyses a sustainable "transformation" or "change" of thinking, as well as an expanded way of thinking. Examples include the so-called "Copernican revolution" in the *Critique of Pure Reason* or the human being who changes her or his moral disposition and way of thinking, initiating a moral revolution.[51] An example relating to Kant's biography can be found in an unpublished reflection. For a long time, Kant was apparently the arrogant urban intellectual who despised "the rabble" because they "know nothing." Reading Rousseau led to a "revolution of his way of thinking." "Rousseau brought me around. This blinding superiority disappeared, I learned to honor human beings [...]".[52]

Many enlighteners saw reason (lower case "r", *not* capitalized) as a universal capacity or competence of humans that could, in principle, be attributed to each

---

[49] See, among others, Jan Heiser and Tanja Prieler, eds., *Die erweiterte Denkungsart. Pädagogische, gesellschaftspolitische und interkulturelle Konsequenzen der Gemeinsinnsmaxime*, Würzburg: Königshausen & Neumann 2017 and my own essays: Denkungsart des Friedens and Auf der Suche nach der eingeschränkten Denkungsart, in: Heiser and Prieler, eds., *Die erweiterte Denkungsart*, 35–52.
[50] Kant, What does it mean to orient oneself in thinking? [1786], in: *Werke*, vol. 8, 131–47, at 146 note.
[51] See, for example, Allen Wood, *Kant and Religion*, Cambridge: Cambridge University Press 2020, ch. 4 (The Change of Heart).
[52] Kant, *Werke*, vol. 20, 44.

Figure 10: Emil Doerstling (1859–1940), Lunch at Kant's house, 1892/93. Social gatherings and discussions facilitate a change of perspective and promote an enlarged mode of thinking.

human being, even to those with whom we do not agree. A systematic philosophical theory of the finite, universal, and indispensable capacity for reason in humans can be found in representatives of the German Enlightenment such as Christian Wolff, Georg Friedrich Meier (1718–1777), Johann Georg Heinrich Feder (1740–1821), Johann Heinrich Lambert (1728–1777), or Kant.[53] This even applies to the extreme case of a mental illness, Kant argues: "We can convince someone only on the basis of his own healthy understanding. If I deny this to him, then it is foolish to reason with him."[54] Reason is considered fallible, which is why it relies on help "from outside," on corrections by other (potentially) rational beings.

Reason was seen as indispensable because otherwise, people would remain confined to arbitrary subjectivity, and we would only exchange feelings that have abandoned any claim to truth (see also the arguments above 2.1 and 2.2). Reason is within the horizon of truth, which is not given but should be sought. Diderot put this as follows: "Skepticism is the first step toward truth." This implied the right to think for oneself and to think freely: "One can demand of me that I

---

53 Norbert Hinske, *Kant als Herausforderung an die Gegenwart*, Freiburg and Munich: Alber 1980, 31–66.
54 Kant, reflection 1578, in: *Werke*, vol. 16, 16.

seek truth, but not that I must find it."[55] Lessing chose the following metaphor: "If God held fast in his right hand the whole of truth and in his left hand only the ever-active quest for truth, albeit with the proviso that I should constantly and eternally err, and said to me: 'Choose!', I would humbly fall upon his left hand and say: 'Father, give! For pure truth is for you alone!'"[56]

3.3 Combating Fanaticism, Prejudices, Superstition, Enthusiasm, and Dogmatism

As previously mentioned, most Enlightenment thinkers were united in their fight against religious fanaticism, prejudice, superstition, enthusiasm, dogmatism, and narrow-mindedness (see 1.1, conception no. 3). Their criticism was usually not directed at religions *per se*, but rather at their perceived distortions. Montesquieu has the Persian Usbek write: "I admit that history is full of wars of religion; but on this point we must be very careful; it is not the multiplicity of religions that produced these wars, but the spirit of intolerance animating the religion that believed itself to be dominant. It is this spirit of proselytism that the Jews picked up from the Egyptians, and then passed on, like a common epidemic, to the Muslims, and the Christians."[57] Most enlighteners did not criticize religions but rather the "spirit of intolerance" and the "spirit of proselytism" (see also 5.1 and 5.2). Proselytism involves attempting, possibly with the help of manipulation and deception, to persuade other people to convert or join one's own religious community.

Most enlighteners found common ground in their fight against fanaticism and superstition. The term fanaticism had been primarily associated with religion since the Reformation.[58] Mainly enthusiasts and followers of sects such as the Quakers were seen as fanatics, who sought recognition for their personal inspirations and private revelations. In many cases, fanaticism, enthusiasm, and exces-

---

55 Translated in Andrew S. Curran, *Diderot and the Art of Thinking Freely*, New York: Other Press 2019, 73. The source is Denis Diderot, *Œuvres complètes*, Paris: Hermann, 1975 ff., vol. 2, 35 and 34. For an introduction to Diderot, see also Daniel Brewer, *The Discourse of Enlightenment in Eighteenth-Century France. Diderot and the Art of Philosophizing*, Cambridge: Cambridge University Press 2006.
56 Gotthold Ephraim Lessing, A rejoinder [1778], in: *Philosophical and Theological Writings*, translated and edited by H. B. Nisbet, Cambridge: Cambridge University Press 2005, 95–109, at 98.
57 Montesquieu, *Persian Letters*, 116–7.
58 See Robert Spaemann, Fanatisch, Fanatismus, in: Joachim Ritter and Karlfried Gründer, eds., *Historisches Wörterbuch der Philosophie*, Basel and Stuttgart: Schwabe 1972, vol. 2, column 904–8 for the following.

sive enthusiasm, or sentimentality had similar meanings. Some made distinctions. David Hume differentiated between "fanaticism," "superstition," and "enthusiasm," with the latter sometimes having a positive connotation. In the French Enlightenment, fanaticism was synonymous with blind belief. The *Encyclopédie* identified it with superstition. During the French Revolution, critics accused the Jacobins of political, ideological, or quasi-religious fanaticism, which finally detached the term from its religious context.

"The Enlightenment's struggle against superstition in the name of reason began in the name of (true) science and (true) faith, assuming their compatibility."[59] Often, belief—in line with Aristotelian virtue ethics—was seen as keeping the "golden mean" between superstition or gullibility on the one hand, and disbelief, or atheism on the other. The witch craze or belief in witches was one of the targets of Enlightenment criticism, as seen in the works of authors like Christian Thomasius. From the mid-18th century onwards, there were also voices that considered all faith a form of superstition. In return, a scientific worldview was at times also accused of being nothing more than superstition. Kant, for example, viewed the "complete subjugation of reason to *facta*" as a dangerous superstition. Most enlighteners were also united in their fight against prejudice. John Locke defined these as "false or doubtful positions, relied upon as unquestionable maxims."[60] People with prejudices were characterized by a specific attitude: they could not tolerate critical objections and were unwilling to examine arguments from a different perspective. The method of comprehensive doubt, as proposed by René Descartes, was meant to help rid oneself of prejudice. Over the course of the 18th century, the term became a fashionable and polemical concept. By the end of the Enlightenment era, nearly all conceivable variations of assessing and judging prejudices had been explored. Some spoke of "legitimate" prejudices that had societal benefits; they attempted to distinguish these from "illegitimate" prejudices. King Frederick II of Prussia ensured that the *Prussian Academy of Sciences* questioned the permissibility of deception of the public and the usefulness of errors and prejudices in 1780. At the opposite end of the spectrum was d'Holbach. In his essay *Essai sur les préjugés* (1770), he argued that prejudice was always harmful and claimed that it needed to be combated by philosophy as the champion of truth. He declared that "all religious and political opinions of humans" were nothing but prejudices. Here again, irreconcilable differences within

---

59 Werner Schneiders, Aberglaube, in: same, ed., *Lexikon der Aufklärung. Deutschland und Europa*, München: Beck 1995, 25–7, with sources. See also Martus, *Aufklärung*, 401.
60 Klaus Reisinger and Oliver R. Scholz, Vorurteil, in: Ritter and Gründer, Hrsg., *Historisches Wörterbuch der Philosophie*, vol. 11, columns 1251–63 with all references and the following quotations. See also Susan Rosa, Prejudice, in: Kors, *Encyclopedia*, vol. 3, 353–8.

Figure 11: Godefroy Engelmann, after a design, *Le dragon missionnaire*, 1686. The "new" mission under Louis XIV, aimed at converting Huguenot "heretics" to Catholicism: a soldier of the king, ironically resembling a Muslim, forces the Huguenot to confess his new faith at point-blank range: Louis XIV is cynically referred to as "the Great."

the Enlightenment movement were evident. D'Holbach's blanket suspicion of every religious and political opinion raised the question of whether there was still a distinction between prejudices, provisional judgments, hypotheses, and true statements. Moreover, if the suspicion is universal, why not apply it to d'Holbach's own position? Considering d'Holbach's attack on religion, some German enlighteners argued that accusing someone of being prejudiced could also be an example of prejudice.

Enthusiasm was generally viewed negatively during the European Enlightenment. Initially, it was associated with religious believers who claimed to have private revelations. Later, the term encompassed various aspects of irrational or seemingly arbitrary ideas. Locke claimed that religious enthusiasts were not willing to acknowledge evidence or arguments independent of their enthusiasm. "[T]his light they are so dazzled with is nothing but an *ignis fatuus* [will-o'-the-wisp], that leads them constantly round in this circle: It is a revelation, because they firmly believe it; and they believe it, because it is a revelation."[61] Enthusiasts, it was asserted, reject any logical, or experience-based verification of their beliefs. Their thinking is seen as circular and dogmatic. Kant warned against "enthusiastic religious delusion," which meant the "moral death of reason without which there can be no religion."[62] According to Kant, enthusiasm is the presumption of wanting to perceive and know something beyond the limits of sensory perception and ignoring the voice of reason, even though thoughts without content are empty. Using the same argument, in the 1780s Mendelssohn lamented the increasing tendency of enthusiastic people to believe in things "that, by their nature, cannot fall under the senses."[63] Similar considerations can be found in Friedrich Gedicke, who recommended ridicule, and satire as a countermeasure. Kant believed that anyone who always adheres to the principle of thinking for themselves would automatically rid themselves of superstition and enthusiasm, "even if he falls far short of having the information to refute them on objective grounds."[64] The quantity of knowledge is not important here. What matters is the ability to comprehend a thought or concept with the help of one's own reason. This is not possible in the case of superstition or enthusiasm.

There were also some enlighteners who expressed somewhat favorable or positive views on enthusiasm. Christoph Martin Wieland believed that the widespread criticism of enthusiasm should be questioned. "Are the efforts of cold-blooded philosophers and Lucianic spirits against what they call enthusiasm and enthusiasm causing more harm than good?" Lessing responded to this question posed in public in 1776, stating that the "enthusiasm of speculation" could also advance philosophy. Even the chiliasm of the Middle Ages had "correct insights into the future."[65]

The terms enthusiasm and fanaticism had roughly the same meaning in England and Germany in the 1700s. It was only later that a more precise differentia-

---

61 Locke, *Essay Concerning Human Understanding*, ch. 19.
62 Winfried Schröder, Schwärmerei, in: Schneiders, ed. *Lexikon der Aufklärung*, 372–3, same, Schwärmerei, in: Ritter and Gründer, ed., *Historisches Wörterbuch der Philosophie*, vol. 8, Immanuel Kant, *Religion within the boundaries of mere reason* [1793], in: Werke, vol. 6, 1–202, at 175.
63 Moses Mendelssohn, *Morning Hours: Lectures on God's Existence* [1785], transl. Daniel Dahlstrom and Corey Dyck, Dordrecht: Springer 2011, 32.
64 Kant, What does it mean to orient oneself in thinking? vol. 8, 146 note.
65 Quoted in Schröder, Schwärmerei, in: Ritter and Gründer, ed., *Historisches Wörterbuch der Philosophie*, vol. 8, column 1480. Lucianic refers to the Syrian satirist Lucian of Samosata (125–180).

3.3 Combating Fanaticism, Prejudices, Superstition, Enthusiasm, and Dogmatism — 93

Figure 12: T. Cook, *A credulous congregation listening to a sermon by a fiery preacher*, engraving after W. Hogarth, 1798. A Church as a Madhouse: "Credulity, Superstition, and Fanaticism. A Medley." The caption, following the first letter of John (1 John 4:1), warns against "false prophets." Evidently, a Muslim (most likely a Turk) wearing a turban is seen looking through a window in amazement at the chaotic scene.

tion was made.[66] Locke rejected enthusiasm as a pseudo-knowledge of immediate revelations, arguing that there could be no genuine experience in this sense. Shaftesbury, in his *A Letter Concerning Enthusiasm* (1708), rejected dogmatic enthusiasm but praised the "noble enthusiasm" as a fervor for the order of nature and virtue.[67] Hume made a distinction between "enthusiasm" and superstition but noted a proximity to political and religious fanaticism. In the German-speaking world, enthusiasm was gradually revalued, especially within the Romantic movement.

Rousseau used the term against scientific or secular currents in the Enlightenment (see 1.1, conceptions no. 4 and 7), because he held that they deified reason and science while remaining morally indifferent. Religious movements of the 18th century, such as the Pietists, the Bohemian Brethren, or the Methodists, also opposed what they saw as the cold rationalism of the Enlightenment and emphasized personal, emotional religiosity, though without the prophetic and ecstatic elements seen in groups like the Camisards. In a familiar fashion, Kant made some distinctions. He defined "genuine enthusiasm" as "passionate participation in the good" and distinguished it from fanaticism, because real enthusiasm "always moves only toward what is ideal and, indeed, to what is purely moral, such as the concept of right." In doing so, Kant brought enthusiasm closer to the feeling of the sublime and to morality.[68]

In the battle against superstition, prejudice, enthusiasm, dogmatism, fanaticism, or fantasies, many enlighteners wanted to draw a line between a collectively shared realm of experience and personal moods and inspirations. The issue was not personal convictions in and of themselves, but the belief that these might not correspond to facts. In general terms, the problem lies in mistaking a subjective notion for something objective. This does not mean that an uncritical cult of the factual must be embraced. As we have seen, some enlighteners already saw the overemphasis on science as a new form of superstition, including thinkers like Thomasius, Rousseau, and Kant (see end of 2.3). In this context, as mentioned earlier, Kant defined a form of superstition as "the complete subjection of reason to facts."[69] However, it remains sensible and necessary to maintain a clear separa-

---

[66] For the following, see Astrid von der Lühe, Fanatismus, in: Schneiders, ed., *Lexikon der Aufklärung*, 116–8; Enthusiasmus, in: Schneiders, *Lexikon*, 97–99; A. Müller, Enthusiasmus, in: Ritter and Gründer, ed., *Historisches Wörterbuch der Philosophie*, vol. 2, column 525–8, Michael Heyd, Enthusiasm, in: Alan Charles Kors, ed., *Encyclopedia of the Enlightenment*, 4 vols., Oxford and New York: Oxford University Press 2003, vol. 2, 1–7.
[67] Shaftesbury, A Letter Concerning Enthusiasm, 28.
[68] Immanuel Kant, The Conflict of the Faculties [1798], in: *Werke*, vol. 7, 1–116, at 86.
[69] Kant, What does it mean to orient oneself in thinking? vol. 8, 145.

tion between the world of sensory experiences and the realm of the metaphysical and the religious (see also Chapter 5).

3.4 Contemporary Context: Jihadists, Fake News, and Filter Bubbles

A look at contemporary discourses demonstrates that certain theories of some enlighteners have remained relevant to this day, such as the separation between the world of sensory experiences and the realm of the metaphysical and religious, or the distinction between knowledge and belief. Here are two interesting examples.

My first example concerns young jihadists who, since the beginning of this century, have made headlines with acts of terrorism, suicide bombings, rapes, beheadings, and other atrocities. The causes of this violence are diverse (see 2.4), but it can be surmised that the very attitudes and beliefs so many European Enlighteners wrote against play a role: religious fanaticism, prejudice, superstition, and dogmatic worldviews. Anthropologist Scott Atran, who has conducted field studies on jihadists and Islamic terrorists, has observed a disturbing lack of religious education among them, even though they are often born-again Muslims.[70] The religious fanatic sanctifies politics and seeks to "establish" the Kingdom of Allah on Earth through violence, also guided by understanding (*Verstand*) or prudence, in an effort to "save" the world. The solution proposed by representatives of reformist Islam and moderate movements in such cases is reminiscent of the European Enlightenment: They propose and advocate more religious, moral, and cognitive education or formation (*Bildung*).

In 2014, Erhan A., a 22-year-old from Germany, and sympathetic to the Islamic State founded by Abu Musab al-Zarquawi in 1999, was interviewed as he contemplated joining the Syrian civil war as a jihadist. His attitude and frame of mind may be typical of many like-minded individuals. In the interview, he explained his simplistic religious worldview, where all people outside his own group are wrong, immoral, and bound for hell—including and especially other Muslims, because, as he put it, "They just don't practice Islam correctly, they pray in the

---

[70] Scott Atran, ISIS is a revolution. All world-altering revolutions are born in danger and death, brotherhood and joy. How can this one be stopped? (2015), https://aeon.co/essays/why-isis-has-the-potential-to-be-a-world-altering-revolution (last accessed October 2, 2025); *Talking to the Enemy. Faith, Brotherhood, and the (Un)Making of Terrorists*, New York: Harper Collins 2010. See also Cavallar, *Islam, Aufklärung und Moderne*, ch. 5.

wrong way, and they don't reject democracy."⁷¹ Being rejected by others—even including devout parents—only reinforces the worldview of these fanatics. Self-critically questioning their own position is out of the question, and they only interact with like-minded individuals who validate and strengthen their ideology. This includes conspiracy theories such as the claim that "the Americans themselves" carried out the 9/11 attacks. The critical search for truth is replaced by a naive belief that they already possess the truth: "Islam is the only true religion. Unfortunately, there is not a single genuine Islamic state anywhere in the world." Violence is justified because it serves a "good cause," and Muslims are obliged to "blindly" follow Allah's laws. These laws are often extracted from the Quran in a straightforward, do-it-yourself manner, without an understanding of hermeneutics, issues of text interpretation, or the traditions of Quranic exegesis. Erhan A. is unable to see even obvious contradictions. "A believer must not kill another believer" (Quran, 4:92) is clearly stated in the Quran. Nonetheless, Erhan is fine with the Islamic State killing other Muslims in the name of the "good cause." In other cases, there is a strict, literal interpretation of the Quran, even if knowledge here is scant. For instance, Erhan justifies beheading IS opponents with a simple "I think it's stated in the Quran *somewhere*."

Reading this or similar interviews or texts leads to the frustrating realization that enlightenment (also with a capital "E", see concept no. 1, conceptions no. 3, 5, and 6) can be compared to an endless uphill struggle against a multi-headed hydra. Prejudice, partial, or complete ignorance, stupidity, superstition, fanaticism, and dogmatism seem to grow "naturally" with each new generation. As Werner Schneiders put it, the goal of enlightenment then boils down to the minimalist attempt to "help humans not to abandon their capacity for rational thinking."⁷²

My second example is perhaps even more sobering. While one could argue that many jihadists belong to societies and cultures that still have not fully mastered processes of modernization and Enlightenment, this certainly does not apply to the country that, according to a widespread narrative, has already realized the best aspects of the Enlightenment (see below 4.3). One can only wonder how a President of the USA, namely Donald Trump (president 2017–2021, reelected 2024), has handled facts, truth, and science. Shamelessly, facts are reinterpret-

---

71 Marie Delhaes and Frederik Obermaier, Ich glaub, das steht irgendwo im Koran. Auch aus Deutschland ziehen junge Menschen für die Terrormiliz IS in den Krieg. Warum? Wir haben mit einem von ihnen gesprochen, *Süddeutsche Zeitung Magazin*, Heft 40, 2014, https://sz-magazin.sueddeutsche.de/politik/ich-glaub-das-steht-irgendwo-im-koran-80691 (last accessed October 2, 2025). The following quotations are taken from this interview.
72 Schneiders, *Hoffnung auf Vernunft*, 179.

ed, denied, or simply invented, for example, a supposed terrorist attack in Sweden in February 2017.[73] These baseless claims are then echoed by parts of the population and media outlets that support the president's views, prioritizing propaganda, and manipulation over critical news. Trump himself revels in repeated attacks on the "liberal press," accusing them without justification of disseminating fake news. The long-term consequences are dire. Too many people live in their echo chambers and filter bubbles, further disconnecting from reality. Relevant social media platforms fill their heads with simplistic ideologies and worldviews, framed in black-and-white templates with adversaries, selective perception, and so-called "alternative facts" (Kellyanne Conway), cultivating a "tunnel vision" that reinforces existing prejudices and stereotypes. Some of these accusations also apply to left-wingers, inside, and outside the US.[74] German essayist Carolin Emcke has warned of this digital brutalization and its detrimental societal effects:

> In the digital realms, we have echo chambers where hatred finds an echo. This includes, as we know, a technically controlled dynamic of escalation on platforms like Facebook or Twitter. The shared public sphere is shrinking. The places where we talk about how we want to live, what kind of society we desire, have become almost invisible.[75]

Throughout the 18th century, under the influence of enlighteners, a public sphere, and a new public culture emerged in Europe, characterized by phenomena such as the revolution of print, public debate culture, a veritable "reading frenzy" among the public, reading societies, the invention of the intellectual, and popular Enlightenment.[76] This public sphere now appears to be disintegrating or dissolving into sectarian, isolated groups marked by a loss of connection to reality and by radical constructivism according to the motto of "everyone creates their own re-

---

[73] https://www.theguardian.com/us-news/2017/feb/19/trumps-sweden-comment-referred-to-rising-white-house-says (last accessed October 2, 2025); https://www.theguardian.com/commentisfree/2017/feb/20/sweden-donald-trump-crime-muslim-immigrants (last accessed October 2, 2025); https://www.welt.de/politik/ausland/article162369453/Schwedische-Regierung-kontert-Trump-mit-harten-Fakten.html (last accessed October 2, 2025).
[74] René Pfister, *Ein falsches Wort. Wie eine neue linke Ideologie aus Amerika unsere Meinungsfreiheit bedroht*, 3rd ed., München: Deutsche Verlags-Anstalt 2022, Alexander Somek, *Moral als Bosheit. Rechtsphilosophische Studien*, Tübingen: Mohr Siebeck 2021, and Helen Pluckrose and James Lindsay, *Cynical Theories. How Activist Scholarship Made Everything about Race, Gender, and Identity – and Why This Harms Everybody*, Durham: Pitchstone Publishing 2020.
[75] Bert Rebhandl, Carolin Emcke: Nicht kleinkriegen lassen vom Hass, *Der Standard*, October 22, 2016, Album A 4.
[76] See the summary in Meyer, *Die Epoche der Aufklärung*, 111–37 with further references.

ality". Ivanka Trump, daughter of US President Donald Trump, posted a tweet in 2013 with a purported quote from Albert Einstein: "If the facts don't fit the theory, change the facts." Einstein never made this claim.[77] Perhaps even more crucial is what Ms. Trump apparently did not understand: the statement is either nonsense or ironic. If ironic, it makes fun of dogmatists who do not form their theories based on perceptions and facts.

What is missing? In extreme cases, there are no traces of anything that can be understood as Enlightenment or enlightenment: enlightenment as a process of critical thinking, Enlightenment through science, and so on. What is missing is at least the attempt to think for oneself and to think coherently (to "think in harmony with oneself"). Irony is lacking, as well as expanded ways of thinking, the consideration of other perspectives and positions, a self-critical reflection on one's own prejudices and dogmatic assumptions, and one's own superstitions. What is missing is a public sphere in which people criticize each other and thereby help each other, as Carolin Emcke has stated:

> There is criticism that is good and helpful because it exposes weaknesses or blind spots in one's own argumentation. You read it and think, 'Oh, I haven't thought about it that way.' And then there is resentment and contempt. Sometimes someone writes: 'People like you are degenerate.' In this case, homosexuals are meant, but often intellectuals in general are implied. The increase in anti-intellectual resentment is disconcerting.[78]

Most enlighteners might have agreed with the statement that "minds are like parachutes; they only function when they are open" (James Dewar). However, this does not mean that truth is always a matter of perspective. Enlightenment should not be equated with indifference, being without a standpoint, or cultural or moral relativism (see 2.3 and 4.2). Otherwise, the following sarcastic remark would also apply to the enlighteners: "They have become so open-minded that their brains are falling out."[79]

---

[77] https://www.ok-magazin.de/people/news/ivanka-trump-falsches-einstein-zitat-48215.html (accessed August 2, 2017); https://www.merkur.de/politik/ivanka-trump-zitierte-einstein-und-blamiert-sich-damit-voellig-zr-8520050.html (last accessed October 2, 2025).

[78] Rebhandl, Carolin Emcke. Yet the Enlightenment is a giddy thing: After the 2024 elections to the European Parliament, Emcke suggested that German democracy should be defended, but the format of pro-con debates should be avoided (she calls it "bullshit"). See Bernd Stegemann, Predigerin der einzigen Wahrheit, June 7, 2024, https://www.cicero.de/kultur/republica-aufritt-von-carolin-emcke-predigerin-der-einzigen-wahrheit (last accessed October 2, 2025); https://www.youtube.com/watch?v=IEbWnXIexNk, after min. 32 (last accessed October 2, 2025).

[79] Do Not Be So Open-Minded That Your Brains Fall Out – Quote Investigator®, April 13, 2014, https://quoteinvestigator.com/2014/04/13/open-mind/ (last accessed October 2, 2025), the quote going back to Walter Kotschnig in 1940.

Chapter 4
Is there a common language of morality? Morality, ethics and law

> No culture on Earth, including that of modern Europe, enjoys more privileged access to rationality than any other.
> —Johann Heinrich Gottlob von Justi[1]

In a lecture on ethics given during the interwar period, Sigmund Freud posed the following question to his audience: "Imagine, gentlemen, you're walking down Kärntner street, and you find ten thousand schillings. I guarantee that no one has seen you pick it up. If you turn it in, you won't receive a finder's fee. How do you decide? Do you take the money to the police—or do you keep it?" Of the twelve students, one wanted to turn in the money, while the others preferred to keep it. For the honest finder, Freud had kind words: "Congratulations on your morality—you fool!"[2]

That sum equals roughly €40,000 today (2024). Honesty as stupidity: This anecdote also serves as a historical document, illustrating the critique of conventional morals in a modern society. Is honesty truly a virtue? Is selflessness a form of foolishness? Is there a distinction between prudence, opportunism, and morality? Is one's conscience autonomous, meaning self-legislated, or heteronomous, derived from something else? Freud himself provided a clear answer to this last question: conscience—which he called the "Superego"—is said to be nothing more than the product of the Oedipus complex. In the Oedipal situation, the son submits to the authority of the father out of fear of castration and internalizes the norms and values of the father, thereby forming the conscience.[3] According to Freud, moral autonomy or self-legislation is an illusion.

Freud's anecdote addressed an age-old moral philosophical problem summarized under the term "Ring of Gyges." The response of most Sophists was like Freud's: Those who adhere to moral principles like impartiality, compassion, selflessness, and universality are naive.[4] Moral relativism and cunning triumphed

---

[1] Quoted in Osterhammel, *Unfabling the East*, 80.
[2] Georg Markus, *Schlag nach bei Markus. Österreich in seinen besten Geschichten und Anekdoten*, 3rd edition, Wien: Amalthea 2011, 179.
[3] Sigmund Freud, *Gesammelte Werke*, 3. Aufl., Frankfurt am Main: Fischer 1963, vol. 9, 188.
[4] Max Klopfer, *Ethik-Klassiker von Platon bis John Stuart Mill. Ein Lehr- und Studienbuch*, Stuttgart: Kohlhammer 2008, 41–44 and Michaela Masek, *Geschichte der antiken Philosophie*, Wien: Facultas 2011, 108–12.

over moral universalism. Freud could see himself as a thinker in the tradition of the Enlightenment, by criticizing and deconstructing supposed prejudices, stereotypes, and traditions, and replacing them with science (see 1.1, conception no. 4). This is the very point where some critics of "the European Enlightenment" start their attacks. Martin Heidegger, for instance, accused this Enlightenment of placing humans at the center and forgetting about 'being' (*Sein*). A one-sided, knowledge-oriented approach, and anthropocentrism, according to Heidegger, contributed to the rise of nihilism in the present.[5]

Nihilistic tendencies in the sense of epistemological and moral relativism are one strong current of contemporary cultures. In a typical Internet post, it is claimed:

> Good and evil are arbitrary human constructs that have been instilled in people as a standard through education and laws. Just as there is no absolute truth, there is no absolute morality. It is a societal consensus created through education and laws. Through its moral rules, humanity aims to distinguish itself from apes. So far, it has done so very poorly. Most often, human morality ends up in human abysses. To justify the infallibility of its morality, humanity then invents gods and declares its own morality to be given by God to bestow it with the aura of absolute truth, to defend it as unassailable, even if it requires taking up arms. Then, murder is no longer murder but morality.[6]

The text contains a range of spurious claims. The implied causal assumptions can all be dismissed as unfounded generalizations without evidence (see 3.3 and 3.4). Did "humanity" truly invent morality to distinguish itself from apes? Are moral norms exclusively the product of education and societal pressure? Psychological speculation—sometimes referred to as "psychobabble"—triumphs over systematic philosophizing, which delineates the limits of our knowledge. The text does not differentiate between customs, traditions, morals, morality, and moral principles. Finally, it contains performative self-contradictions (see the beginning of 2.1). For the author, there is no "absolute truth," yet he claims true knowledge about the underlying motives of the human species. The author asserts that universal ("absolute") morality is an illusion, yet he refers to this very morality, as in the last

---

5 The debate between Heidegger and Ernst Cassirer (who defended the Enlightenment) in Davos in 1929 became famous. See Martin Heidegger, *Kant und das Problem der Metaphysik* [1929], in: *Gesamtausgabe*, vol. 3, ed. F. W. von Herrmann, Frankfurt am Main: Vittorio Klostermann 1991, 274–96, Ferrone, *Enlightenment*, 43–7 as well as Thomas Mertens, Am Ausgang des Neukantianismus: Cassirer und Heidegger in Davos 1929, in: Robert Alexy, ed., *Neukantianismus und Rechtsphilosophie*, Nomos: Baden-Baden 2002, 523–40.

6 Jürgen Vogel, Moral ist ein willkürliches Menschenkonstrukt, August 2, 2016, https://www.faz.net/aktuell/feuilleton/buecher/sachbuch/philosophin-bettina-stangneth-ueber-boeses-denken-14363243.html (last accessed October 2, 2025).

sentence, making a clear distinction between murder and morality and the implicit claim that murder is *not* morally acceptable, as opposed to legitimate self-defense, for example. In other words, the text is a collection of metaphysical claims that are not justified but simply asserted as true and valid. There is no awareness that these required justifications are not only extremely difficult but might not even be possible. The text is probably symptomatic of a prevailing *zeitgeist* that is apparently widespread but largely ignorant of philosophical problems.

4.1 Foundations of Morality in the Age of Enlightenment

Most enlighteners were convinced of the universality and objectivity of norms and morality. They did not deny, in the words of Usbek in the *Persian Letters*, that people can be unjust "because it is in their interest, and they prefer their self-interest to the benefit of others." However, most enlighteners probably understood that any criticism of institutions, injustices, character flaws, and errors always presupposes a standard of what is morally right and good. That is why Usbek is also convinced "that justice is eternal, and independent of human conventions." He is certain that "deep in the hearts of all men lies a principle which fights on our behalf."[7] Montesquieu, Shaftesbury, Rousseau, Kant, and others referred to this inner compass, sometimes in line with tradition, as virtue, the consciousness of natural justice, moral sense, or conscience. Many enlighteners distinguished between a kind of instinctive conscience and a cultivated or reflective conscience which would be the result of moral education or formation.[8]

Enlighteners were familiar with the argument that moral norms and conscience could be relative, in the sense that they may not be universally valid and objective but have their roots in historical, personal, cultural, or social circumstances that are purely coincidental. Even before the Enlightenment, intellectuals had grappled with forms of moral relativism. The discovery of new non-European cultures, such as through contacts with China via Jesuit missionaries, further exacerbated this philosophical problem.

There are several possible reasons why most enlighteners never endorsed full-blown moral relativism. One reason might have been that they sometimes per-

---

7 Montesquieu, *Persian Letters*, 114.
8 For Montesquieu, see Michael Hereth, *Montesquieu zur Einführung*, Hamburg: Junius 1995, 64–6 and 154–8. See also Catherine Volpilhac-Auger, *Montesquieu: Let There Be Enlightenment*, transl. by Philip Stewart, Cambridge: Cambridge University Press 2022, 44, 207 and 219 and Tricoire, *Die Aufklärung*, 119–20. Tricoire claims that this conception of conscience can be traced back to scholastic moral philosophy.

sonally experienced blatant injustice. Enlighteners often had to contend with the traditional social hierarchy of the *ancien régime*, as well as with societal and religious prejudices. Religious minorities were often subject to severe discrimination. A relatively mild injustice was experienced by Voltaire, who, as a commoner, had adopted the "de" in his name in 1726. Chevalier Guy Auguste de Rohan-Chabot (1683–1760) wanted to teach the popular poet and social climber a lesson, so he had some ruffians beat him with sticks at night. To the amusement of those present, Rohan is said to have cynically shouted, "Don't hit his head; something good may come out of it yet!"[9] Voltaire was humiliated, sought revenge, but the privileges of the nobility were greater than his anger. Noble friends refused to help Voltaire, and Rohan eventually obtained a royal warrant or *lettre de cachet* that sent Voltaire to the Bastille without trial, and then into exile in Great Britain.

The discourses on tolerance made by many enlighteners often drew from other concrete experiences of injustice. Aristocratic and royal arbitrariness in the case of Voltaire was relatively mild compared to the Calas case and other judicial murders of the time. Jean Calas (1698–1762) was a French Protestant and merchant whose eldest son had hanged himself out of despair. Although the son had completed a law degree, he had not been allowed to take the final exam because he did not belong to the Catholic faith: the first injustice. Father Calas was then accused of having strangled his own son, supposedly because he was planning to convert to Catholicism. Jean Calas was tortured, sentenced to death, and executed in a gruesome manner: the second injustice. Voltaire and others launched a public campaign for the posthumous rehabilitation of Jean Calas. Part of Voltaire's campaign was his work *Traité sur la tolérance* (1763). The case was eventually reopened, King Louis XIV annulled the sentence, and Calas was posthumously exonerated.

Olympe de Gouges experienced other forms of injustice, namely the discrimination against illegitimate children, against women in general, and the injustice of slavery. Her critique was inspired by her awareness of universal moral principles. In her *Réflexions sur les hommes nègres* (1788), de Gouges wrote that many of her contemporaries saw Africans as "brutes, cursed by Heaven. As I grew up, I clearly realized that it was force and prejudice that had condemned them to that horrible slavery, in which Nature plays no role, and for which the unjust and powerful interests of Whites are alone responsible". She asked, "When will we turn our attention to changing [their dreadful lot], or at least to easing it? I know nothing about the Politics of Governments; but they are fair. Now the

---

9 Vinaire's Blog. Where Eastern thought meets Western technology, VOLTAIRE: Paris: Oedipe | Vinaire's Blog, October 15, 2023, and also quoted in Geier, *Aufklärung*, 107.

Figure 13: Daniel Nikolaus Chodowiecki (1726–1801), *Jean Calas bids farewell to his family*, engraving, 1885. Calas is seated in the center of the dungeon, comforting his children. His desperate wife is in the back on the right in a wicker chair. The 64-year-old was broken on the wheel and then burned at the stake. Voltaire made sure that the affair became known throughout Europe.

Law of Nature was never more apparent in them. People are equal everywhere" (see also 4.4 below).[10]

Atrocities of the religious wars prior to the European Enlightenment were preserved in collective memories and contributed to the rise of Enlightenment ideas. Among them was the St Bartholomew massacre in 1572, the sack of Magdeburg during the Thirty Years War, and the atrocities committed by the troops of Oliver Cromwell in the town of Drogheda in Ireland in 1649.[11] By the end of the

---

[10] Olympe de Gouges, Reflections on Negroes (1788), in: Hilda L. Smith and Berenice A. Carroll, eds., *Women's Political and Social Thought. An Anthology*, Bloomington, Indiana: Indiana State University Press 2000, 133–4, at 133.

[11] See Robertson, *The Enlightenment. The Pursuit of Happiness*, 85–94. Tricoire, *Die Aufklärung*, 41, 99–129 and 247 doubts that the religious wars played a major role. He claims that the Enlightenment was "invented" when philosophers looked for answers to disputes in the field of moral theology among Christian denominations.

17th century, early enlighteners in the German-speaking territories of the *Holy Roman Empire* were speaking out against the witch hunts and witch trials. Among them was Thomasius. Points of criticism included the use of torture, or the shaky evidence that harm had been caused by alleged witches. Debates on this issue among skeptics (they were not always enlighteners) and their opponents extended throughout the entire 18th century and ended relatively late in the so-called "Bavarian Witch War" (1766–1770).[12]

Other minority groups in early modern Europe also experienced injustices, including the Huguenots in France after the 1680s when the protections granted by the Edict of Nantes gradually disappeared (see also 4.3), Jews all over Europe, and the dissenters in England. The Jewish Enlightener Moses Mendelssohn is a case in point. As a Jew, he was only allowed to enter Berlin through a single gate. For the most part, basic civil rights were denied to him. Mendelssohn also spoke out against internal Jewish intolerance, making use of the argument that Jews themselves were constantly confronted with Christian intolerance. This gave them an additional reason to be more mindful of possible injustices.

> Alas, my brothers! Up to now you have felt the oppressive yoke of intolerance all too harshly and perhaps believed yourselves to have found a kind of satisfaction in having granted to you the power to press an equally harsh yoke down on your subordinates! Revenge seeks an object, and if it can do no harm to others, then it gnaws at its own flesh. [...] Love, and you will be loved![13]

In the field of ethics and moral philosophy, the European Enlightenment surprises with a multitude of positions.[14] Even classifications or categorizations are difficult. Adam Smith, in his *Theory of Moral Sentiments*, grappled with the same problem, eventually distinguishing between three basic ethical theories: either self-love, sentiment/feeling or reason were the crucial faculties of mind that recommended virtue.[15] There were, among others, Christian-oriented theonomous ethics, virtue ethics, Kantian autonomous ethics, conscience ethics, ethics of compas-

---

12 Günter Jerouschek, Hexenverfolgung/Hexenprozesse, in: Schneiders, ed., *Lexikon der Aufklärung*, 178–9 and Robertson, *The Enlightenment. The Pursuit of Happiness*, 14–21.
13 Moses Mendelssohn, From the Preface to *Vindiciae Judaeorum* (1782), in: *Writings on Judaism, Christianity, and the Bible*, ed. by Michah Gottlieb, Waltham, Massachusetts: Brandeis University Press 2011, 40–52, at 52.
14 See Michael Albrecht, Ethik/Moralphilosophie, in: Schneiders, ed., *Lexikon der Aufklärung*, 112–4, David Fate Norton and Manfred Kuehn, The Foundations of Morality, in: Haakonssen, *The Cambridge History of Eighteenth-Century Philosophy*, 939–86, and Ulrich Dierse, Tugend, in: Haakonssen, *The Cambridge History of Eighteenth-Century Philosophy*, 415–8.
15 Smith, *Theory of Moral Sentiments*, VII.iii.2.

sion, and ethics of sentiment. There were followers of the "British egoists" Thomas Hobbes (1588–1679) and Bernard de Mandeville, and the followers of Christian Wolff. There was Hume's historically informed theory of enlightened self-interest. Initially, approaches with longer traditions were continued, including forms of religious ethics, natural law, and virtue ethics. Gellert, for instance, advocated an interesting form of religious ethics. He was skeptical of reason and accused defenders of philosophy and of moral autonomy of thinking in an unhistorical manner. "Through the instruction we receive from youth in the truths of religion, our reason makes them its own without us knowing it. We find them in our memory when we begin to think for ourselves, and so we think that we owe them solely to the light of reason."[16] Gellert's argument is an interesting combination of "tradition and modernity." The defense of Christian revelation and ethics is traditional, while the reference to a form of the unconscious and the emphasis on historically developed forms of consciousness are modern. He argues that the defenders of autonomous morality or natural religion overlook how much the enlighteners still draw from a resource provided by the Christian tradition. Christian Wolff's ethics, on the other hand, were clearly rationalist and influenced the discussion in Germany: human reason was capable of distinguishing between good and evil. The goal of all actions was the perfection of one's own self and finding comprehensive happiness.

According to Shaftesbury, the moral sense ensured humans could distinguish between good and evil actions. Hume, on the other hand, strongly opposed rationalist justifications and stated, "Reason is, and ought only to be the slave of the passions and can never pretend to any other office than to serve and obey them."[17] According to Hume, morality is based on compassion or sympathy. For some time, Lessing advocated a form of ethics based on compassion, long before Schopenhauer. "*The most compassionate person is the best person*, most inclined toward all social virtues and all forms of generosity."[18] In this way, he continued the English moral sense theory. Society is held together by compassion, empathy, and sympathy for others. In France, several materialistic moral theories were developed. Helvétius believed that the goal of all actions was self-pleasure. Human reason was entirely determined by self-love, passion, and biological factors. The philosopher and reformer Jeremy Bentham, on the other hand, declared the prin-

---

16 Gellert, Moralische Vorlesungen. Moralische Charaktere, in: *Gesammelte Schriften*, vol. 6, 41.
17 David Hume, *A Treatise of Human Nature* [1739–40], ed. with an Analytical Index by Sir Lewis Amherst Selby-Bigge, second edition by Peter Harold Nidditch, Oxford: Clarendon Press 1992, III.3.3.
18 Lessing, Briefwechsel über das Trauerspiel, letter to Friedrich Nicolai, November 1756, in: *Werke*, ed. Herbert G. Göpfert, vol. 4, 159–65, at 163.

ciple of utility as the ultimate yardstick. According to Bentham, morality contributed to the greatest happiness or pleasure of the greatest number of people.

A common denominator of moral theories in the European Enlightenment can perhaps be formulated as follows: Most enlighteners asserted that "virtue consists in subordinating one's own well-being to the common good, being charitable to one's neighbor, benefiting humanity, and practicing love for humanity, thus also promoting the happiness of all when promoting one's own interest."[19] In his famous speech at the University of Halle in 1721, Christian Wolff declared:

> And because the Chinese stressed so strongly the idea that one must continually advance along the path of virtue and not rest at any degree of perfection less than the very highest degree, which of course no one can attain, it is my opinion that their philosophers, too, subscribed to the view that man cannot achieve happiness unless he seeks to attain more perfection day by day.[20]

This statement combines key Enlightenment concepts: virtue, perfection, happiness, and an enlarged, cosmopolitan way of thinking that respects Chinese ethics instead of condemning them as atheist and un-Christian (see also 4.4). Wolff also repeats a familiar doctrine of Greek ethics, especially Stoicism: true happiness can only be achieved if we strive for virtue or morality. By the end of the century, even Kant arrives at a similar conclusion. Kant is sometimes regarded as a cheerless stickler whose life and philosophy focused on moral duty and explicitly excluded happiness (*Glückseligkeit* as opposed to *Glück* or luck). True to the motto: "Do your moral duty and stop whining!" This is a slight distortion, to put it mildly. According to Kant, we are allowed to pursue our own bliss or happiness. Promoting the happiness of others is therefore not an unconditional requirement:

> [A] maxim of promoting others' happiness at the sacrifice of one's own happiness, one's true needs, would conflict with itself if it were made a universal law. Hence this duty is only a *broad* one; the duty has in it a latitude for doing more or less, and no specific limits can be assigned to what should be done.[21]

Kant claims that because we can and should see ourselves as ends in themselves, we should also look after our own well-being. This is grounded in our duty or obligation to preserve ourselves as moral persons. In principle, my interests, or inclinations are therefore no less valuable or inferior to those of other people. Promot-

---

19 Kondylis, *Die Aufklärung*, 518–25, especially 522. See also Dierse, Tugend, 416 and Robertson, *The Enlightenment. The Pursuit of Happiness*, 1–14.
20 Quoted in Robertson, *The Enlightenment*, 167.
21 Immanuel Kant, The metaphysics of morals [1797], in: *Werke*, vol. 6, 203–493, at 393.

ing the happiness of others is therefore a broad duty whose limits cannot be defined *a priori*; it requires judgment, sensitivity to context, and awareness of the "sensibilities" (*Empfindungsart*) of others. True happiness *might* be achieved if we strive for virtue or morality—yet there is no guarantee for this. Kant adds that we should become *worthy* of this happiness by way of our virtue/morality and our moral life-conduct.[22]

By the end of the 18th century, three major shifts had occurred. First, some enlighteners arrived at a reevaluation of atheism. The traditional view held that atheists were incapable of moral action because they denied God as the ultimate moral legislator. However, Pierre Bayle argued that atheism did not necessarily lead to immorality. There were numerous discussions in the 18th century on the possibility of a "virtuous atheist." Kant, at the end of the era, believed that virtue consisted in respect for the moral law for its own sake. Those who subjected themselves to "free self-coercion," based on their own realization that the moral law (the categorical imperative) was reasonable, were acting morally. With this, Kant separated ethics from moral theology, claiming that "the doctrine of virtue stands on its own (even without the concept of God)."[23] Thus, even the atheist was capable of moral sentiments, dispositions, and actions (see also below 4.3).

Secondly, by the end of the century "competing *systematic normative theories*" had been developed. They included utilitarianism, Kantian deontological ethics, and virtue ethics. The third major change was that moral theories increasingly emphasized the internal dimension of the nature of moral obligation, namely "deliberative practical reasoning."[24] These three changes link the European Enlightenment with the present.

4.2 Qualified Normative Universalism

In the previous section, I provided examples of clear injustices. They challenge the claim that moral norms are always and necessarily mere inventions of societies, or that conscience, virtue, or morality are products of upbringing. First, we should differentiate between general universal moral principles such as justice, human dignity, and impartiality on one hand, and the specific norms influenced by soci-

---

[22] See Georg Cavallar, *Auf dem Weg zur Moral. Immanuel Kant und die Fahrprüfung des Denkens*, Wien: Leykam, 2024 154–5, 80–88 and 127–34 for more.
[23] See Jonathan Israel, *Radical Enlightenment. Philosophy and the Making of Modernity 1650–1750*, Oxford: Oxford University Press 2001, 331 ff. and passim; Kant, Religion, vol. 6, 183.
[24] Stephen Darwall, Norm and Normativity, in: Haakonssen, *The Cambridge History of Eighteenth-Century Philosophy*, 987–1025, at 988.

ety, religions, and culture on the other. Qualified normative universalism asserts that there is a "core set of universal moral norms," while also acknowledging a gray area "where culture-specific moral norms, as well as cultural, and individual differences in the application of norms in specific situations, should be considered."[25] Moral relativism is justified within this gray area. However, extending this relativism to the level of general moral principles, to the fundamental level, is not justified. The qualified normative universalism presented here is further supported by the phenomenon that the ideas of human dignity or impartiality can be found in different historical periods, cultures, religions, and worldviews. In the era of globalization, it gains additional plausibility through the endorsement of many non-European intellectuals and ordinary people who, based on rational arguments, align themselves with this allegedly "European" normative universalism, often stemming from their own traditions, or injustices experienced in their own societies.

In my opinion, the most comprehensive foundation for qualified normative universalism can be found in Kant's ethics, when properly understood. Kant incorporated many elements of his predecessors in ethical theory. For example, Pierre Bayle distinguished between a religious or theological basis of morality and a secular foundation that kept moral theology, revelation, and ethics apart. Kant's distinction between autonomy, as self-legislation of practical reason, and heteronomy is hinted at in Bayle's work. Bayle wrote: "Reason dictated to the ancient sages that it was necessary to do what is good for the love of the good itself, that virtue was its own reward, and that it belonged only to a vicious man to abstain from evil for fear of punishment."[26] According to Bayle, moral reasoning is a process of abstraction that enables us to overcome our own contingencies and limitations, such as prejudices, or particular interests. "But as Passion and Prejudice do but too often obscure the Ideas of natural Equity, I should advise all who have a mind effectually to retrieve them, to consider these Ideas in the general, and as abstracted from all private Interest, and from the Customs of their Country."[27] Personal reflection examines whether a particular action would be generally agree-

---

[25] Gertrud Nunner-Winkler, Moralischer Universalismus – kultureller Relativismus. Zum Problem der Menschenrechte, in Johannes Hoffmann, ed., *Universale Menschenrechte im Widerspruch der Kulturen*, Frankfurt am Main: Verlag für Interkulturelle Kommunikation 1994, 79–103, at 80. See also Heiner Bielefeldt, *Philosophie der Menschenrechte. Grundlagen eines weltweiten Freiheitsethos*, Darmstadt: Primus Verlag 1998, 25–201.
[26] Pierre Bayle, *Various Thoughts on the Occasion of a Comet-State* [1682], translated with Notes and an Interpretive Essay by Robert C. Bartlett, Albany: State University of New York Press 2000, § 178.
[27] Bayle, *Philosophical Commentary*, part I, ch. 1, 69.

able and investigates the underlying principle impartially and without passion. Bayle considers this general principle of reciprocity to be a "universal Ray of Light" to which every person should adhere.[28] This is very close to a key feature of Kantian ethics, namely formal, or abstract impartiality and reciprocity.

Bayle also opposed an instrumental understanding of morals, according to which the allegedly "good" or "true" end or purpose justifies any means. A specific example for Bayle were the arguments of some theologians such as Bossuet, who claimed that the true religion could and should be enforced with violence. According to this reasoning, violence was suddenly transformed into something morally good and beneficial, which Bayle declared to be "abominable confusions." This mindset, he argued, could not be universalized, or turned into a general rule or law. According to the standards of natural morality, violence remains nothing more than violence, even when attempts are made to relativize it with purportedly good or useful ends or purposes. The teachings of Christ would be reversed, and all "boundaries" that separate virtue from vice would be erased, "by making Murder, and Robbery, and Felony, and Tyranny, and Rebellion, and Calumny, and Perjury, and all Crimes generally, when practiced against a heterodox Party, lose the Character of Evil, and become Virtues of a most necessary Obligation."[29] Another example of the influences of the European Enlightenment on Kant's ethics is the role of moral sense. Kant incorporated the moral sense theory of British enlighteners, especially Hume and Smith, into his own ethics, which is to this day usually portrayed as predominantly rational. While, according to Kant, moral sense can no longer be considered the foundation of morality, it does play a crucial role in discussions about what motivates agents to realize moral principles.[30]

The crucial distinction between understanding and reason is fundamental to Kant's ethics (see 1.2). This can be illustrated using Friedrich Schiller's drama *Don Carlos* (1787). Friedrich Schiller (1759–1805) was a German polymath who embraced and contemplated central Enlightenment motifs. In one scene, Marquis Posa endorses ideas of many enlighteners, such as the rule of law, tolerance, and the liberation from oppression. His confident and famous statement is, "Sire, grant us freedom of thought!" In his *Letters on Don Carlos*, Schiller subjected Marquis Posa's moral attitudes and dispositions to a sharp critique. While the Marquis had noble moral goals, namely the "liberation of an oppressed people,"

---

[28] Bayle, *Philosophical Commentary*, 70.
[29] Bayle, *Philosophical Commentary*, part I, ch. 4, 90–1.
[30] Birgit Recki, *Ästhetik der Sitten. Die Affinität von ästhetischem Gefühl und praktischer Vernunft bei Kant*, Frankfurt am Main: Klostermann 2001 and Frazer, *Enlightenment of Sympathy*, especially 112–38. See also Birgit Recki, *Die Vernunft, ihre Natur, ihr Gefühl und der Fortschritt. Aufsätze zu Immanuel Kant*, Paderborn: mentis 2006.

Figure 14: Pierre Bayle (1647–1706) was a French philosopher, lexicographer, and early representative of the Enlightenment. As a Huguenot, he fled to the Dutch Republic in 1681. His major work is the *Dictionnaire Historique et Critique* where he hid controversial claims in the footnotes. His skeptical philosophy and his advocacy of tolerance influenced subsequent enlighteners.

and his sentiment was "cosmopolitan," he must be criticized because he used his friend Don Carlos for his own—albeit noble—purposes. Even a morally acceptable end does not justify immoral means. Every person should always be respected as an end in themselves. According to Schiller, Marquis Posa violated these moral principles. Schiller intended his example to demonstrate that "the most selfless, purest, and noblest person, out of enthusiastic attachment to their concept of virtue and the happiness to be produced, very often acts just as arbitrarily with individuals as the most selfish despot."[31] The moral idealist as a potential despot: Schiller criticizes, in an enlightened manner, the kind of Enlightenment that prioritizes understanding (*Verstand*), prudence, and calculation or seeks to subject all actions to "rational ends." In Kant's ethics, this prudential thinking corresponds with the so-called hypothetical imperatives: a maxim underlying an action is supposedly morally good when the desired end is good. The categorical imperative of reason, on the other hand, states that every person should be respected as an end in themselves and should never be used merely as a means to an end.

Another formulation of the categorical imperative concerns the universalizability of maxims.[32] The fundamental idea can be explained using an example provided by Kant himself. Is it morally permissible to borrow money with the intention of not repaying it? Kant's position has been variously interpreted over the last two and a half centuries. According to a prevalent interpretation, Kant was an advocate of rule utilitarianism: a general rule or maxim is morally acceptable when it is generally beneficial or enables a rational form of coexistence. In concrete terms, the maxim of borrowing money with no intention to repay cannot be universalized because this would render promises ineffective as a social norm. Ultimately, no one would trust the dishonest person, and a meaningful institution—namely money lending—would likely disappear from society. Kant's primary argument takes a different form, although these considerations of utility may also play a role. Kant's transcendental argument seeks to demonstrate a logical contradiction. What does a consciously false promise mean? Promising something is self-commitment. The person making a promise thereby refrains from making the fulfillment of that promise dependent on considerations of prudence. The promise has the form: "I promise you x" without the restrictive addition of

---

[31] Friedrich Schiller, Briefe über Don Karlos, in: *Schillers Werke. Nationalausgabe*, hrsg., Herbert Meyer, Weimar: Böhlau 1958, vol. 22, 137–77, at 151, 170. See also Volker C. Dörr, Friedrich Schiller und die Aufklärung, in: Hofmann, ed., *Aufklärung*, 229–46.

[32] Immanuel Kant, Groundwork of The metaphysics of morals [1785], in: *Werke*, vol. 4, 385–463, at 402 and 422. This section follows my article Nazis, Lügen, Anne Boleyn und ein sonderbarer Philosoph: Kants Ethik im Philosophieunterricht, in: Violetta L. Waibel and Margit Ruffing, eds., *Akten des 12. Internationalen Kant-Kongresses Natur und Freiheit*, Berlin: Akademie Verlag 2018, vol. 5, 3845–53. See also Otfried Höffe, *Immanuel Kant*, München: Beck 1983, 192–6. Robert B. Louden, Making the law visible: the role of examples in Kant's ethics, in: Jens Timmermann, ed., *Kant's Groundwork of the Metaphysics of Morals. A Critical Guide*, Cambridge: Cambridge University Press 2010, 63–81 discusses the use of examples in Kant's moral philosophy.

"but only if it is beneficial to me." A consciously false promise boils down to making a commitment without intending to honor it. The crucial criterion is the contradiction in one's own maxim. Therefore, it cannot be universalized. The categorical imperative serves as an evaluative process to determine whether maxims pass the test of universalizability.[33]

Similarly, and long before Kant, Pierre Bayle described the test of abstraction and universalization with the following words. We should always ask ourselves:

> "Whether this or that Practice be just in itself; and whether, might the Question now be put for introducing it in a Country where it never was in vogue, and where it were left to our choice to admit or reject it; whether, I say, we should find upon a sober Inquiry, that it's reasonable enough to merit our Suffrage and Approbation? I fancy an Abstraction of this kind might effectually disperse a great many Mists which swim between the Eyes of our Understanding."[34]

Kantian ethics endorses qualified normative universalism. Apart from "sober inquiry" and personal "approbation," the key concept is the faculty of judgment. It has two tasks. Firstly, it assesses the moral quality of maxims and actions based on these maxims, investigating whether they correspond with the categorical imperative and pass the test of universalization. Secondly, the faculty of practical judgment applies the categorical imperative in concrete situations, while being sensitive to context and empirical factors.[35] For example, if it is my duty to promote the happiness of other people, it is not evident *a priori* how, when, and to what extent I am obliged to do this. Kant calls this a "wide duty" (see 4.1). Strict duties are different. The duty not to torture, rape, or murder other human beings, based on respect for their human dignity, does not allow for exceptions and is unconditional. Even here, however, the faculty of judgment is required. Qualified normative universalism asserts that there are strict duties when it comes to the core set of universal moral norms or principles. Yet it also acknowledges a gray area in which wide duties apply, or where the application of norms in specific situations allows for differences. An example is the behavior toward the elderly in traditional societies as opposed to our conduct toward them in industrialized societies, where specialized care, and homes are available.

---

[33] This follows Höffe, *Immanuel Kant*, 193–4. There is, of course, a bulk of secondary literature on this topic. For an introduction, see Mark Timmons and Sorin Baiasu, eds., *Kant on Practical Justification: Interpretive Essays*, Oxford: Oxford University Press 2013.
[34] Bayle, *Philosophical Commentary*, part I, ch. 1, 69–70.
[35] Kant, Groundwork, in: *Werke*, vol. 4, 389. See also *Critique of practical reason* [1788] V, 3–163, at 67: "[…] practical judgement, by which what is said in the rule universally (*in abstracto*) is applied to an action *in concreto*."

4.3 Rule of Law and Justifications for Tolerance

As in the case of morality, concrete legal practices and experiences with absolutism, aristocratic privileges, royal arbitrariness, and legal discrimination often served as starting points for change. Examples of formative experiences of injustice include the revocation of the Edict of Nantes in 1685 (see 3.1) or the Calas case (see 4.1). Other examples can be readily found. The *Carolina* (1532), the Carolina Code issued by Emperor Charles V in the Holy Roman Empire, remained in force for a long time, and included provisions for torture and a limited role for the defense. In 1772, Susanna Margaretha Brandt (1746–1772) was executed in Frankfurt for infanticide. The court showed little understanding of the young woman's social circumstances, and the fact that the child's father was unwilling to marry her was not addressed. The trial was conducted in secret and in written form. The city's oligarchy held sway. Defense attorney Marcus Christof Schaaf argued primarily for mitigating circumstances but could not prevent the death sentence. This case likely served as an inspiration for Goethe's drama *Faust* (started in 1772, finally published in 1808). Another inspiration might have been the execution of Katharina Maria Flint (1739–1765) from Stralsund. Swiss educator and educational reformer Johann Heinrich Pestalozzi (1746–1827) addressed this brutal legal reality in his treatise *On Legislation and Infanticide* (1783). He unequivocally placed the blame not on young women but primarily on the legal system and prevailing mentalities. "All principles, customs, laws, rights, freedoms, practices, prejudices, and opinions, for the sake of which fertile people are to remain infertile, are the unambiguous sources of this universal state infanticide (*Staatskindermord*)."[36]

Since Montesquieu's *The Spirit of the Laws* (1748), from the mid-18th century onwards voices demanding judicial reforms grew. One groundbreaking work was the bestseller *On Crimes and Punishments* (1764) written by Italian lawyer, politician, and philosopher Cesare Beccaria (1738–1794). In part, he was able to build upon the natural law considerations of earlier authors such as Samuel Pufendorf. Beccaria's starting point was a secularized approach involving a strict separation of the religious and legal spheres. The focus was no longer on the confession and sincere repentance of the accused, offering them the chance to save their souls. Beccaria excluded this religious dimension for methodological reasons and formulated a secular social contract. People come together for the purpose of general security, agree on common legal norms for coexistence, and punish those who violate this contract. Beccaria's new standard for the severity of punishment was

---

[36] Quoted in Martus, *Aufklärung*, 774.

the harm caused by the criminal to society.[37] The book became a resounding success, was translated multiple times, and influenced Enlightenment figures such as Voltaire and the Founding Fathers of the United States.

These enlighteners were also adept marketing strategists. A competition organized by the Bern *Economic Society* in 1777 caused a sensation, criticizing torture, arbitrary judicial decisions, unequal application of legal norms, and the class-based nature of the legal system. In Spain's American colonies, litigants, some of them poor, enslaved, and illiterate, sued superiors at an increasing rate. There was a faster rise of civil suits initiated by slaves, native peasants, and women. Over the long term, "these litigants generated, through their actions as much as through the arguments they brought into court, a turn toward a law-oriented culture, distinguishable from the justice-oriented culture of the early modern period."[38] This new law-oriented culture emphasized concepts of freedom, legal custom, merit, the concept of law as a separate formal system distinct from moral philosophy, theology and metaphysics, and the modern concept of natural individual rights rather than older natural law.

In the following paragraphs, I would like to focus on selected aspects of what I refer to as "the successful Enlightenment": the conception of human rights, the foundations of the modern state based on the rule of law (*Rechtsstaat*), justifications for tolerance, the fight against slavery, and approaches to global justice.

Human rights are primarily individual rights that are seen as inherent to all individuals by virtue of their humanity. They are based on human dignity and the principle of equality, they protect spheres of freedom of action and are considered universal and indivisible.[39] A genuinely modern form of human rights emerged in the late Middle Ages and early modern period in Europe. It brought together sev-

---

[37] Cesare Beccaria, On Crimes and Punishments (1764), in: *On Crimes and Punishments and Other Writings*, ed. Richard Bellamy, Cambridge: Cambridge University Press 1995, 22–24, 31 and passim. See also Martus, Aufklärung, 771–8 as well as Randall McGowen, Law and Enlightenment, in: Fitzpatrick et al., eds., *The Enlightenment World*, 502–14 and Frederick Rosen, Utilitarianism and the reform of the criminal law, in: Mark Goldie and Robert Wokler, eds., *The Cambridge History of Eighteenth-Century Political Thought*, Cambridge: Cambridge University Press 2006, 547–72 (covers Montesquieu, Beccaria, Bentham and the debates on the death penalty).

[38] Bianca Premo, *The Enlightenment on Trial. Ordinary Litigants and Colonialism in the Spanish Empire*, Oxford: Oxford University Press 2017, 224. See also Premo, *The Enlightenment*, 3, 15–6, 67–75 and 141–5.

[39] See Cavallar, *Islam, Aufklärung und Moderne*, 84–9 with references. A narrative and explanation different from my own is presented by Israel, *Enlightenment that Failed*, 301–17. Israel dismisses alternative interpretations such as those by Lynn Hunt and Dan Edelstein and claims—surprise, surprise!—that the true founding fathers of universal and equal rights were the representatives of Radical Enlightenment (see Israel, *Enlightenment that Failed*, 302–4).

eral traditions, especially that of natural law. Starting in the 17th century, natural law was transformed into a secular rational law, as exemplified by figures including Samuel Pufendorf and John Locke. This transformation involved a systematic separation between theology, natural law, and positive law. The focus now shifted to individuals as legal persons with personal rights and responsibilities. Many enlighteners came to advocate religious freedom, understood as equal legal freedom irrespective of religious belief (see the section below on tolerance). Variants of enlightened absolutism implemented elements of these modern human rights and the modern rule of law.[40] One case in point is the reforms of Leopold II (1747–1792) when he was Grand Duke of Tuscany.[41] However, the most impressive example is most likely the American Revolution of 1776–1787. Two aspects are of central importance here.[42]

Firstly, the revolution was a rupture in history. The revolutionaries repositioned the dimensions of the past, present, and future. They abandoned the traditional focus on the past and emphasized an open future centered on citizens' ability to shape it in accordance with the triad of "Life, Liberty, and the Pursuit of Happiness." The present was seen as a new beginning that, in line with the idea of perfection, could lead to a better future. This project of the American Revolution was grounded in the time semantics of the Enlightenment, and the turn toward history (see the end of 1.2). These time semantics are illustrated by the transformation of the protest of the American colonists. Until 1776, they still invoked the established "rights of Englishmen," the historically evolved tradition of the English constitution, royal charters, and the "time before 1763." This changed, at the latest, with the pamphlet and bestseller *Common Sense* by Thomas Paine (1737–1809) and the *Declaration of Independence* (1776 which no longer appealed to the past, but instead to the secularized natural law doctrines of the Enlightenment, a universalist conception of reason, and an open future.

Secondly, the American Revolution was the breakthrough of modern constitutionalism and thus a "historical novelty" (Dieter Grimm). Between 1776 and 1787,

---

40 See Derek Beales, Philosophical kingship and enlightened despotism, in: Goldie and Wokler, eds., *Eighteenth-Century Political Thought*, 497–524 and Meyer, *Die Epoche der Aufklärung*, 95–109.
41 The standard biography is Adam Wandruszka: *Leopold II. Erzherzog von Österreich, Großherzog von Toskana, König von Ungarn und Böhmen, Römischer Kaiser*, 2 vols., Wien and München: Herold 1963 and 1965.
42 This follows Volker Depkat, Angewandte Aufklärung? Die Weltwirkung der Aufklärung im kolonialen Britisch Nordamerika und den USA, in: Wolfgang Hardtwig, ed., *Die Aufklärung und ihre Weltwirkung*, Göttingen: Vandenhoeck & Ruprecht 2010, 205–41. See also Gordon S. Wood, The American Revolution, in: Goldie and Wokler, eds., *Eighteenth-Century Political Thought*, 601–25, who claims: "The American Revolution transformed thinking about politics" (Wood, The American Revolution, 601).

constitutions for individual states, and at the federal level were debated. The federal constitution of 1787 then departed from the British constitutional tradition in key aspects, as well as from the theories of classical and early modern republicanism and liberalism.[43] The result was a constitution *oriented toward the future.* Amendments made development and potential improvement possible, based on critically reflected experience. The American democratic rule of law was established "as a sort of enduring experiment in democracy that could unfold as a collective learning process."[44]

Is this not an overly rosy picture of US political history since 1776? Yes, at least partially. Max Horkheimer and Theodor Adorno, under the influence of 20th-century totalitarianisms, referred to the contradictions of modernity and a particular form of Enlightenment as the *Dialectic of Enlightenment* (see Introduction, Assumption 4). On the one hand, political Enlightenment contained significant potential for emancipation, a potential for rational improvement that could be realized in the future. However, this emergence of rationality in the sense of reasonable universalizability was often overshadowed by a release of prudence, means-end-thinking, and understanding (*Verstand*). "Enlightenment, therefore, contained not only a historically effective potential for emancipation but also opened up new, much more effective, and far-reaching forms of domination and control, oppression, and exclusion, violence, and destruction through the interest-guided instrumentalization of reason."[45]

In the terminology of Kant and others, understanding (*intellectus, Verstand*) would triumph over reason (*ratio, Vernunft*) as the ability to form universal ideas or principles such as human dignity (see 1.2). While this dialectic of the Enlightenment has largely been neglected in US research on the Enlightenment, it can indeed be observed in historical developments since 1776. There were gaps between the aspirations of the constitution and social reality. The doctrine of universal and equal human rights remained contested and divisive. The Enlightenment which centered around understanding or *Verstand* (*verständige Aufklärung*, Hegel) provided the pragmatic rather than principled "justification" of the treat-

---

[43] For more details, see Depkat, Angewandte Aufklärung, 226–32 and Wood, The American Revolution, 610–6. Nathaniel Wolloch, *Moderate and Radical Liberalism. The Enlightenment Sources of Liberal Thought*, Leiden and Boston: Brill 2022 covers the transition from the late Enlightenment to early 19th century liberalism, especially John Stuart Mill.
[44] Depkat, Angewandte Aufklärung, 232. Key concepts such as democracy, the rule of law, sovereignty, common good or citizenship in Enlightenment philosophy are the focus of Michael Mosher and Anna Plassart, eds., *A Cultural History of Democracy in the Age of Enlightenment*, London et al.: Bloomsbury Academic 2021.
[45] Depkat, Angewandte Aufklärung, 232.

Figure 15: The *United States Constitution* of 1787, which famously begins *We the People*.

ment of Native Americans or African Americans, with reference to concepts such as "civilization" or "progress." This was evident in the *Indian Removal Act* (1830), which legitimized the forced relocation of Indians to areas west of the Mississippi. They were denied the status of humanity or the right to be citizens. The US Americans' self-perception as an "enlightened nation" was helpful in this exclusion.

Despite justified criticism of the perversion and limited application of universal ideas, in part provided by the enlighteners, two aspects should be kept in mind. Firstly, this criticism has drawn precisely on those sources of rational deliberation that most Founding Fathers of the American Constitution also drew upon. Any criticism of one or several conceptions or currents of the Enlightenment which are centered around understanding or *Verstand* always presupposes the normative benchmark of rational justification, criticism, and enlightenment (first, third, and fifth conception). Secondly, a *dynamic* constitution made sure that the potential of universal, abstract and formal norms and principles was never exhausted, and allowed for a "democratization of democracy." In many cases, although this was apparently not the intention or desire of the Founding Fathers, it could not be prevented. The "openness of the constitution allowed those excluded from the promise of happiness in the *Declaration of Independence* to demand civil and political rights for themselves by appealing to the values of the American Revolution and applying the procedures of American democracy."[46] The fight against slavery and the slave trade, and various civil rights movements such as the early women's movement in the 1790s are cases in point. In the *Declaration of Sentiments* (1848) we find a self-assured rephrasing of the *Declaration of Independence:* "We hold these truths to be self-evident that all men and women are created equal."[47]

The US-constitution should be seen as an exception rather than as a typical example of Enlightenment political thought.[48] In general, politics were supposed to promote the common good (*bonum commune*), follow the natural order of things, and facilitate the moral improvement of subjects. Most enlighteners did not promote liberal ideas (which became more dominant in the 19th century), but opted for the enlightened, virtuous monarch and the *despotism éclairé*, or enlightened despotism. Theories were often paternalistic, emphasizing a prince's task or even duty to discipline and educate morally her or his subjects rather than provide spheres of freedom or autonomy. Proponents of popular rule or democracy were rare. They were not endorsed by enlighteners, except perhaps for Rousseau (*Du contrat social*, 1762). Influenced by the Levellers, British evangelicals like Richard Price (1723–1791) and the scientist and theologian Joseph Priestley (1733–1804) can be credited with having developed the first modern full-blown democratic theories.

---

46 Depkat, Angewandte Aufklärung, 235, 239 as well as 236–8 (on feminist Enlightenment).
47 The Declaration of Sentiments of the Seneca Falls Convention, 1848, in: Karen O'Connor, ed., *Women's Leadership. A Reference Handbook,* Los Angeles: Sage 2010, vol. 1, 62.
48 This paragraph follows Tricoire, *Die Aufklärung,* 175–98.

Human rights approaches could take on various forms. German Protestant theologian, prolific writer, and part-time innkeeper Carl Friedrich Bahrdt (1741–1792) developed a highly controversial, innovative, and unique theory.[49] Bahrdt asserted familiar natural rights, such as freedom of opinion and the press and the right to life. Yet he also claimed a human right to sexual satisfaction (*"Recht zur Befriedigung des Geschlechtstriebes"*), which apparently applied to both women and men (Bahrdt is not explicit here). He postulated this right within his discussion of the right to divorce, criticizing theologians who adhered to the traditional doctrine that marriage was indissoluble. Bahrdt qualified the right: It only applies to heterosexual relationships. Secondly, a man who makes use of this right must not "harm other human and natural rights and freedoms, that is, so long as he follows nature and satisfies his drives with the free will of a person of the other sex, without harming public morals [*öffentliche Sittlichkeit*]".[50] There are four possible sources of Bahrdt's unique an original right to satisfaction of the sexual drive: The natural law tradition, some currents of Protestant theology, libertinism and Spinozist authors, and finally Bahrdt's own way of life. He became an *enfant terrible*, among other things for living with his mistress and making at least two of his maids pregnant. Apart from sex, he loved singing, drinking and making fun of political authorities. He wrote more than 130 books and pamphlets to finance his lifestyle and pay back his debts. Bahrdt lost two jobs at German universities, mainly because of his unorthodox views.

According to a widespread interpretation, the Enlightenment saw the breakthrough of more secular human rights theories with a focus on individual freedom and legal equality. These new theories are said to have gone beyond previous

---

[49] Carl Friedrich Bahrdt, *Rechte und Obliegenheiten der Regenten und Unterthanen in Beziehung auf Staat und Religion*, Riga: Johann Friedrich Hartknoch 1792. See also Bahrdt, *The Edict of Religion. A Comedy and The Story and Diary of My Imprisonment*, ed. John Christian Laursen and Johan van der Zande, New York et al: Lanham 2000 and John Christian Laursen, "From Libertine Idea to Widely Accepted: the Human Right to Sexual Satisfaction. A Research Program for the Study of the Idea from Carl Friedrich Bahrdt to the Present", in: Lorenzo Bianchi, Nicole Gengoux and Gianni Paganini, eds., *Philosophie et libre pensée – Philosophy and Free Thought*, Paris: Champion 2017, 491–510 as well as "Die Pflichten des Bürgers gegen den Staat – und des Staates gegen die Bürger. Carl Friedrich Bahrdt über das Recht auf freie "Befriedigung des Geschlechtstriebes", in: Sonja Schierbaum and Dietrich Schotte, eds., *Untertan – Staatsbürger – Mensch. Beiträge zur Kritik und Rechtfertigung bürgerlicher Rechte in der deutschen Aufklärung*, Basel: Schwabe Verlag 2024, 163–192.
[50] Bahrdt, *Rechte und Obliegenheiten*, 12, translated in Laursen, From Libertine Idea to Widely Accepted, 493.

natural law approaches.⁵¹ The interpretation should be qualified, for various reasons.⁵² First, conceptions of individual natural rights were already developed by the Second Scholastic and the School of Salamanca of the 16ᵗʰ century. Secondly, natural law theories of the 17th century until the 1760ies were state-centered, emphasizing social stability and duties rather than individual freedoms. Finally, natural rights were understood as derivatives of natural law, not as their center. The doctrine of individual, "subjective" rights was embedded in a framework of natural law.⁵³ Enlightenment theories usually did not go beyond the metaphysical and theological assumptions implied in this framework. In the 1760ies, French Physiocrats like François Quesnay (1694–1774) returned to the older natural law theories of the Second Scholastic and postulated that natural laws were valid not only in the state of nature, but also in civil society. The laws of nature or natural laws were evident and intelligible, part of the natural order (*ordre naturel*), attributed to God, and everyone had to obey them. French *philosophes* like Diderot, Raynal and Condorcet picked up this new conception, added the right of resistance to oppression, and sometimes used the terms "rights of humanity" and "human rights".⁵⁴

Many enlighteners famously argued for religious tolerance. The concept of tolerance or toleration encompasses different conceptions or dimensions. The first conception refers to the phenomenon that members of different faiths or denominations are tolerated by the ruler, the state, or the religious majority.⁵⁵ This usually meant that the ruler refrained from imposing their own faith on those with different beliefs. Toleration meant "that the authority (or majority) grants the mi-

---

51 See for instance Richard Tuck, *Natural rights theories. Their origin and development*, Cambridge: Cambridge University Press 1979.
52 See Tricoire, *Die Aufklärung*, 149–54 and Cavallar, *Rights of Strangers*, 80–4 for the following.
53 Knud Haakonssen, *Natural Law and Moral Philosophy*, Cambridge: Cambridge University Press 1996, 315 and 322.
54 Dan Edelstein, *On the Spirit of Rights*, Chicago and London: University of Chicago Press 2019, 74–90.
55 For an introduction, see especially Rainer Forst, *Toleration in Conflict. Past and Present*, Cambridge: Cambridge University Press 2013. Also helpful are Elisabeth Holzleither, Toleranz. Geistesgeschichtliche Perspektiven eines umstrittenen Begriffs, *Polylog*, 21 (2009), 35–50, Rainer Forst, ed., *Toleranz. Philosophische Grundlagen und gesellschaftliche Praxis einer umstrittenen Tugend*, Frankfurt am Main und New York: Campus 2000 and Jürgen Habermas, *Zwischen Naturalismus und Religion: philosophische Aufsätze*, Frankfurt am Main: Suhrkamp 2005, 258–78. See Friedrich Vollhardt, ed., *Toleranzdiskurse in der Frühen Neuzeit*, Berlin: de Gruyter 2015 as well as Jon Parkin and Timothy Stanton, ed., *Natural Law and Toleration in the Early Enlightenment*, Oxford: Oxford University Press 2013 on the various conceptions of tolerance in the European Enlightenment.

nority the permission to live in accordance with its convictions so long as it—and this is the crucial condition—does not question the predominance of the authority (or majority)."[56] The edicts of tolerance from the 16th to the 18th century did not grant the human right of religious freedom but were dependent on the benevolence and whim of the ruler. France is a typical example. In the *Edict of Nantes* (1598), King Henry IV granted religious tolerance and full civil rights to the Huguenots. The aim of this "permission conception" of tolerance (Rainer Forst) was to ensure or restore domestic peace, tranquility, and to prevent the disaster of a civil war. Accordingly, French statesman Cardinal Richelieu (1585–1642) refrained from suppressing Protestantism, expressing his belief that "the conversion of the Reformed is a work we must await from Heaven."[57] This policy was based not on principle but on prudence. Its pragmatism relied on the intellect (*Verstand*) rather than on impartial reason. In 1685, Louis XIV revoked the edict, and the Calvinist Protestants in France lost all religious and civil rights. Hundreds of thousands fled to Protestant territories. For many enlighteners, the lesson was clear: royal arbitrariness and religious intolerance should be rejected.

Over the course of the early modern period, other conceptions of tolerance emerged in Europe. The second conception, the respect conception of tolerance, is based on the mutual and respectful interaction of citizens in a heterogeneous society governed by the rule of law.[58] Adam Smith assumed that religious pluralism and a kind of free market in religious groups and denominations could be beneficial. The "zeal of religious teachers" could be mitigated or "become altogether innocent where the society is divided into two or three hundred, or perhaps into as many thousand small sects, of which none could be considerable enough to disturb the public tranquility." Theologians and priests would then be driven to subscribe to "candor and moderation," and abstain from theological squabbles. Eventually they might focus on what really matters, namely "pure rational religion, free from every mixture of absurdity, imposture, or fanaticism, such as wise men have in all ages of the world wished to see established."[59] This was in line with what many enlighteners thought about the issue (see 5.1 and 5.2). Thirdly, tolerance can also be interpreted as a moral virtue in dealing

---

56 Forst, *Toleration in Conflict*, 27.
57 Quoted in Robertson, *The Enlightenment. The Pursuit of Happiness*, 91.
58 Forst, *Toleration in Conflict*, 29–31.
59 Adam Smith, *An Inquiry into the Nature and Causes of the Wealth of Nations* [1776], ed. by R. H. Campbell, A. S. Skinner, Oxford: Clarendon Press 1976, V.i.g.III.8, 792–3. See also Robertson, *The Enlightenment. The Pursuit of Happiness*, 90–1. Some scholars argue that Forst's respect conception cannot be found among Enlightenment thinkers. I want to thank Chris Laursen for pointing this out to me.

with others. This requires participants "to respect one another and to adopt one another's perspectives."⁶⁰ This form of tolerance is an aspect of the enlarged way of thinking (see 3.2) and, at the same time, the opposite of religious or political fanaticism (3.3). Many enlighteners developed toleration conceptions of the second and third type.

Different arguments were made for tolerance as a virtue (the third meaning). The appeal to Christianity or a religious standpoint was especially common among theologians and in the early Enlightenment. They could draw upon considerations made since the time of theologian Augustine of Hippo (354–430): tolerance is a consequence of love; only God has the right to judge believers and unbelievers; conscience should not be coerced; and true faith should come about through understanding. However, before the early Enlightenment these forms of tolerance had very narrow boundaries. This was the case with Augustine, who, in his struggle against the Donatists, reinterpreted many of the arguments in a way that called for intolerance and the fight against heretics and schismatics. Similarly, Italian theologian and philosopher Thomas Aquinas (around 1225–1274) placed "eternal salvation" at the center, subordinating "earthly well-being" and even "bodily life" to it. This allowed him to justify the persecution of heretics.⁶¹

The situation changed with the early Enlightenment, which was influenced by natural law and a natural theology shaped by Christianity. The thoughts of figures such as Samuel Pufendorf, John Locke, Leibniz, Christian Thomasius, and the French jurist Jean Barbeyrac (1674–1744) had little to do with liberal individualism that emphasized the religious rights of the individual. Instead, they were concerned with "questions about the relationship between God and His creation and its implication for human life and the institutions through which it is lived."⁶² Locke explicitly referred to the New Testament and the example of Christ. He argued that someone who lacks "charity, meekness, and goodwill in general toward all mankind, even to those that are not Christians, he is certainly yet short of being a true Christian himself."⁶³ True Christian faith, according to Locke, lies in an at-

---

60 Jürgen Habermas, *Between naturalism and religion. Philosophical essays*, transl. Ciaran Cronin, Cambridge: Polity Press 2008, 258.
61 Forst, *Toleration in Conflict*, 66–70. See Forst, *Toleration in Conflict*, 404–15 on the various religious and theological arguments in favor of toleration in early modern European history.
62 Jon Parkin, Preface: Rethinking Toleration via Natural Law, in: Parkin and Timothy Stanton, *Natural Law and Toleration*, x–xxi, at xi.
63 John Locke, *Two Treatises of Government and A Letter Concerning Toleration*, ed. and with an Introduction by Ian Shapiro, New Haven and London: Yale University Press 2003, 215. New interpretations of Locke's conception of toleration are contained in Parkin and Stanton, ed., *Natural Law and Toleration*, 35–137.

titude of charity and respect that renounces violence and dominion. Forms of religious justifications for tolerance were common in the European Enlightenment.

It is mistaken to claim that genuine tolerance in the second and third meaning presupposes secularization understood as the loss of religion. However, this assertion is still made today. Here is a typical example: "Enlightenment notions of tolerance are predicated on an indifference to existential or religious experience."[64] On the other hand, it is true that in the European Enlightenment, conceptions of tolerance were considered that no longer primarily relied on theological or religious arguments. Toleration conceptions do not require secularization in the sense of turning away from religion. However, secularization processes must have occurred, namely the functional differentiation of religious and secular spheres (such as the state or the sciences) and the emancipation of the secular from the religious sphere (see also Chapter 5).[65]

The first modern arguments for tolerance developed from this kind of secularization. It was deemed necessary because the government was not supposed to meddle in the beliefs of individual citizens. Locke made a distinction between personal virtue and the state's duty of tolerance. The separation of church and state obliges the government not to interfere in matters of spiritual salvation. Therefore, tolerance extends even to pagans, Jews, and Muslims.[66] Other enlighteners argued with the help of the concept of justice—understood as impartiality—and a proposed change of perspective. An early example is Pierre Bayle, who also fell victim to religious discrimination and intolerance in the Catholic France of Louis XIV. Louis's motto was *"un roi, une foi, une loi"* (one king, one faith, one law), and he used suppression, and violence against the Huguenots, eventually revoking the *Edict of Nantes*. Theologians like Bossuet supported this approach, believing that the true religion could and should be enforced to achieve a religiously homogeneous kingdom (see also 4.1 and 5.2). As the son of a Huguenot pastor from southern France, Bayle fled via various routes to Rotterdam where he obtained a professorship. There, he also faced religious intolerance and discrimination due to

---

64 Stephen Eric Bronner, *Reclaiming the Enlightenment: Toward a Politics of Radical Engagement*, New York: Columbia University Press 2004, 141. The volume of Parkin and Stanton, eds., *Natural Law and Toleration* shows that this is an inaccurate assessment of the early Enlightenment.

65 See especially José Casanova, *Public Religions in the Modern World*, Chicago and London: University of Chicago Press 1994, Anna Tomaszewska, Hasse Hämäläinen, eds., *The Sources of Secularism. Enlightenment and Beyond*, Palgrave Macmillan 201, Anton M. Matytsin and Dan Edelstein, eds., *Let There Be Enlightenment. The Religious and Mystical Sources of Rationality*, Baltimore: Johns Hopkins University Press 2018, Annelien de Dijn, The Politics of Enlightenment: From Peter Gay to Jonathan Israel, in: *The Historical Journal*, 55, 3 (2012), 785–805 and my own *Islam, Aufklärung und Moderne*, 37–44.

66 Locke, *Two Treatises of Government and A Letter Concerning Toleration*, 250.

his provocative writings, this time from his Huguenot community. "The victims of intolerance were not themselves inclined to be tolerant. [...] Like St Augustine, they did not object to persecution in principle; it was just that the wrong people were doing the persecuting."[67]

Bayle combined the argument of impartiality with the epistemological argument based on the limits of reason (see above 2.3).[68] Bayle claimed that if we followed impartial considerations, non-Christian religions, especially Jews, and Muslims, should be tolerated. According to Bayle, it is not clear why the Pope can send missionaries to India, while hypothetical Turkish missionaries would be forbidden to do the same in France. Muslims, too, might be convinced that they are teaching "the true Religion to those who are in Error, and promoting the Salvation of their Neighbor, whose Blindness they lament."[69] If the principles of reciprocity and generalization were consistently applied, Turks would also have the right to peacefully carry out missionary activities in Europe. "We must not forget the Command against having double Weights and double Measures, nor that with what measure we mete it shall be measured to us again."[70] Bayle connected this argument of impartiality with the argument based on the limits of reason. Reason is finite and, due to fundamental boundaries, cannot decide metaphysical issues or discussions beyond experience about the one "true religion" or a "higher truth." Reason and faith, philosophy and theology, are separate, and provide different answers to different questions. Bayle does not challenge the claim of faith to truth. He merely disputes that this claim can be proven with the help of reason or experience. The source of faith is inner conviction. According to Bayle, it is not irrational but supra-rational—it surpasses the capacity of reason and is beyond that reason (If it was irrational, it would be superstition). It is still open to debate whether Bayle was an atheist, Spinozist, a radical sceptic, or a follower of fideism.[71]

---

67 Robertson, *The Enlightenment. The Pursuit of Happiness*, 116.
68 My interpretation follows the excellent Forst, *Toleration in Conflict*, 237–65. See also John Christian Laursen and Cary J. Nederman, eds., *Beyond the Persecuting Society. Religious Toleration Before the Enlightenment*, Philadelphia: University of Pennsylvania Press 1998 as well as John Christian Laursen and María José Villaverde, eds., *Paradoxes of Religious Toleration in Early Modern Political Thought*, Lanham: Lexington Books 2012.
69 Pierre Bayle, *A Philosophical Commentary*, part II, ch. 7, 212.
70 Bayle, *A Philosophical Commentary*, 213.
71 Forst, *Toleration in Conflict*, 243 sees Bayle as a fideist. See also Bayle, *A Philosophical Commentary*, 257, 482, 492–3. Bayle's fideism is a contentious issue among experts. Israel, *Radical Enlightenment*, 332–41 pegs him as a secret follower of Spinozism. Gianluca Mori, "Bayle, Saint-Evremond, and Fideism: A Reply to Thomas M. Lennon", *Journal of the History of Ideas*, 65 (2004), 323–334 argues that Bayle's fideism should not be taken "at face value". See also his "Bayle et

The 18th century saw a wealth of conceptions of tolerance, which, however, did not always reach the level of Bayle's analyses. Voltaire's famous *Traité sur la tolérance* (1763), and the article "Tolerance" in his *Philosophical Dictionary* (1764), summarized the most common arguments of the theological and philosophical tradition since Augustine, in addition to those of the enlighteners since Spinoza, Bayle, and Locke for the public.[72] Yet Voltaire's *Treatise* for toleration and against superstition and religious fanaticism lacks originality. Voltaire knew how to provoke and contributed to a new narrative: the Greeks and Romans practiced religious tolerance and did not persecute. The rest of the world, from the Muslims to the Japanese, is probably more tolerant than the Christians, who tend to misinterpret, or misunderstand their religion. Priests and theologians, especially of the Catholic sort, have turned the humanism of Jesus' teachings into superstition, intolerance, and bigotry. However, Voltaire also admits that many European countries such as "Germany", England or even France, and religious groups have become more tolerant in recent decades.[73]

Lessing's dramatic poem *Nathan the Wise* (1779) has remained popular to this day. The famous ring parable contained therein has at least two core elements Firstly, the judge recommends that the three sons, who stand for the three monotheistic religions and can no longer recognize the real ring, turn to moral practice. Religious squabbles, fights, and wars should turn into the peaceful competition of religions, which should try to outdo each other in tolerance, virtue, and active humanism. Secondly, all three religions can be interpreted as containing the core of natural or rational religion within themselves (see also 5.2). However, due to the limits of reason, it remains unclear which of the historical faiths is

---

Hume devant l'athéisme", *Archives de philosophie*, 81 (2018), 749–774. Antony McKenna, "Pierre Bayle, rationalism and religious faith: self-evident truths and particular truths", *Etica & Politica / Ethics & Politics*, 20 (2018), 163–181 and *Études sur Pierre Bayle*, Paris: Champion 2015 also sees Bayle as a clandestine atheist.

72 Forst, *Toleration in Conflict*, 286–93 and Robertson, *The Enlightenment. The Pursuit of Happiness*, 123–6. See Antony McKenna, "Pierre Bayle: free thought and freedom of conscience", *Reformation & Renaissance Review*, 14 (2012), 85–100 and Gianluca Mori, "Bayle's two consciences and the paradox of the "conscientious persecutor", *Journal of the History of Philosophy*, 59 (2021), 559–582 on Bayle's conception of toleration.

73 Voltaire, *Treatise on Toleration* [1763–5], translated by Desmond M. Clarke, London: Penguin Books 2016, chs. 7 and 8 on the Greeks and Romans, ch. 13 on the partial tolerance of Judaism, ch. 4 on the Japanese, and ch. 14 on Jesus Christ.

more likely to develop toward this rational religion. Only God can make a competent judgment at the end of history.[74]

More recent studies point out that the many enlighteners' conceptions of toleration were deficient or flawed. A closer look reveals that indeed many theories of toleration were full of inconsistencies, weaknesses, blind spots, ambiguities, or paradoxes.[75] John Locke can be taken as an example. Tolerance did not extend to Catholics and atheists. Regarding Catholics, this limitation partly had political reasons, such as the revocation of the *Edict of Nantes* in France or the danger of a Catholic heir to the English throne. Moreover, according to Locke, Catholics "deliver themselves up to the protection and service of another prince," namely the Pope in Rome, and that, according to Locke, was incompatible with the sovereignty of the magistrate, prince, or government where they happened to live. "For by this means the magistrate would give way to the settling of a foreign jurisdiction in his own country, and suffer his own people to be listed, as it were, for soldiers against his own government."[76] For Locke, the same applies to Muslims, because they "blindly" obey the Ottoman emperor. As for atheists, Locke followed the traditional view that moral laws require the sanctioning authority of a divine ruler; otherwise, they would be ineffective. People who deny the existence of God would, in turn, question the ultimate binding force of morality. "Promises, covenants, and oaths, which are the bonds of human society, can have no hold upon an atheist. The taking away of God, though but even in thought, dissolves all." [77] According to Locke, atheism would thus endanger society, and the state. In the end, toleration only applied to a very limited section of Europe's population. In a similar vein, Voltaire argued against the "godless" and followers of allegedly unenlightened religions that did not conform to his concept of deism. On top of that, he was full of prejudices against, and contempt for the Jews and Jewish religion.[78]

---

74 Forst, *Toleration in Conflict*, 301–7 and Robertson, *The Enlightenment. The Pursuit of Happiness*, 126–30. See also Rudolf Langthaler, *Kant – ein Kritiker Lessings? Übereinstimmungen und Differenzen im Kontext von Aufklärung und Religion*, Berlin: de Gruyter 2021.
75 See John Christian Laursen and María José Villaverde, eds., *Paradoxes of Religious Toleration in Early Modern Political Thought*, Lanham et al.: Lexington Books, 2012 for a full and excellent analysis.
76 John Locke, *Two Treatises of Government and A Letter Concerning Toleration*, ed. and with an Introduction by Ian Shapiro, New Haven and London: Yale University Press 2003, 245.
77 Locke, *Two Treatises of Government*, 246.
78 See Forst, *Toleration in Conflict*, 291–3, Adam Sutcliffe, Myth, Origins, Identity. Voltaire, the Jews and the Enlightenment Notion of Toleration, in: *The Eighteenth Century*, 39 (1998), 107–26 and Caroline Christian Boggis-Rolfe, *Tolerance and intolerance in the writings of Voltaire: The instance of the Jews*, Dissertation University College London 2006.

The toleration conceptions of many Enlightenment thinkers indeed had their limits. However, it should not be forgotten that thinkers like Bayle or Kant took decisive steps forward in this regard. The discussions about atheism reached a new quality with the writings of Bayle (although only a few enlighteners followed him). Probably his most significant change was the separation between moral disposition and religion. Bayle detached morality from its connection with religion, suggesting that morality is an independent capacity, irrespective of religion. Christians in the past had demonstrated their capacity for atrocious crimes despite their fear or reverence for God. Conversely, Bayle argued that heathens and atheists could perform good deeds. Morally good actions, according to Bayle, were probably not always attributable to belief in God but rather to a specific "temperament" based on factors such as education, self-interest, or the voice of reason. Every individual could arrive at rational, universally valid moral insights, such as the realization that what is morally good should be done "for the love of the good itself" and not out of fear of punishment, and "that virtue was its own reward." Fanaticism, intolerance, and superstition were considered worse than atheism.[79]

Kant continued these reflections of Bayle and other enlighteners regarding universal morality, seen as the first element of genuine toleration (see also 4.2). Autonomous morality, or morality as the independent capacity of practical reason to give itself an ultimate principle of morally right action, should be distinguished from values that are religiously grounded. Only those norms or maxims that can be rationally and generally justified are valid or legitimate. The second element of this new conception of tolerance is the dignity of all human beings, to be respected as ends in themselves. The third element is the extension of the concept of respect to the political or state level. Kant went beyond the "permission conception" of tolerance by arguing that only those legal norms that can find mutual recognition and justification in a republic of free and equal citizens are legitimate.[80] So the discussions about tolerance at the end of the European Enlightenment reached a level of reflection that is still relevant for contemporary debates.

By the end of the 18th century, the following mainstream arguments had been made in favor of toleration.[81] Firstly, the enlighteners claimed that conscience could and should not be forced. Minds should only be changed by mild persuasion and rational arguments. In the words of Thomas Jefferson (1743–1826): "Reason

---

[79] All references in Forst, *Toleration in Conflict*, 243–7.
[80] This is based on Forst, *Toleration in Conflict*, 314–29 and 434–6.
[81] See the summary in Robertson, *The Enlightenment. The Pursuit of Happiness*, 111–5.

and free inquiry are the only effectual agents against error."[82] Secondly, enlighteners argued for the separation of faith and religion from the state or government. This also implied a distinction between personal convictions and the sphere of the law and the duties of citizens and their actions. Thirdly, many enlighteners followed the example of the Dutch humanist, philosopher and theologian Erasmus of Rotterdam (1466–1535), claiming that many religious issues were "things indifferent" or *adiaphora*.[83] They did not touch the essence or core of Christianity or religion in general. The fourth argument was epistemological. Most enlighteners argued that there are clear limits of our understanding, and that nobody could be a hundred percent sure of one's religious or metaphysical convictions (see 2.3). Finally, enlighteners sometimes also referred to pragmatic or consequentialist arguments. Toleration was not only good and valuable, but might also lead to more trade, prosperity, domestic tranquility, and peace.

In conclusion, we should avoid the simplistic narrative that the enlighteners single-handedly ushered in a new and bright era of tolerance and freedom of religion. There were many people outside the Enlightenment movement who made significant contributions. A case in point are the so-called *politiques*, namely moderate Catholics, Protestants or Huguenots who did not advocate toleration in principle but saw it as an expedient and indispensable policy. In addition, there were political changes that helped to promote religious toleration—and these changes sometimes took place independently of the debates of the *philosophes* or other enlighteners. An illustrative example is the United Provinces of the Dutch Republic, founded in 1581. To be sure, some religious minorities like the Arminians, also known as Remonstrants, were discriminated against, and suffered many restrictions. Yet government policy became more tolerant after the 1630s, with governors playing a crucial role. Among them was William III, prince of Orange, who became king of Great Britain after the Glorious Revolution.[84] We have seen that some enlighteners' conceptions of toleration were deficient, yet their overall achievement is still impressive. There was room for the respect conception of tolerance that rejected the centuries-old conception of permission. In addition, many arguments were no longer based on prudence but on moral or legal principles.

---

[82] Thomas Jefferson, Notes on the State of Virginia [1785], in: *Political Writings*, ed. Joyce Appleby and Terence Ball, Cambridge: Cambridge University Press 2004, 394.
[83] Quoted in Robertson, *The Enlightenment. The Pursuit of Happiness*, 113.
[84] This follows Robertson, *The Enlightenment. The Pursuit of Happiness*, 94–8.

4.4 Slavery, Human Rights, and Cosmopolitanism

In recent decades, authors have pointed at the responsibility of the European Enlighteners for advocating or defending slavery, the slave trade, colonialism, and racism.[85] An almost "classic" example of racism has already been mentioned (see Assumption 5 on David Hume). Among others, critics point at the discrepancy between universalist rhetoric and outcomes. In fact, within European Enlightenment were numerous voices that considered slavery and the slave trade as a business like any other, with no moral qualms. Some enlighteners remained silent or mentioned the alleged benefits of slavery, such as slaves leading a better life on North American plantations than in their African homelands. Among the proponents of slavery, the frequent reference to the economic benefits for the public is particularly noteworthy. The African traders' association, for instance, argued that the end of the slave trade and slavery as an institution would have devastating consequences because "the effects of this trade to Great Britain are beneficial to an infinite extent."[86] Slave traders from Nantes, as well as Liverpool, one of Europe's most important slave ports, made similar arguments. In cases like these, prudence, and self-interest once more triumphed over impartial reasoning. Indeed, the slave trade was a significant economic driver and had certainly not outlived its usefulness by the end of the 18th century. The abolition or elimination of the slave trade and slavery was likely an economic stupidity. As German historian Jürgen Osterhammel put it, "Slavery was not abolished because it obstructed economic progress but because it was no longer politically and morally defensible."[87] Anti-slavery sentiments and societies emerged in Britain and France in the 1770s. By the end of the century, most people in these countries apparently saw slavery as immoral, cruel, and downright wrong.

The reasons for this eventual abolition of slavery and the slave trade were diverse. Four factors likely played a central role. The first was the criticism leveled

---

85 See Andreas Eckert, Aufklärung, Sklaverei und Abolition, in: Hardtwig, ed., *Die Aufklärung und ihre Weltwirkung*, 243–62, Robin Blackburn, Slavery, emancipation and human rights, in: Kate E. Tunstall, ed., *Self-Evident Truths? Human Rights and the Enlightenment*, New York: Bloomsbury 2012, 137–55, Jürgen Osterhammel, *Sklaverei und die Zivilisation des Westens*, 2nd ed., München: Carl Friedrich von Siemens Stiftung 2009, Tricoire, *Aufklärung*, 305–16, Outram, *The Enlightenment*, 67–83, and Joel Quirk and David Richardson, Anti-slavery, European Identity and International Society, in: *Journal of Modern European History*, 7 (2009), 68–92.
86 Quoted in Eckert, Aufklärung, Sklaverei und Abolition, 248–9. See also Outram, *The Enlightenment*, 70–2 and 80–2 and Justin Roberts, *Slavery and the Enlightenment in the British Atlantic, 1750–1807*, Cambridge: Cambridge University Press 2013.
87 Osterhammel, *Sklaverei*, 54.

by religiously motivated abolitionists, nonconformists and Evangelicals in England. From the 1780s onwards, they garnered broad public support for their campaign. German historian Andreas Eckert calls this "the first international human rights movement."[88] The abolitionists deemed slavery a sin and appealed to people's compassion. They employed peaceful and mass-influencing methods for their campaign, such as petitions, posters, magazines, or consumer boycotts. "Slavery was doomed the moment the sighs of distant and invisible slaves seemed to echo with every spoonful into the sugar bowl."[89] Secondly, the abolitionists managed to turn their campaigns into an issue of British politics. They successfully instigated a parliamentary inquiry into the slave trade and slavery. The struggle was facilitated by the opportunity to use a universal moral concern for political goals. The hero of this story is the British politician and born-again Anglican William Wilberforce (1759–1833). He campaigned against the slave trade for twenty years until the *Slave Trade Act* of 1807 was passed.[90] Over the long term, England's political, and social elites benefited from the abolition movement. Britain could justify its maritime supremacy with the claim that the country fought against the slave trade. Thirdly, the abolitionists could draw on a wealth of natural law and other European traditions that criticized slavery. This criticism dated back at least to Jean Bodin and his main work, *Les six livres de la République* (1576).

In the 18th century, a growing number of authors emerged, both male and female, who reiterated the central argument that slavery violated natural rights. Among them were figures such as Montesquieu, Diderot, Rousseau, Condorcet, the physiocrat and Catholic theologian Abbé Nicolas Baudeau (1730–1792), the Catholic priest, bishop and republican Abbé Henri Jean-Baptiste Grégoire (1750–1831), Olympe de Gouges, and the Scottish lawyer George Wallace (1727–1805). The latter stated in 1760 that "every one of those unfortunate men who are pretended to be slaves has a right to be declared free, for he never lost his liberty, he could not lose it, his prince had no power to dispose of him. Of course, the sale was *ipso jure* void."[91] The idea of inalienable and natural rights could hardly be expressed more precisely. A fourth factor, often neglected in narratives, was the resistance of the slaves themselves and so-called black abolitionism. In this

---

88 Eckert, Aufklärung, Sklaverei und Abolition, 252. See also Tricoire, *Die Aufklärung*, 305–7.
89 Osterhammel, *Sklaverei*, 60.
90 For an introduction see Christopher Leslie Brown, *Moral Capital: Foundations of British Abolitionism*, Chapel Hill: University of North Carolina Press 2006. Brown cautions us against creating a one-sided narrative of "abolition and emancipation as the work of a noble few," in: Brown, *Moral Capital*, 334.
91 George Wallace, *A System of the Principles of the Laws of Scotland*, Edinburgh 1760, 94–5, quoted in Blackburn, Slavery, 144–5.

context, the Haitian Revolution (1791–1804) deserves to be mentioned.[92] People of color demonstrated that narratives about their alleged inferiority were untenable, as they managed to achieve and maintain their political freedom. As is often the case, it is difficult to weigh the significance of these four factors—and possible other factors. Yet it is plausible to assume that in the 18th century, the arguments of many enlighteners played a crucial role.

Cosmopolitanism is the theory that all people, regardless of ethnicity, religion, or political affiliation, belong to, or should belong to a global community.[93] It has become quite common to distinguish between various forms of cosmopolitanism. Nowadays, people usually refer to the political variant of cosmopolitanism that advocates a specific type of global legal order, such as a world state or a world republic. During the Enlightenment era, authors like Christian Wolff, the French peace advocate Charles-Iréné Castel, abbé de Saint-Pierre (1658–1743), the Prussian international lawyer Emer de Vattel (1714–1767), Rousseau, Kant, and the Prussian author and revolutionary Anacharsis Cloots (1755–1794) presented various plans Within political cosmopolitanism, a republican version can be found which was developed in two main forms: Intellectuals and philosophers like the Scottish poet and vegetarian John Oswald (around 1760–1793), Karl Wilhelm Frie-

---

[92] See especially Robin Blackburn, *The Overthrow of Colonial Slavery*, London: Verso 1988, The Role of Slave Resistance in Slave Emancipation, in: Seymour Drescher and Pieter C. Emmer, eds., *Who Abolished Slavery? Slave Revolts and Abolitionism: A Debate with Joao Pedro Marques*, New York: Berghahn Books 2010, 169–78. This contrasts with Israel, *Enlightenment that Failed*, 729–68 with the dubious emphasis on the allegedly unique role of radical enlighteners such as Diderot, d'Holbach, and Condorcet.

[93] See the introductions in Louden, *The World We Want*, 93–123, Robertson, *The Enlightenment. The Pursuit of Happiness*, 600–54, and Anthony Pagden, *The Enlightenment and Why it Still Matters*, Oxford: Oxford University Press 2013, 247–314. Here is a brief selection of relevant publications on this topic: Andrea Albrecht, *Kosmopolitismus. Weltbürgerdiskurse in Literatur, Philosophie und Publizistik um 1800*, Berlin und New York: de Gruyter 2005, Rebecka Lettevall and Kristian Petrov, ed., *Critique of Cosmopolitan Reason: Timing and Spacing the Concept of World Citizenship*, Oxford: Peter Lang 2014, Pauline Kleingeld, *Kant and Cosmopolitanism: The Philosophical Ideal of World Citizenship*, Cambridge: Cambridge University Press 2012, Joan-Pau Rubiés and Neil Safier, eds., *Cosmopolitanism and the Enlightenment*, Cambridge: Cambridge University Press 2023 and my own studies: *Imperfect cosmopolis: studies in the history of international legal theory and cosmopolitan ideas*, Cardiff: University of Wales Press 2011, Jean-Jacques Rousseau über Kosmopolitismus und kosmopolitische Erziehung, in: *Allgemeine Zeitschrift für Philosophie*, 37, 3 (2012), 281–304, *Kant's Embedded Cosmopolitanism: History, Philosophy and Education for World Citizens*, Kantstudien-Ergänzungshefte Bd. 183, Berlin, Boston: de Gruyter 2015, Between Cosmopolis and Apology: Kant's Dynamic and Embedded Religious Cosmopolitanism, *Interdisciplinary Journal for Religion and Transformation in Contemporary European Society*, 1, 1 (2015), 128–51, *Theories of Dynamic Cosmopolitanism in Modern European History*, Oxford: Peter Lang 2017.

DE LA LITTÉRATURE DES NÈGRES,

OU

Recherches sur leurs facultés intellectuelles, leurs qualités morales et leur littérature; suivies de Notices sur la vie et les ouvrages des Nègres qui se sont distingués dans les Sciences, les Lettres et les Arts;

Par H. GRÉGOIRE,

Ancien évêque de Blois, membre du Sénat conservateur, de l'Institut national, de la Société royale des Sciences de Göttingue, etc., etc., etc.

Whatever their tints may be, their souls are still the same.
Mrs ROBINSON.

A PARIS,
CHEZ MARADAN, LIBRAIRE,
RUE DES GRANDS-AUGUSTINS, N°. 9.
M. DCCC. VIII.

Figure 16: Henri Grégoire (1750–1831), *De la littérature des nègres*, title page, 1808. As a member of the *Society of the Friends of the Blacks*, the Catholic bishop advocated racial equality. His encyclopedia on black literature also served this purpose.

drich von Schlegel (1772–1829), or Rousseau proposed an alliance of republics, while Cloots favored a world republic with departments but without individual states.[94]

Economic or commercial cosmopolitanism, namely the notion "that the economic market should become a single global sphere of free trade," is still associated with authors like Adam Smith and other representatives of the Scottish Enlightenment.[95] Natural law or moral cosmopolitanism, tracing its roots to ancient and medieval sources, is the oldest form of cosmopolitanism. It either asserts that all humans, by virtue of their humanity, already form a global community, or that rationally defensible norms, as well as the principles of humanism, should be applied globally, and extended to all people. This moral cosmopolitanism is an extension of ethical universalism or human rights universalism, which has been discussed earlier (see 4.1, 4.2 and the beginning of this section).

Cultural cosmopolitanism was a new form of cosmopolitanism that emerged during the European Enlightenment. This cosmopolitanism holds the view "that humanity expresses itself in a rich variety of cultural forms, that we should recognize different cultures in their particularity, and that attempts to achieve cultural uniformity lead to cultural impoverishment."[96] Representatives of the European Enlightenment such as Johann Gottfried Herder or Georg Forster can serve as examples. Both showed a cosmopolitan attitude, understood as openness to foreign cultures which did not amount to cultural or moral relativism. Forster, as one author put it, likely embodied the enlightened ideal of "moving toward" people with different backgrounds.[97] Herder's reference point was a common humanity, centered around the concepts of *Bildung, Humanität,* and *Kultur.* For both,

---

[94] On Rousseau see Georg Cavallar, Jean-Jacques Rousseau über Kosmopolitismus as well as Jean-Jacques Rousseau (1712–1778), in: Bardo Fassbender and Anne Peters, eds., *The Oxford Handbook of the History of International Law*, Oxford: Oxford University Press 2012, 1114–7. See Francis Cheneval, Der kosmopolitische Republikanismus erläutert am Beispiel Anacharsis Cloots, *Zeitschrift für philosophische Forschung*, 58, 3 (2004), 373–96 and Frank Ejby Poulsen, Anacharsis Cloots and the Birth of Modern Cosmopolitanism, in: Lettevall and Petrov, ed., *Cosmopolitanism*, 87–118 on Cloots.

[95] Pauline Kleingeld, Six Varieties of Cosmopolitanism in Late Eighteenth-Century Germany, *Journal of the History of Ideas*, 60, (1999), 505–24, at 515. See Georg Cavallar, Kosmopolitismus in der Philosophie der Britischen Aufklärung, in: Matthias Lutz-Bachmann et al., eds., *Kosmopolitanismus. Zur Geschichte und Zukunft eines umstrittenen Ideals*, Frankfurt am Main: Velbrück Wissenschaft 2010, 163–89 on British cosmopolitanism.

[96] Kleingeld, Six Varieties of Cosmopolitanism, 51.

[97] Quoted in Greif, Forster, 125. See also Frazer, *Enlightenment of Sympathy*, 139–67 on Herder's cosmopolitan ethics, described as a "pluralist version of reflective sentimentalism" (167).

humanity's common potential can, and has been realized in a variety and diversity of cultures.[98]

Forms of religious cosmopolitanism will be discussed in a later section (see 5.2). Another form of cosmopolitanism is epistemological or cognitive. Kant and other enlighteners referred to the "citizen of the world" or the "world citizen" who attempts to overcome the "egoism of reason," which lies in the unwillingness to test one's own judgments with the help of the judgments of others. The ideal frame of mind involves one of the three principles of general human reasoning, the enlarged mode of thinking mentioned earlier (see 3.2). Adam Smith explained this change in perspective with the concept of the "impartial spectator." The prerequisite for a cosmopolitan perspective is the willingness to transcend the "subjective private conditions of judgment." A person with an expanded or cosmopolitan mode of thinking "reflects on his own judgment from a *universal standpoint* (which he can only determine by putting himself into the standpoint of others)."[99] This mindset can be considered cosmopolitan when it attempts to view other cultures, religions, or ethnicities from this "universal standpoint" of impartiality. [100]

The average enlightener was not—although this is a popular stereotype—a rootless rationalist who felt at home "nowhere" and loved the Tartars "so as to be spared having to love his neighbors," as Rousseau cynically noted.[101] More widespread was a form of cosmopolitan patriotism: Intellectuals were embedded in their own society, religion, culture, and state, which were often criticized but not necessarily and comprehensively rejected.[102] The enlighteners laid the philosophical foundations of an approach that I have termed dynamic cosmopolitanism. In a nutshell, it can be argued that various forms of cosmopolitanism have existed in Europe since ancient Greek and Roman times. However, these were mostly conceived as static: people were members of a moral or natural global community. During the early modern period, a new form of cosmopolitanism emerged—its dynamic version. It asserted that this community did not exist (and if it did, only in its embryonic form) and, therefore, could and should be

---

98 Robertson, *The Enlightenment. The Pursuit of Happiness*, 648–51 and same, *Humanität, Bildung, Kultur*: Germany's civilising values, in Sarah Colvin, ed., *The Routledge Handbook of German Politics and Culture*, London and New York: Routledge 2015, 20–33.
99 Immanuel Kant, *Critique of the Power of Judgment* [1790], in: *Werke*, vol. 5, 165–485, at 295; see also Logic [1800], in: vol. 9, 1–150, at 57.
100 See also Cavallar, *Islam, Aufklärung und Moderne*, ch. 3 and 173–6.
101 Rousseau, *Emile*, 39.
102 Louden, *The World We Want*, 211, Pauline Kleingeld, Kant's Cosmopolitan Patriotism, in: Sharon Byrd and Joachim Hruschka, eds., *Kant and Law*, Aldershot, Burlington: Ashgate 2006, 473–90, Robertson, *The Enlightenment. The Pursuit of Happiness*, 750–5.

established, promoted, and perhaps realized in the future by individuals and their collective efforts.[103]

In his seminal work on how European travelers, adventurers, missionaries, administrators, and enlighteners engaged with Asian cultures, Jürgen Osterhammel has argued that typical postcolonial narratives, theories, and assumptions must be qualified. His main argument is "that the Enlightenment's discovery of Asia entailed a more open-minded, less patronizing approach to foreign cultures than suggested by those who see it as a mere incubation period of Orientalism."[104] By the end of the century, this cosmopolitan stance and inclusive Eurocentrism was replaced by arrogance, feelings of superiority, and exclusive Eurocentrism, and came to dominate the nineteenth century. As usual, qualifications and nuances are essential. German political economist Johann Heinrich Gottlob von Justi (1717–1771), for instance, offers a fine example of epistemological or cognitive cosmopolitanism. His *Comparisons of the European with the Asiatic and Other Supposedly Barbaric Governments* (1762) is an impressive critique of exclusive Eurocentrism.

> So highly do we esteem our reason, our knowledge, our understanding, that we look down on all other nations that do people the Earth as on so many miserable creeping worms; and in truth, we treat them no better. We consider ourselves lords of the Earth; we seize without compunction the lands belonging to all those that inhabit the three other parts of the world; we dictate to them the laws of their lands, appear before them as their masters; and, if they dare put up the least resistance, we exterminate them utterly.[105]

In good Enlightenment fashion, Justi wants to encourage his readers to change their perspectives, and assess without bias non-European justice systems, for instance, those of the Khoikhoi (usually referred to as the Hottentots) or the Siamese. Montesquieu's *Persian Letters* (1721) and similar publications can also be seen as examples of cognitive cosmopolitanism. Authors try to change their perspectives, are skeptical toward their own culture, traditions, religion, values, and practices, and try to practice the enlarged way of thinking (see 3.2). Other publications that assumed an outsider's perspective to describe, discuss, criticize or satirize European manners and customs were the *Lettres juives* (*Jewish Letters*, 1736) by the French writer Marquis d'Argens (1704–1771), *The Citizen of the World* (1762) by

---

103 See Cavallar, *Dynamic Cosmopolitanism*, 1–30.
104 Osterhammel, *Unfabling the East*, x. Another useful study is Bettina Brandt and Daniel Purdy, eds., *China in the German Enlightenment*, Toronto, Buffalo and London: University of Toronto Press 2016.
105 Quoted in Osterhammel, *Unfabling the East*, 78. For an interpretation, see Brown, *Moral Capital*, 77–81.

the Anglo-Irish writer Oliver Goldsmith (1728–1774), and *Marokkanische Briefe* (*Moroccan Letters*, 1784) by the Bavarian author Johann Pezzl (1756–1823).¹⁰⁶ Many Jesuit missionaries wrote extensively and often enthusiastically about Chinese culture, religion, and society, among them Joachim Bouvet (1656–1730) and Jean-Baptiste du Halde (1674–1743). Some even lavishly praised Chinese government, economics, and moral standards.¹⁰⁷ It can be argued that these and other writers were, in some way or another, prejudiced, racist, or ethnocentric. Yet there are differences among travelers, travel writers, enlighteners, and intellectuals in general. Some were, for instance, more biased than others. Some managed to critically reflect upon their own assumptions, distanced themselves from them, and learned "to see their own culture through foreign eyes."¹⁰⁸ Fine examples are the English writer and medical pioneer Lady Mary Wortley Montagu (1689–1762) and Georg Forster.

Figure 17: Plate from Joachim Bouvet, *Etat present de la Chine* (1697).

"It is to the Enlightenment that we also owe the modern conception of the global society."¹⁰⁹ This is probably too sweeping a claim, as it tends to trivialize cosmopolitan approaches that existed before the European Enlightenment. Addition-

---

106 Robertson, *The Enlightenment. The Pursuit of Happiness*, 605–6.
107 Robertson, *The Enlightenment*, 621–6.
108 Robertson, *The Enlightenment*, 611 and Robertson, *The Enlightenment*, 611–21 on Montagu and Forster.
109 Pagden, *The Enlightenment*, viii. See also Pagden, *The Enlightenment*, 323.

ally, it overlooks how often declarations of cosmopolitanism remained superficial. Sometimes, it merely indicated a pro-European attitude or a rejection of narrow-minded patriotism. As with other normative theories, it should not be forgotten that the approaches of many enlighteners were quite deficient, and their cosmopolitan stances were often unconvincing.[110] A more accurate statement is probably that in the 18th century, cosmopolitan theories of modern European history reached a culmination point and have remained influential up to the present day.

Currents of cosmopolitanism among some enlighteners often coexisted with, or even overlapped, with downright racist theories. Kant is probably the most famous case in point.[111] Enlighteners did not invent racism, but they often provided philosophical arguments supporting it. The 18th century saw the birth of modern antisemitic theories. Even authors who spoke up in favor of Jewish emancipation, legal equality and integration like Abbé Henri Grégoire were full of positive, but also negative stereotypes about the Jewish "national character".[112] Yet it should also be emphasized that racist prejudices against other Europeans such as the Scots, the Irish or the Eastern Europeans were also widespread. Sometimes theories of civilization were not racist, but followed the four stages theory, the assumption that human societies pass through four distinct states, namely hunting, shepherding, agriculture, and finally the age of commerce. This theory implied that allegedly backward, superstitious, wild or immature groups, societies or whole continents could be eventually civilized.

4.5 Contemporary Relevance: Moral Relativism and Moral Universalism

Since the European Enlightenment, there has been a diversity of ethical positions, such as utilitarianism, ethics of compassion, or forms of moral criticism. To this

---

110 For an example, see the debates whether Kant was, by present-day standards, a cosmopolitan or not. For introductions, see Pauline Kleingeld, Kant's Second Thoughts on Race, *The Philosophical Quarterly*, 57 (2007), 573–92, Parekh, *Black Enlightenment*, 19–22 and 50–79, and my discussion in *Kant's Embedded Cosmopolitanism*, 10–2.
111 This paragraph follows Tricoire, *Die Aufklärung*, 277–96.
112 Henri Baptiste Grégoire, *Essai sur la régénération physique, morale et politique des juifs* (Essay on the physical, moral and political regeneration of the Jews), Metz: Claude Lamort 1789, English translation in 1791 and Alyssa Goldstein Sepinwall, A Friend of the Jews? The Abbe Gregoire and Philosemitism in Revolutionary France, in: Jonathan Karp and Adam Sutcliffe, eds., *Philosemitism in History*, Cambridge: Cambridge University Press 2011, 111–27. "Even as it professed to support the Jews, the *Essai* functioned as Catholic apologetic, aiming to prove the truth of Christianity to readers" (Sepinwall, A Friend of the Jews?, 116).

day, issues of demarcation persist. What falls within the realm of normative universalism, and what belongs to the sphere of cultural relativity? The answers are —hopefully—clear in cases like slavery or genocide, but difficulties arise in areas such as end-of-life care and assisted dying. What exactly is meant by the phrase "dying with dignity?" Where exactly are the boundaries of freedom of speech? When is it abused? Should tolerant people be intolerant with those who are apparently intolerant? In which cases is prudence appropriate, and when should a principled approach take the lead?

The question of the origins of human morality also remains controversial. Since the 18th century, a plethora of scientific disciplines, such as evolutionary biology, psychology, and empirical anthropology, have proposed answers. The prevailing insight is that humans are exposed to numerous external factors, such as society or culture, and may be largely determined by them. This often leads to moral relativism: moral norms and principles are "nothing more than" products of societal, cultural, or psychological factors. A typical statement is the following: "Mr. Kant's *a priori* assumptions are rejected by modern philosophy because they are wrong. Through modern sciences, we know that Kant was wrong."[113] However, the talk of "modern philosophy" and "modern science" is undifferentiated. Neither provides a unanimous judgment. For instance, scholars from different disciplines have developed the theory of a "universal moral grammar," which posits that certain moral principles are, analogously to linguistic structures, "innate" or *a priori*, independent of cultures. Cultural differences only arise in the concrete manifestation of these formal structures depending on the social environment.[114]

There are substantial objections against this theory of universal moral grammar. However, this is by no means a problem. What is crucial is understanding the fundamental difference between a scientific, empirical paradigm on the one hand, and a philosophical, hermeneutical approach on the other. In the natural sciences, humans are perceived as natural beings and subjected to analysis as objects from an external standpoint. This is one version of the Enlightenment, name-

---

[113] Jürgen Vogel, https://www.faz.net/aktuell/feuilleton/buecher/sachbuch/philosophin-bettina-stangneth-ueber-boeses-denken-14363243.html (last accessed October 2, 2025).

[114] John Mikhail, "Universal moral grammar: theory, evidence and the future, *Trends in Cognitive Sciences*, 11, 4 (2007), 143–52, Marc Hauser, *Moral Minds: How Nature Designed Our Universal Sense of Right and Wrong*, Ecco press 2006. This approach is criticized by Nalini Elisa Ramlakhan, An Argument in Favour of a Universal Moral Grammar and Its Weaknesses, *International Journal of Arts & Sciences*, 4, 27 (2011), 91–106. See also Nicolas Baumard, Jean-Baptiste André and Dan Sperber, A mutualistic approach to morality: The evolution of fairness by partner choice, *The Behavioral and brain sciences*, 36, 1 (2013), 59–122 and the reply of Nalini Ramlakhan and Andrew Brook, Sense of fairness: not by itself a moral sense and not a foundation of a lot of morality, *The Behavioral and brain sciences*, 36, 1 (2013), 96–7.

ly Enlightenment through science relying on empirical data (see 1.1, conception no. 4). According to the hermeneutical approach, actions and judgments are sought to be clarified and reconstructed "from within."[115] It is the perspective of reason that views freedom, equality, and human dignity as problematic but possible concepts. Humans are not approached as objects of inquiry but as acting subjects. In the words of Heiner Bielefeldt, concepts like human dignity assume that mutual respect for humans as responsible subjects is "inescapable" in the sense that normative reflections and communication cannot be abandoned—they are "always already" implied and present.[116] The result might be a performative self-contradiction (see 2.1).

Both perspectives, empirical analyses and hermeneutical reconstruction, are complementary but fundamentally different. Consequently, there is tension between them. It is crucial to acknowledge the epistemological limits of an empirical approach (see 2.3). Failure to do so turns the scientific paradigm and its perspective into a reductionist, naturalistic metaphysics. This approach would ignore the boundaries of knowledge and would cease to be science, becoming, in the words of Jürgen Habermas, nothing more than "bad philosophy."[117] Some modern philosophers such as John Rawls, Jürgen Habermas, Birgit Recki, Heiner Bielefeldt, Brigitte Falkenburg, or Rainer Forst do not simply assert that Kant was "wrong." It is more accurate to claim that they are engaged in building upon Kant's philosophy in creative and novel ways. If the empirical paradigm is turned into something absolute and no longer complements but seeks to abolish the hermeneutic paradigm, this must evoke protests from philosophers in the name of moral common sense and epistemological considerations.

The topic of tolerance provides a fitting example. To this day, the insight of many enlighteners remains valuable, because they emphasized that "only a generally valid justification of toleration which rests on higher-level conceptions of reason and morality could lead to a generally intelligible, binding, and fair form of toleration." This conception of tolerance, grounded in the recognition, equality,

---

115 Heiner Bielefeldt, *Auslaufmodell Menschenwürde? Warum sie in Frage steht und warum wir sie verteidigen müssen*, Freiburg im Breisgau: Herder 2011, 91. See also Bielefeldt, *Auslaufmodell Menschenwürde?*, 90–104 and Kate E. Tunstall, ed., *Self-Evident Truths? Human Rights and the Enlightenment*, New York: Bloomsbury 2012 (especially the essays by James Tully and Seyla Benhabib), Hans Joas, *The sacredness of the person: a new genealogy of human rights*, Washington, D. C.: Georgetown University Press 2013 and Vincenzo Ferrone, The Rights of History: Enlightenment and Human Rights, *Human Rights Quarterly*, 39 (2017), 130–41.
116 Bielefeldt, *Auslaufmodell Menschenwürde?*, 91.
117 Jürgen Habermas, *Glauben und Wissen*, Frankfurt am Main: Suhrkamp 2001, 20.

and autonomy of individuals, makes sense in modern pluralistic societies. Contemporary philosophers like Rainer Forst can connect their own systematic considerations to these traditions of the European Enlightenment.[118] Reducing debates to unquestioned naturalistic assumptions would be of little help.

Many enlighteners have navigated a path between dogmatic and relativistic tendencies. An ultimate philosophical justification for morality should be eyed with suspicion, as should unqualified normative relativism. Nevertheless, attempts at justification should not be abandoned, even if they only succeed partially and provisionally. The moral and legal philosophies of the European Enlightenment reached a level of reflection that can still serve as models for contemporary discussions. Denis Diderot's unpublished manuscript *Rameau's Nephew* (written between 1761 and 1774) is a case in point.[119] In this imaginary philosophical debate, a character called *Moi* ("Me", probably Diderot himself) meets *Lui* ("Him"), modeled around Jean-François Rameau (1716–1777), the nephew of the composer of the same name. For many contemporaries, Jean-François was a libertine, a parasite, a loser, and a self-contradicting clown. Both characters take materialism and atheism for granted. They discuss the possibility of morality in modernity. "If God does not exist, is there really a basis for morality? Is it possible to be virtuous? And what, if anything, separates humankind from the amorality and potential ruthlessness of the animal world?"[120] *Moi* defends a version of secular and benevolent humanism *avant la lettre*. *Lui*, by contrast, is more radical. He claims that what is commonly considered virtue or moral behavior amounts to nothing more than a refined form of vanity and narcissism. Or it seems that this is *one* of the positions he endorses. As one commentator put it, "The boisterous ramblings of *Lui* enact a succession of possibilities in which nothing is excluded."[121]

Elements of Enlightenment philosophy also provide the tools to question and combat this cynical and hedonistic worldview. Is Rameau's claim that we live in a dog-eat-dog world, where "people of all stations prey on each other" like all other

---

[118] The quotation in Forst, *Toleration in Conflict*, 241. Forst's own approach, inspired by figures like Bayle and Kant, views the "right to justification" as the focal point of the concept of tolerance; see the second part of his book.

[119] Denis Diderot, *Rameau's Nephew. Le Neveu de Rameau. A Multi-Media Edition*, ed. Marian Hobson, translated by Kate E. Tunstall and Caroline Warman, 2nd ed., Cambridge: Open Book Publishers, 2016. My interpretation follows Curran, *Diderot*, 188–99 and Lloyd, *Enlightenment Shadows*, 127–39.

[120] Curran, *Diderot*, 192.

[121] Lloyd, *Enlightenment Shadows*, 128.

Figure 18: Louis-Michel van Loo (1707–1771), Portrait of Denis Diderot (1713–1784), 1767. Diderot was a prominent *philosophe* and contributor to, and, together with Jean Le Rond d'Alembert, chief editor of the *Encyclopédie*. He wrote works of fiction and non-fiction, and about 7,000 articles for the famous encyclopedia.

species[122] an appropriate description based on facts, or just one of many other possible interpretations? Can *Lui's* assertion that virtue is "nothing but" vanity be substantiated, or is it little more than psychobabble? Does not Rameau's criticism of virtue as a form of hypocrisy, or his denouncing of "abject poverty"[123] imply a standard of morality? In the sense of: true virtue is beyond hypocrisy, vanity, narcissism, and disrespect for the needs of others? *Rameau's Nephew* challenges any brand of humanism, and even the authority of reason and philosophy. But this challenge does not have to end in the defeat of the humanist "Enlightenment project"—provided it ever existed.[124]

Many convictions held by the Enlightenment thinkers cannot be shared today: an often naively conceived notion of human nature; teleological assumptions about the development of the individual and humanity as a whole; and the belief that improving institutions—such as education and training—would, in the long run, also enhance moral dispositions. Robert Louden summarized this conviction of many enlighteners as follows:

> Humanity would become moralized through and by means of the growth of education, participation in democratic polities dedicated to the rule of law, free trade between nations, and the establishment of an effective international justice system. In the process of becoming moralized, support for Enlightenment ideals would itself become stronger and more widespread across the human species.[125]

There is little evidence today that a dynamic process of this kind has taken place. In particular, the claim that political or social institutions directly impact internal dispositions must be approached with caution.

Despite its limitations, the moral and legal philosophies of the enlighteners should not be condemned *tout court*. Particularly valuable is the effort to establish universal moral and legal principles that are not grounded in theology, naturalism, or ideology. The humanism of the Enlightenment fundamentally differed from classical, ancient humanism. The latter, succinctly summarized with reference to Plato and Aristotle, can be described as follows: "According to the teachings of classical humanism, the essence of humanity, that of *all* humans, can only be *realized, portrayed, represented* by a *few* (male) specimens for whom others do

---

122 Diderot, *Rameau's Nephew*, 42.
123 Diderot, *Rameau's Nephew*, 42.
124 See, for instance, Schmidt, What Enlightenment Project?
125 Louden, *The World We Want*, 128. The concepts of human nature, humankind and humanity in some philosophies of the European Enlightenment are the topic of Stefanie Buchenau, and Ansgar Lyssy, eds., *Humankind and Humanity in the Philosophy of the Enlightenment. From Locke to Kant*, London et al.: Bloomsbury Academic 2023.

4.5 Contemporary Relevance: Moral Relativism and Moral Universalism — 143

Figure 19: Engraving by Daniel Chodowiecki in the *Elementarwerk* (Elementary Work) by the theologian and educator Johann Bernhard Basedow (1774), from J.B. Basedow's *Elementarwerk*, edited by Theodor Fritzsch, third volume, Leipzig 1909. Basedow (1724–1790) was the most prominent representative of the Philanthropists, a reform pedagogical movement in the German-speaking territories of the Holy Roman Empire. Instruction takes place in the countryside or in a garden, where children are allowed to touch, hear, smell, and comprehend. A child experiences the pain of a thorn prick. It was a new form of education aimed at bringing about long-term positive changes in society.

the work."[126] This elitist humanism is at least partially questioned, sometimes even overcome, in the European Enlightenment.

Vincenzo Ferrone writes, "The best part of the intellectual heritage of the late Enlightenment undoubtedly consists in the definitive formulation of human rights

---

[126] Hauke Brunkhorst, Klassischer und moderner Humanismus. Die Rolle der Intellektuellen in Europa, in: Richard Faber and Brunhilde Wehinger, eds., *Aufklärung in Geschichte und Gegenwart*, Würzburg: Königshausen & Neumann 2010, 35–44, at 35. See also Richard Faber, Streit um die Humanität. Polyphonie und Kalophonie des Aufklärungs-Zeitalters, in: Faber and Wehinger, *Aufklärung*, 15–34 on Enlightenment humanism. It should be noted, however, that the term "humanism" had a different meaning until the middle of the 19th century, see Robertson, *The Enlightenment. The Pursuit of Happiness*, xvi.

and their use as the spearhead of the West."[127] I agree with the first part of the sentence, but the second part is questionable. In my opinion, this once again points to the danger of instrumentalizing morality or law, even when they can legitimately claim universal validity. Human rights doctrines can then become a continuation of politics by other means, used as a "weapon" or "spearhead" in a polemical battle or military confrontation against other cultures.

Modern human rights doctrines can in part be seen as an achievement of the European Enlightenment. However, it is essential to continue this Enlightenment tradition with inter- or transcultural discourses. Otherwise, there is a risk that the Enlightenment, as a polemical term, "turns into a quasi-culturalist category or even serves as a means of Western cultural self-assurance in contrast to supposedly unenlightened cultures and religions"[128] (see the Introduction, Assumption 1). This would fuel the "clash of civilizations," directly contradicting the concept of enlightenment as an intercultural phenomenon and the emancipatory conception of enlightenment (see 1.1).

"Is there a common language of morality?" was the key question of this chapter. The answer: Quite possibly. In the spirit of some enlighteners, one could add that it is our task to bring this language to light and contribute to its cultivation. This includes the minimal normative standards of human dignity, human rights, tolerance, and democratic rule of law. In this sense, the Enlightenment was also a century of humanism.

---

[127] Ferrone, *Die Aufklärung*, 11. This statement is missing in the English translation, namely Ferrone, *The Enlightenment*.
[128] Heiner Bielefeldt, *Menschenrechte in der Einwanderungsgesellschaft. Plädoyer für einen aufgeklärten Multikulturalismus*, Bielefeld: transcript 2007, 197.

Chapter 5
Faith and hope: Religion, critique of religion, and the religious Enlightenment

> Pure reason does not undermine religion, but rather its aberrations. You will lose prejudices and retain religion
> —Andreas Riem, *On Enlightenment* (1788)[1]

5.1 Hostility Toward Religion?

According to a widespread cliché, the European Enlightenment was hostile to religion and was secular and atheistic (see Assumptions 2 and 6). For example, German-American Peter Gay, one of the most influential historians of the European Enlightenment, claimed in the 1960s that, despite all their differences, the Enlightenment thinkers agreed on a "single passion": "The passion to cure the spiritual malady that is religion, the germ of ignorance, barbarity, filth, and the basest self-hatred."[2] Unfortunately, this cliché is still perpetuated today, most recently by Anthony Pagden, who asserts that the European Enlightenment was "profoundly anti-religious."[3] According to a corresponding and polemical narrative, the European Enlightenment was the crucial step from a traditional, religious, ignorant, and fanatical past to an enlightened, secular (and atheist) present characterized by science, reason, humanity, and progress.[4]

German philosopher Ernst Cassirer questioned this assumption or rather prejudice back in the 1930s, stating, "If we attempt to test this traditional view with concrete historical facts, we soon come to entertain the gravest doubts and reservations so far as German and English thought of the Enlightenment is con-

---

[1] Andreas Riem, *On Enlightenment: Is It and Could It Be Dangerous to the State, to Religion, or Dangerous in General? A Word to be Heeded by Princes, Statesmen, and Clergy* [1788], in: James Schmidt. ed., *What is Enlightenment? Eighteenth Century Answers and Twentieth Century Questions*, Berkeley, Los Angeles, London 1996, 168–87, at 172.
[2] Peter Gay, *The Enlightenment: An Interpretation, vol. 1: The Rise of Modern Paganism*, New York: Norton 1966, 373.
[3] Pagden, *The Enlightenment*, xi.
[4] A corresponding narrative can be found among some conservative or right-wing intellectuals: The Enlightenment is seen as the crucial step towards a godless, secular and horrible present which deifies science and reason. For more on this perspective, see Paul Avis, *Theology and the Enlightenment. A Critical Enquiry into Enlightenment Theology and Its Reception*, London: T&T Clark 2023.

cerned."⁵ Recent research has largely confirmed Cassirer's more nuanced judgment. Most enlighteners criticized religious fanaticism, superstition, intolerance, and related manifestations. They often attacked Christian denominations or state churches. However, a blanket rejection of religion and Christianity cannot be attributed to them.⁶ Werner Schneiders emphasizes the simple fact that there can also be a theistic, theological, or religious criticism of religion, which has existed throughout history. This is because one can "also fight against certain forms of religion, theology, and the church for religious reasons, and one can also advocate a sharp distinction between knowledge and faith for religious reasons."⁷

As in related cases, it is not appropriate here to think in dubious binary oppositions and alternatives: This world or the otherworldly, human or divine, anthropology, or theology, autonomy, or theonomy, reason, or faith, secular philosophy of history, or theological philosophy of history. Although thinking in binary oppositions is still widespread today, it does little to aid our understanding of the European Enlightenment. It is evident that many Enlightenment thinkers believed in a "both and."

The evidence for binary opposition is limited, as the example of Anthony Pagden illustrates. He discusses French materialists like d'Holbach and La Mettrie, as well as Voltaire, and especially Hume. Voltaire, however, can be characterized as a typical deist, and Hume as a skeptic who considered a rational justification of belief impossible and therefore described "our most holy religion" as "founded on *Faith* not on reason." Voltaire can be considered mainstream, while the atheistic materialists like d'Holbach and La Mettrie were outsiders among mainstream enlighteners and usually fiercely opposed, also by deists like Voltaire. Pagden mistak-

---

5 Ernst Cassirer, *The Philosophy of the Enlightenment* [1932], updated edition, Princeton: Princeton University Press 2009, 134.
6 Apart from Cassirer, *The Philosophy of the Enlightenment*, 134–96 see also Louden, *The World We Want*, 15–26, Beutel, *Kirchengeschichte*, Charly Coleman, Religion, in: Daniel Brewer, ed., *The Cambridge Companion to the French Enlightenment*, Cambridge: Cambridge University Press 2014, 105–21, same, *The Virtues of Abandon. An anti-individualist History of the French Enlightenment*, Stanford, Calif.: Stanford University Press 2014, 9–12, Outram, *The Enlightenment*, 114–129, but also 99–113, Karlfried Gründer and Karl Heinrich Rengstorf, *Religionskritik und Religiosität in der deutschen Aufklärung*, Tübingen: Max Niemeyer 2011, especially the longer essay by Hans Erich Bödeker, Die Religiosität der Gebildeten, in: Gründer and Rengstorf, *Religionskritik und Religiosität*, 145–95; David Sorkin, *The Religious Enlightenment. Protestants, Jews, and Catholics from London to Vienna*, Princeton: Princeton University Press 2008; Avis, *Theology and the Enlightenment*, especially 137–208; Anna Tomaszewska, ed., *Between Secularization and Reform. Religion in the Enlightenment*, Leiden and Boston: Brill 2022.
7 Schneiders, *Hoffnung auf Vernunft*, 11. See also Schneiders, *Hoffnung auf Vernunft*, 11–2, 16, 23, and 166–7.

enly equates the fight against religious intolerance and superstition with the fight against Christianity and religion in general.[8]

The European Enlightenment was primarily a process of self-reflective enlightenment of reason and understanding, a critique of prejudices, superstitions, and fanaticism with an open outcome (see 1.1, conceptions 3, 5, and 6). If the "true" Enlightenment is characterized as atheistic or politically radical—as by Jonathan Israel, for example—at least two problems arise. First, the essence of "genuine" or "real" Enlightenment is defined, which raises the objection that this might be nothing but a metaphysical claim. In a second step, the interpreter is then compelled to label "about ninety percent of Enlightenment thinkers as not genuine or inconsistent, as half-hearted, or compromising Enlightenment thinkers."[9] This is not a convincing approach (see also 5.3).

A widespread "secularist self-perception," especially in present day Europe, also hinders an unbiased interpretation of the religious dimensions of the European Enlightenment.[10] The narrative goes like this: European history, or even world history itself, is reconstructed as a continuous progress from naive, dogmatic, and intolerant faiths, and religions to a secularized, rational, and scientifically oriented modernity. This triumphant modernity has learned to separate religion from science and politics, has privatized religion, and—in some accounts—has eventually abolished it. In this narrative, the European Enlightenment is a crucial step toward extensive or complete secularization.

This narrative is problematic. It contains historical distortions and simplifications and is prone to turn into a teleological construction of history situated in the realm of metaphysics. Unhistorical theories of secularization tend to overlook the division of the world into religious and secular spheres during the European High

---

[8] See Pagden, *The Enlightenment*, 79–124, especially 80, 122 (with the Hume quotation), and 82.
[9] Schneiders, Hoffnung auf Vernunft, 16. This is evidently the outcome of Jonathan Israel's approach. See, for example, his review essay "Enlightenment! Which Enlightenment? [2006], in: Ryan Patrick Hanley and Darrin M. McMahon, eds., *The Enlightenment. Critical Concepts in Historical Studies*, 5 volumes, London and New York: Routledge 2010, Vol. 1, 307–27. According to Israel, the "true," consistent, and uncompromising representatives of the European Enlightenment were the minority of materialistic atheists and Spinozists; most Enlightenment thinkers simply do not fall into this category. Ironically, Schneiders articulated his critique 16 years *before* Israel's review essay.
[10] José Casanova, Eurozentrischer Säkularismus und die Herausforderung der Globalisierung, in: Wilhelm Guggenberger, Dietmar Regensburger and Kristina Stöckl, eds., *Politik, Religion und Markt: Die Rückkehr der Religion als Anfrage an den politisch-philosophischen Diskurs der Moderne*, Innsbruck: Innsbruck University Press 2009, 19–40, the quotation in: Casanova, Eurozentrischer Säkularismus, 26, and his key work *Public Religions*. See also Cavallar, *Islam, Aufklärung und Moderne*, 37–8.

Middle Ages, as well as the attempts at that time to shift the boundaries between them.[11] Harold J. Berman and Charles Taylor have argued that secularization as differentiation began with the papal revolutions and reforms in the High Middle Ages. It was an "attempt to secularize the religious," to bring it into the *saeculum*.[12] This eventually led to a reassessment and valorization of the secular sphere. One path involved expanding Christian life beyond the monastery walls. Reform movements, the Reformation, Pietism, and Neology, which advocated a new form of religiosity, serve as examples. Many representatives of the religious Enlightenment, among them Kant, believed that the Kingdom of God could be prepared in this world. Kant referred to it as the "Kingdom of God *on earth*" or the "ethical community," promoted through our moral efforts.[13] The binary opposition of "this world" and the "otherworldly" was thus qualified.

The thesis of an anti-Christian and anti-religious Enlightenment must be vigorously challenged (see also 1.1, conception no. 6). Swedish-born intellectual historian Helena Rosenblatt turns the relevant claims of figures like Paul Hazard or Peter Gay upside down: "It is becoming increasingly evident that in a great many places in Europe, the Enlightenment was not at war with Christianity. Rather, it took place within the Christian churches themselves."[14] The cliché of an irreligious Enlightenment hostile to Christianity is also contradicted by numerous events. The Swiss pastor and philosopher Johann Caspar Lavater (17411801), for example, encountered Charles Bonnet's *La palingénésie philosophique* in 1769. In this work, the Genevan naturalist Bonnet (1720–1793) argued that the development of living beings indicated the existence of the Christian God. Lavater

---

11 Casanova, *Public Religions*, 15 and *Säkularismus*, 21.
12 The classical studies are Harold J. Berman, *Law and Revolution. The Formation of the Western Legal Tradition*, Cambridge, Mass. and London: Harvard University Press 1983 and Charles Taylor, *Sources of the Self. The Making of the Modern Identity*, Cambridge, Mass., and London: Harvard University Press 1989. The quotation is in Casanova, *Säkularismus*, 21.
13 Kant, Religion, vol. 6, 151–2, 175 note, 192, The Conflict of the Faculties, vol. 7, 68, 74. Refl. 1396, vol. 15, 608 offers perhaps the most concise formulation: "The kingdom of God on earth: that is the ultimate destiny of humanity." See also my study *Dynamic Cosmopolitanism*, 17–27. In contemporary language, "religion" refers to a "set of beliefs," while religiosity pertains to the "subjective attitude of a believer towards these beliefs," see Gerhard Alexander and Johannes Fritsche, Religion und Religiosität im 18. Jahrhundert. Eine Skizze zur Wortgeschichte, in: Gründer and Heinrich Rengstorf, *Religionskritik und Religiosität*, 11–24, at 11.
14 Helena Rosenblatt, The Christian Enlightenment [2006], in: Hanley und McMahon, *The Enlightenment*, vol. 4, 342–58, at 342. See also William J. Bulman and Robert G. Ingram, eds., *God in the Enlightenment*, New York: Oxford University Press 2016, Madeleine Pennington, *Quakers, Christ, and the Enlightenment*, Oxford: Oxford University Press 2021, Fillafer, *Aufklärung habsburgisch*.

programmatically titled his translation *Mr. Carl Bonnet's Philosophical Investigation of the Evidences for Christianity*. He claimed to have undertaken the translation with enthusiasm, shedding "tears of joy over the certainty of my religion."[15] A copy was sent to the Jewish Enlightenment thinker Moses Mendelssohn, accompanied by a public dedication letter. Lavater bluntly urged Mendelssohn to either refute Bonnet's argument for the superiority of Christianity or, as a German Socrates, convert from Judaism to Christianity. Lavater intentionally placed Mendelssohn in an uncomfortable position: Silence, conversion, or an open attack on Christianity were not genuine options. The dispute was avidly followed by the interested public throughout Europe. "The first great cultural conflict between Christianity and Judaism begins, with strong anti-Semitic aggressions also being staged in the media."[16] Several elements stand out: neither Bonnet nor Lavater accepted a clear separation between natural science and theology. Lavater engaged in what Montesquieu had condemned as proselytizing a few decades earlier. Little evidence of the spirit of tolerance is discernible; religion is not considered a private matter, and this controversy takes place at the end of the century of the Enlightenment.

Recent academic research has shown that even the familiar contrast between allegedly conservative Catholicism and progressive Enlightenment thinkers should be seen in a more nuanced light. There were various forms of the Catholic Enlightenment, for instance, within Benedictine monasteries, or the reform movement of Jansenism. The goal here was again an enlightened religiosity that criticized, for example, the excessive cult of relics, superstition, or belief in witches. As German philosopher, historian, and theologian Ulrich L. Lehner argues, the "enlightened monks" of the Benedictines promoted "a modern and strong belief in individual freedom, tolerance, human rights, nonviolence, and the conviction that the church, but especially monastic life, had to modernize, and adapt to society."[17]

---

15 Quoted in Geier, *Aufklärung*, 192, where this episode is narrated; see Geier, *Aufklärung*, 191–98.
16 Geier, *Aufklärung*, 198.
17 Ulrich Lehner, *Enlightened Monks. The German Benedictines 1740–1803*, Oxford: Oxford University Press 2011, 2. Lehner is a prolific writer. See also Ulrich Lehner and Michael Printy, *Brill's Companion to the Catholic Enlightenment in Europe*, Leiden: Brill 2010, Ulrich Lehner and Jeffrey Burson, *Enlightenment in Catholic Europe. A Transnational History*, Notre Dame, Ind.: University of Notre Dame Press 2014, Lehner, *The Catholic Enlightenment. The Forgotten History of a Global Movement*, *The Inner Life of Catholic Reform: From the Council of Trent to the Enlightenment*, New York: Oxford University Press 2022. See also, among others, Daniel J. Watkins, *Berruyer's Bible. Public Opinion and the Politics of Enlightenment Catholicism in France*, Montreal and Kingston, London and Chicago: McGill-Queen's University Press 2021 on the attempt of the French Jesuit Isaac-Joseph Berruyer to combine Enlightenment ideas with Catholic theology.

Generalizations do not do justice to the actual heterogeneity of the Enlightenment, which encompassed various currents ranging from proponents of natural religion, a religion of feeling, freethinkers, deism, atheism, indifference, agnosticism, skepticism, reform movements within Christian theology such as Neology, to the largely neglected apologetic literature (which sought to justify or defend the Christian faith). Cassirer referred to "the wealth and confusing diversity of the literature of religion and theology in the eighteenth century."[18] In fact, the French materialists, and atheists were a small group, mostly rejected, and opposed by other enlighteners. They were by no means representative of "the Enlightenment." It can be generalized that most Enlightenment thinkers opposed religious fanaticism, dogmatic attitudes, sectarian polemics, and intolerance in matters of religion (Introduction, Assumption 6, and 1.1, conception no. 6). However, religion or Christianity was not universally rejected. Rather, the focus of most enlighteners was on the reform of the religious, attempting to overcome sectarian polemics, to cultivate religious inner life, to promote tolerance, or to emphasize the moral content of religions, especially of Christianity. In the words of Albrecht Beutel, "confessionally diverse Christianity felt compelled and empowered to develop trans-confessional ethical foundations (reason, natural law, natural religion)," primarily because of the religious wars of the 17th century and the historical fact of a religiously fragmented Europe.[19]

The starting point for many considerations was the existence of different forms of belief and denominations. The various denominations in Europe were the result of the Reformation and religious disputes and wars that had shaken the early modern period. This historical experience likely led many early enlighteners to criticize the narrow-mindedness and dogmatic fixation of many believers and church leaders. Montesquieu did not see religions themselves as the causes of these wars, but rather the "spirit of intolerance that fills those who consider themselves followers of the state religion" and the "spirit of proselytism" (see also 3.3). By this, he meant the attempt to persuade members of other religious groups to

---

18 Cassirer, *The Philosophy of the Enlightenment*, 137. For an overview see Robertson, *The Enlightenment. The Pursuit of Happiness*, 220–60.

19 Beutel, *Kirchengeschichte*, 23. See also Louden, *The World We Want*, 16–25 and Martus, *Aufklärung*, 771. The countless works that defended the rationality, reasonableness, and divinity of Christianity against "freethinking," especially atheist attacks in the 17th and 18th centuries, are grouped under the terms "Apologetics" or "apologetic literature." See Friedrich Vollhardt, Verweltlichung der Wissenschaft(en)? Zur fehlenden Negativbilanz in der apologetischen Literatur der Frühen Neuzeit, in: Lutz Danneberg, ed., *Zwischen christlicher Apologetik und methodologischem Atheismus. Wissenschaftsprozesse im Zeitraum von 1500–1800*, Berlin: de Gruyter 2002, 67–93, especially 77–88.

convert to one's own religious community, perhaps through manipulation, and deception. In his *Persian Letters*, Montesquieu has a Muslim character write about Catholic Christianity, stating that there are "an infinite number of scholars, for the most part dervishes, who among themselves raise thousands of new questions about religion. [...] those that produce some new propositions are immediately called heretics."[20] Disputes of this nature are not only politically dangerous as they can plunge a state into disorder or even civil wars. Since they relate to metaphysical and theological issues, they also cannot be solved—according to a common assumption—through reasoning or rational argumentation (see 2.3).

I have argued in my Introduction that most enlighteners were not hostile to religion but rather sought its reform. Sectarian differences were to be overcome with the concept of a "natural religion" or the "religion of reason."" Perhaps the hypothesis can be formulated that many Enlightenment thinkers until around 1750 were *still religious*, as evidenced by the theological justification of morality, adherence to proofs of God's existence, and belief in the afterlife, divine justice, and providence.[21] Their confrontation with French atheism and materialism necessitated a nuanced examination. Many later enlighteners were religious despite—or precisely because of—this engagement with atheism, although not in a traditional, orthodox sense. Rousseau, Spalding, Smith, and Kant can serve as examples (see 5.3). Rousseau broke with the *philosophes* of the *Encyclopédie* in February 1758, writing an open letter to d'Alembert. Yet there was a radical break, even within the religious Enlightenment: Christianity was no longer taken for granted; it could be analyzed, criticized, rejected, defended, reformed, or justified. After all, the European Enlightenment was an "age of criticism" (see 1.2). Natural philosophy gradually separated itself from theology. Sir Isaac Newton (1643–1727), probably the century's foremost scientist, might be a case in point. He subscribed to experimental science, and was a Christian, though he did not believe in the doctrine of the Trinity.[22] Another example is the Swiss and French liberal Henri-Benjamin Constant (1767–1830). In his *De la religion* (1824–1834), he argued that there is a universal need for religion among humans,

---

20 Montesquieu, *Persian Letters*, 39.
21 See Thomas Ahnert, Fortschrittsgeschichte und Religiöse Aufklärung. William Robertson und die Deutung außereuropäischer Kulturen, in: Hardtwig, ed., *Die Aufklärung und ihre Weltwirkung*, 101–22 and Christine Vogel, Von Voltaire zu Le Paige—Die französische Aufklärung und der Jansenismus, in: Hardtwig, *Aufklärung*, 77–99 for examples.
22 Robertson, *The Enlightenment. The Pursuit of Happiness*, 56–64, Curran, *Diderot*, 159–60, Meyer, *Die Epoche der Aufklärung*, 143, Outram, *The Enlightenment*, 106 and 112–3.

and that every religion can be reformed over time. His arguments are in turn based on the ideas of progress and perfectibilité.[23]

The so-called Pantheism Controversy (*Pantheismusstreit* or *Spinozismusstreit*) of German society of the 1780s showcased the diversity of positions. The writer Friedrich Heinrich Jacobi (1743–1819) can be best described as a representative of a fideist position. In his view, the example of Spinoza demonstrated that reason was incapable of proving the existence of God. This would inevitably lead to pantheism, materialism, determinism, and ultimately atheism. The only way out was to renounce philosophy and take a "leap" into faith. Moses Mendelssohn advocated a form of theistic rational religion (see below). Other participants in the debate, such as Goethe, and Herder, found some merit in pantheism. Kant also participated, emphasizing the boundary between knowledge and belief, and distanced himself, along with Jacobi, Biester, and Hamann, from Spinoza, and Spinozism. Novalis attempted a synthesis of Spinozistic pantheism with traditional Christianity.[24] Probably starting with this Pantheism Controversy and with the next generation, namely with the early Romantics and German Idealism, there was a break with the basic tenets of Christianity and the variants of natural religion that had dominated the European Enlightenment.[25] This was a European-wide trend.

---

23 For an introduction, see John Christian Laursen, "Religious progress and perfectibility in Benjamin Constant's enlightened liberalism", *History of European Ideas*, 50 (2024), 34–49. I wish to thank Chris Laursen for pointing out the importance of Constant to me.
24 Heinrich Scholz ed., *Die Hauptschriften zum Pantheismusstreit zwischen Jacobi und Mendelssohn*, Berlin: Reuther & Reichard 1916, Jonathan Israel, *Democratic Enlightenment. Philosophy, Revolution, and Human Rights 1750–1790*, Oxford: Oxford University Press 2011, 687–721 and Benjamin D. Crowe, On "The religion of the visible Universe": Novalis and the pantheism controversy, in: *British Journal for the History of Philosophy*, 16 (2008), 125–146.
25 Schneiders, *Hoffnung auf Vernunft*, 166–7 and Frederick Beiser, *German Idealism. The Struggle against Subjectivism, 1781–1801*, Cambridge, Mass.: Harvard University Press 2002, 362: "Jacobi's *Briefe* was a sensation. It shocked the orthodox, and it provoked the *Aufklärer*. But, worst of all, it backfired. It was avidly read by the young, who were inspired by it. Rather than heeding Jacobi's warnings about Lessing's secret religion, the new generation was drawn to it." See also by Beiser *The Romantic Imperative. The Concept of Early German Romanticism*, Cambridge, Mass.: Harvard University Press 2003 on the early German romantics.

5.2 Critique of Theology and State Churches, and Natural Religion

Most enlighteners were united in their criticism of those theologians who attempted to subordinate philosophy to theology and describe it as the "handmaiden" of theology. The German Enlightenment, from Thomasius to August Friedrich Müller, Christian Wolff and Kant, insisted on the primacy of philosophy. Wolff, for example, transformed the assumption of philosophy as the "handmaiden" of theology into its opposite. Only philosophy, by enlightening the mind, shed light on the other sciences and thus on theology. "I therefore used to say jokingly that worldly wisdom was the handmaiden of the higher faculties insofar as the woman had to grope in the dark and would often fall if the handmaiden did not shine for her."[26]

Criticism of religious fanaticism, religious and theological prejudice, and religious intolerance was widespread (see 3.3). During the 18th century, historical criticism of the Bible intensified. One example is the *Letters on the Study and Use of History* (1736, published in 1752) by Henry St. John Viscount Bolingbroke (1678–1751). He simply questioned biblical historical narratives as reliable sources of historical events. In general, positions were again diverse. There were Christian apologists, but also those who weakened or undermined Christianity as a whole with their criticism of Christianity as it was practiced, of erroneous forms of Christianity, or of denominations different from their own.[27] To this day, it is difficult to assess the extent to which the repeated professions of faith in Christianity, in one's own denomination, or in natural religion were mere lip service, hypocrisy, self-censorship, compromises with state censorship, or sincerely meant. The literature repeatedly contains claims that the confessions were "hypocritical" or "feigned."[28] Here, too, a good dose of enlightened skepticism is in order. Claims of this kind are just that: assumptions that are very difficult, perhaps even impossible, to prove using circumstantial evidence. A fascinating example is Baruch Spinoza. He has been labeled as a covert atheist and materialist, as a pantheist (the

---

26 Christian Wolff, Ausführliche Nachricht von seinen eigenen Schriften [1726], in: *Gesammelte Werke*, vol. 9, ed. Hans Werner Arndt, Hildesheim: Olms reprint 1973, 536. See the articles in Haakonssen, *The Cambridge History of Eighteenth-Century Philosophy*, part III (641–813) on the relationship between philosophy and theology, revealed and natural religion, arguments for the existence of God, and theodicy.
27 Andreas Urs Sommer, Kritisch-moralische exemplar-Historie im Zeitalter der Aufklärung. Viscount Bolingbroke als Geschichtsphilosoph; in: *Saeculum. Jahrbuch für Universalgeschichte*, 53 (2002), 269–310 and Skepsis und Aufklärung, 93, James Dybikowski, The Critique of Christianity, in: Martin Fitzpatrick et al., eds., *The Enlightenment World*, London: Routledge 2004, 41–56.
28 See for example Sommer, Skepsis und Aufklärung, 93.

most frequent label), as a "God intoxicated man" (Novalis), and as a Christian. All this is questionable. It is *probably* safe to claim that Spinoza was a very unorthodox and eccentric religious thinker, a panentheist with existential metaphysics and theology *sui generis*.[29]

Many enlighteners referred to the concept of a "natural religion" or "rational religion." Two versions can be distinguished. The basic idea of the first variant was that all historical forms of belief contain a core of universal and reasonable religious convictions. Robert Louden calls this the "common morality thesis." This core had to be uncovered. The aim was not to abolish religion, but to bring about a renewal or inner transformation of religion.[30] An early example is the "father of deism," Lord Edward Herbert of Cherbury (1583–1648), who asserted a system of "common notions," which "at least as it concerns theology, has been clearly accepted by every normal person, and does not require any further justification." Among these "common notions," he included belief in God and belief in virtue as the most important elements of religious practice.[31] During the European Enlightenment, there were numerous approaches to determining the nature of this core set of beliefs. In most cases it amounted to belief in God, the conviction that a moral way of life was the actual worship of God, voluntarism (the assumption that people choose, and are entitled to choose, their own beliefs), and the central importance of religious tolerance. Most Enlightenment thinkers did not construct an opposition between faith and knowledge, faith, and reason, faith, and unbelief, but between faith, and *superstition*.[32] For Locke, a religious community or church was a free association based on choice and formed by people, "a voluntary society of men, joining themselves together of their own accord, in order to the public worshiping of God, in such a manner as they judge acceptable to him, and effectual to the salvation of their souls."[33] Religion should be a humanistic re-

---

[29] See the excellent book Clare Carlisle, *Spinoza's Religion. A New Reading of the Ethics*, Princeton and Oxford: Princeton University Press 2021, especially 5–12 and 62–70. The most appropriate label for Spinoza is panentheism, the "view that whatever is, is in God." (Carlisle, *Spinoza's Religion*, 63).

[30] Cassirer, *The Philosophy of the Enlightenment*, 158 and 182.

[31] Quoted in Peter Gay, ed., *Deism. An Anthology*, Princeton: Van Nostrand 1968, 32. Deism is notoriously difficult to define. According to the conventional definition, deists believe in an aloof and impersonal deity that does not interfere in human affairs. Tricoire argues that English deism is not very different from traditional Christian theology. He distinguishes between a moderate deism endorsed by the English deists and Rousseau and a radical wing, with Voltaire as the most prominent representative; see Tricoire, *Die Aufklärung*, 233–8.

[32] See Cassirer, *The Philosophy of the Enlightenment*, 161.

[33] John Locke, *Two Treatises of Government and A Letter Concerning Toleration*, ed. and with an Introduction by Ian Shapiro, New Haven and London: Yale University Press 2003, 220.

ligion in which human dignity took center stage. David Hume had Cleanthes say: "The proper office of religion is to regulate the hearts of men, humanize their conduct." For Thomas Paine, religious and moral duties coincided and consisted of "doing justice, loving mercy, and endeavoring to make our fellow-creatures happy."[34] This amounted to a "religious universalism" or a "cosmopolitan religiosity," at least in theory. In terms of implementation, much was flawed—*quod erat expectandum*. Rousseau, the German neologists, and Kant were also representatives of this model of "reforming historical forms of faith."

A second form of rational religion was advocated by Voltaire. He rejected historical forms of faith, including Christian denominations, as they had led to fanaticism, intolerance, and superstition. In their place, he put forward a deistic religion of reason, which he presented as the only reasonable alternative. It was largely undogmatic and "lean" in terms of content. "We condemn atheism, we revile barbarous superstition, we love God and the human race: these are our dogmas."[35] German philosopher and deist Hermann Samuel Reimarus (1694–1768) held a similar position. He contrasted his own deistic "reasonable practical religion" with revealed religions. According to Reimarus, even Christianity had distanced itself from its rational origins with an uncritical obedience to scripture and authority. In the *Apologie oder Schutzschrift der vernünftigen Verehrer Gottes*, which was published by Lessing after his death as *Fragmente eines Ungenannten* in 1774–78, Reimarus denied the possibility of a rational belief in revelation. Reimarus and Lessing both spoke out in favor of a public and free discussion about faith and revelation.[36] Some of the representatives of the first variant can perhaps also be assigned to this second form of rational religion.

The justifications for this natural religion varied. In almost all cases, a starting point was sought outside of Christian revelation and the Bible. For Thomas Paine, it was creation. "Search not the book called the scripture, which any human hand might make, but the scripture called the Creation."[37] For Moses Mendelssohn, the existence of God and the immortality of the soul were some of the insights that could be grasped by reason without revealed religion. He achieved fame in the

---

[34] Quoted in Louden, *World We Want*, 22 and 20. For an introduction, see J. C. D. Clark, *Thomas Paine. Britain, America, and France in the Age of Enlightenment and Revolution*, Oxford: Oxford University Press 2018, especially 81–3 and 331–55.
[35] Voltaire, *Proféssion de foi des théistes*, quoted in: Forst, *Toleration in Conflict*, 287.
[36] Hermann Samuel Reimarus, Von Duldung der Deisten. Fragment eines Ungenannten, ed. Gotthold Ephraim Lessing, in: *Werke*, ed. Herbert G. Göpfert, vol. 7, 313–476, especially 344 and the summary in Forst, *Toleration in Conflict*, 399–401.
[37] Thomas Paine, *The Age of Reason*, in: *The Thomas Paine Reader*, ed. Michael Foot and Isaac Kramnick, New York: Penguin 1987, 421.

Figure 20: Daniel Nikolaus Chodowiecki (1726–1801), *Die aufgeklärte Weisheit als Minerva schützt die Gläubigen aller Religionen*, engraving, 1791. Minerva, the Roman goddess of knowledge, gives light, and at the same time protects the religions and denominations that come together in peaceful harmony.

German-speaking world with his writing *Phaedon, oder über die Unsterblichkeit der Seele in drey Gesprächen* (1767). The later work *Morgenstunden oder Vorlesungen über das Daseyn Gottes* (1785) defended the so-called ontological proof of God's existence against objections.[38] With David Hume, empiricism, and Kant's *Critique of Pure Reason* (1781), these objections had become difficult to counter. Hume's and Kant's core claim was that theoretical knowledge of God is impossible because knowledge always relates to sensory perceptions (see 2.3).

Kant also broke new ground in the philosophy of religion. First, he used the claim that theoretical knowledge in the field of religion and metaphysics is impossible (because knowledge always relates to sensory perceptions) against dogmatic atheists and materialists ("There is no God"). In the sphere of theoretical knowledge, we simply do not know which proposition is true (*"non liquet"*). Secondly, he endeavored to provide a new justification of religious belief via practical reason or morality (see 4.2). Humans are entitled to happiness, provided they follow their moral obligations outlined in the categorical imperative. Since life is often a valley of tears, especially for the virtuous, happiness proportionate to virtue can only be guaranteed by an all-knowing, just, and all-powerful being, namely God. Third, using the assumption of two concentric circles, Kant argued that there was room for more than just a moral religion "within the limits of mere reason." This was the path that many enlighteners had taken: religion coincided with morality. Kant claimed that there was also a sphere outside these boundaries of reason (an outer concentric circle).[39] This was the sphere that transcended reason and referred to revelation and its mysteries. Kant thus rejected what he saw as a reductionist understanding of religion which was limited to charity, morality, or beliefs that could be rationally reconstructed.

---

38 Anselm of Canterbury had argued that from the concept of God ("that beyond which nothing greater can be conceived"), the reality of God could be inferred with logical stringency. This argument has been controversial since Thomas Aquinas and was subjected to a thorough critique by Kant. See for example Allen W. Wood, *Kant's Rational Theology*, Ithaca and London: Cornell University Press 1978.

39 Kant's arguments are much more sophisticated than my summary. For introductions see Eberhard Jüngel, Zum Titel und den beiden Vorreden, in: Otfried Höffe, ed., *Die Religion innerhalb der Grenzen der bloßen Vernunft*, Berlin: Akademie-Verlag 2011, 29–42 and Burkhard Nonnenmacher, Der Begriff sogenannter Gnadenmittel unter der Idee eines reinen Vernunftglaubens, in: Höffe, *Religion*, 211–29. Reliable introductions are Rudolf Langthaler, *Kant über den Glauben und die Selbsterhaltung der Vernunft: Sein Weg von der Kritik zur eigentlichen Metaphysik—und darüber hinaus*, Freiburg and München: Karl Alber 2018, Lawrence Pasternack, *Kant on Religion within the Boundaries of Mere Reason*, London, New York: Routledge 2014 and especially Wood, *Kant and Religion*.

One result of Enlightenment processes was probably more individualized and personalized forms of religion. This is suggested by many testimonies from the late Enlightenment period. For example, a friend wrote to a certain Luise Mejer in 1779: "Luise, should you die, just believe that I will not take a single step without the firm conviction that your spirit surrounds me, and that I will lose nothing in you in this world like the sensual."[40] This is a far cry from conventional Christian orthodoxy. But the statement could be typical of some currents of the time, which encompassed esotericism, pantheism, and belief in spirits.

Many enlighteners advocated religious belief for pragmatic reasons. The anecdote of the deist Voltaire, who believed that it would be very useful if his fellow human beings believed in God and divine punishment, became famous. "I want my attorney, my tailor, my valets, even my wife to believe in God; I fancy then that I'll be robbed and cuckolded less often."[41] Unless this argument is merely ironic and sarcastic, it can be interpreted along the lines of a widespread utilitarian thinking of the 18th century. According to this brand of utilitarianism *avant la lettre*, religion had a social and moral function. In many cases, this utilitarian aspect might have been dominant. A pluralistic and more individualistic conception of religion was intended to prevent religious disputes, religiously motivated wars, and civil wars. "Enlightenment intellectuals sought to develop a more pluralistic and less divisive concept of religion that would enable people to live in peace with one another."[42] Among other things, this new conception was simply more useful for society.

In some cases, the result was what can be described as religious cosmopolitanism. This is the assumption that believers of different religions, religious communities, or denominations are or should be members of a single religious community. It was based on the concept of natural or rational religion, namely the conviction that all historical forms of faith contain a core of universal and reasonable religious beliefs. According to dynamic religious cosmopolitanism, the hope was that in the future *una religio in varietate rituum*, a single faith manifested in different rites (Nicholas of Cusa, 1401–1464), would prevail. The historical background to these forward-looking considerations was the new semantics of time in the Enlightenment era. Like the philosophers of history, or later the Founding Fa-

---

40 Anne Conrad, Umschwebende Geister und aufgeklärter Alltag. Esoterik als Religiosität der Spätaufklärung, in: Monika Neugebauer-Wölk and Holger Zaunstöck, eds., *Aufklärung und Esoterik*, Hamburg: Felix Meiner 1999, 397–415, at 397 with more passages.
41 Voltaire, "A," in Entretien 16, Sur des choses curieuses, in *L'A, B, C, Dialogue curieux* (1762), 159, quoted in: *The Quotable Voltaire*, ed. Garry Apgar and Edward M. Langille, Lewisburg, Pennsylvania: Bucknell University Press 2021, 126.
42 Louden, *World We Want*, 25.

Figure 21: Nicolas de Largillière (1656–1746), Portrait of Voltaire (1694–1778) [at the age of twenty-four (?)], 1718–1724. François-Marie Arouet, better known by his pen name Voltaire, was a prolific writer of novels, plays, philosophical texts, and histories. He has become the most famous of the French *philosophes*, advocating religious freedom, toleration, and the separation of church and the state.

thers of the United States of America (see 4.3. above), some Enlightenment theologians, for instance the Neologians in Protestantism, repositioned the levels of time past, present, and future in relation to each other. They abandoned the traditional orientation toward the past and focused on an open future that was to be shaped by believers who aimed at human perfection and their moral vocation or *Bestimmung*. The present was seen as a new beginning. The true church consisted of a new church of the future, not a return to early Christianity or the original Lutheran congregation.[43] For the Neologian Johann Friedrich Wilhelm Jerusalem (1709–1789), for example, true Christianity was to be found at the end of history, not at the beginning.[44] German theologian and church historian Johann Salomo Semler (1725–1791) also claimed that Christianity was characterized by a continuous increase in moral and religious knowledge.[45] Christianity was valuable because it contained the "germ" of future improvement, which consisted of an authentic "private religion", a "religion of all people," which was primarily concerned with love of God and of neighbors.[46] In *Über historische, gesellschaftliche und moralische Religion der Christen* (1786), Semler distinguished between public and private religion. The latter took personal conscience as a guideline; it was independent of the religious languages of the church communities; and the moral, religious, and spiritual message of Christ was at its center. Theology was subject to error and shortcomings but also had the potential to grow continuously.[47]

The European Enlightenment is sometimes accused of having propagated an anti-religious education. Again, this must be qualified. Firstly, sweeping statements of this kind are not helpful and do not do justice to the diversity of positions. Secondly, it is necessary to look at the issue from a historical perspective. It is undoubtedly true that the European Enlightenment—compared to earlier

---

[43] See Sommer, *Sinnstiftung durch Geschichte*, 108–9 and Cavallar, *Dynamic Cosmopolitanism*, 17–27.
[44] See Sommer, *Sinnstiftung durch Geschichte*, 140–1.
[45] Johann Salomo Semler, *Ob der Geist des Widerchrists unser Zeitalter auszeichne?*, Halle: Hemmerdeschen Buchhandlung 1784 and Semler, *Neue Versuche die Kirchenhistorie der ersten Jahrhunderte aufzuklären* [1788], ed. Dirk Fleischer, Nordhausen: Bautz 2010, Beutel, *Kirchengeschichte*, 130–32, Emanuel Hirsch, *Geschichte der neuern evangelischen Theologie* [1954], Neuausgabe von Albrecht Beutel, vol. 4, Waltrop: Spenner 2000, 49–89, Gottfried Hornig, *Johann Salomo Semler. Studien zu Leben und Werk des Hallenser Aufklärungstheologen*, Tübingen: Niemeyer 1996, Douglas McGaughey, Kants theologischer Kontext: Eine Stichprobe, in: Otfried Höffe, ed., *Die Religion innerhalb der Grenzen der bloßen Vernunft*, Berlin: Akademie-Verlag 2011, 271–82, at 273–4.
[46] Semler, *Ob der Geist des* Widerchrists, 211.
[47] Hirsch, *Geschichte der neuern evangelischen Theologie*, 53–59, Hornig, *Johann Salomo Semler*, Martin Laube, Die Unterscheidung von öffentlicher und privater Religion bei Johann Salomo Semler. Zur neuzeittheoretischen Relevanz einer christentumstheoretischen Reflexionsfigur, *Zeitschrift für Neuere Theologiegeschichte*, 11, 1 (2004), 1–23, at 5–15.

eras—weakened the importance of religious education. Among others, this has to do with what Robert Louden called the "morality thesis": "Religion's proper purpose is moral as opposed to theological."[48] Finally, unbiased readers today will be surprised at how often and with what vehemence religious education was advocated as part of general education, even during Enlightenment.[49]

5.3 Radical Enlightenment? Jonathan Israel and the example of Kant

A critique is radical when it goes "back to basics," ignores any kind of authority, and examines the foundations of our knowledge, of our moral, and aesthetic judgments. The only authorities left are one's own reason, the reason of others, and rational arguments. I argue here that Kant offered this radical approach. In doing so, I distance myself from Jonathan Israel's interpretation, which identifies the Radical Enlightenment elsewhere, namely in a group of materialists and atheists (allegedly) following Spinoza, with d'Holbach, or Diderot as typical examples.

Israel distinguishes between a moderate and a Radical Enlightenment. The moderate mainstream was in favor of a gradual reform of society by partially rejecting "the ideas, habits, and traditions of the past." The orientation was theistic, critical of Christianity, but not hostile, rationalist, but not materialistic. According to this characterization, Kant belonged to the moderate Enlightenment.[50] For Jonathan Israel, the hallmarks of the Radical Enlightenment were philosophical materialism, atheism, and secularization in the sense of a complete rejection of religion. According to the radical enlighteners, all traditions, especially in the spheres of religion and politics, were not to be reformed or improved, but completely abolished. This Radical Enlightenment "rejected all compromise with the past and sought to sweep away existing structures entirely." According to Israel, this included religious ideas such as providence or revelation, the divine right of kings or institutions such as the churches or the existing social order.[51] The radical enlighteners favored democratic republicanism, "philosophical-scientific reason," univer-

---

[48] Louden, *The World We Want*, 20.
[49] Louden, *The World We Want*, 38–9 with quotes.
[50] Jonathan *Israel, Enlightenment Contested. Philosophy, Modernity, and the Emancipation of Man 1670–1752*, Oxford: Oxford University Press 2006, 11, *Democratic Enlightenment*, 7, *Radical Enlightenment*, 445–562.
[51] Israel, *Radical Enlightenment*, 11, *Democratic Enlightenment*, 7 and Winfried Schröder, Radikalaufklärung in philosophiehistorischer Perspektive, in: Jonathan Israel and Martin Mulsow, eds., *Radikalaufklärung*, Berlin: Suhrkamp 2014, 187–202, at 191.

sal and equal human rights, tried to enlighten human minds, developed new "modes of thought," were cosmopolitan, secular, and endorsed normative universalism.[52] The radical enlighteners were all Spinozists and were attacked by the Enlightenment mainstream.

The term itself may be a useful concept. There was, for instance, a radical and underground movement parallel to the moderate and mainstream early German Enlightenment, and they often interacted.[53] However, like many others, I disagree with the way Israel defines and employs the concept in his research and is fixated on Spinoza's impact.

Since the publication of his first work in 2001, Israel's critics have raised sharp objections, among them his overemphasis on the influence of Spinoza; Israel's causal explanations and teleological constructions; and his tendency to arbitrarily reinterpret enlighteners who do not fit into his binary scheme. Johnson Kent Wright summarizes this criticism as follows: "In the eyes of his critics, Israel's interpretation of the Enlightenment is a kind of academic juggernaut, careening destructively through the discipline, in the service of a false idol—Spinoza, supposed demiurge of modernity—and an unsustainable principle—the idea of an umbilical connection between metaphysical monism and political radicalism."[54] I am going to limit my objections to the aspect of the alleged radicalism of the Radical Enlightenment. Firstly, it is dubious whether radicalism in Israel's

---

52 Israel, *Enlightenment that Failed*, 9, 28, 31, 29, 929 and passim. A succinct definition of Radical Enlightenment runs: "Rejection of religious authority tied to democratic republicanism and universal and equal human rights." (28).

53 See for instance Martin Mulsow, *The Hidden Origins of the German Enlightenment*, transl. by H. C. Erik Midelfort, Cambridge: Cambridge University Press 2023, same, *Enlightenment Underground: Radical Germany 1680–1720*, tr. H. C. Erik Midelfort, Charlottesville and London: University of Virginia Press 2015, Carl Niekerk, ed., *The Radical Enlightenment in Germany. A Cultural Perspective*, Leiden and Boston: Brill Rodopi 2018, and some essays contained in Jonathan Israel and Martin Mulsow, eds., *Radikalaufklärung*, Berlin: Suhrkamp 2014.

54 Johnson Kent Wright, Review essay of Jonathan Israel, Democratic Enlightenment, *H-France Forum*, vol. 9, 1 (2014), 1–25, http://www.h-france.net/forum/forumvol9/Israel1.pdf (last accessed October 2, 2025). See also the criticisms of Anthony J. La Vopa, A New Intellectual History? Jonathan Israel's Enlightenment, *The Historical Journal*, 52 (2009), 717–38 as well as Israel and Mulsow, eds., *Radikalaufklärung*, especially the contributions by Wiep van Bunge, Winfried Schröder and Martin Mulsow. Israel's numerous critics are listed in Israel, *Enlightenment that Failed*, 13, footnote 28. Israel attempts to rebut these criticisms in Israel, *Enlightenment that Failed*, 923–42. See also Steffen Ducheyne, ed., *Reassessing the Radical Enlightenment*, Abingdon: Routledge 2017, Marta García-Alonso, ed., *Les Lumières radicales et le politique: études critiques sur les travaux de Jonathan Israel*, Paris: Champion 2017 and Andreas Pecar and Damien Tricoire, *Falsche Freunde: War die Aufklärung wirklich die Geburtsstunde der Moderne?*, Frankfurt am Main: Campus 2015.

sense only ever appeared in connection with philosophical monism. In his interpretation, the religious background of Spinoza's philosophy and his early followers is either ignored or trivialized. Most likely, Spinoza was a panentheist, and an unorthodox and eccentric religious thinker, but not a materialist, and atheist.[55] Spinozism is much more moderate than, for example, Pierre Bayle's radical critique of knowledge or Hume's skepticism and Kant's criticism. Texts can be cited as neither Spinozistic nor monistic and are far more radical in their self-reflexive criticism of metaphysics and reason than writings from the same period. Examples include the text *Symbolum sapientiae/Cymbalum mundi* by an anonymous author, and *Lettre de Thrasybule à Leucippe*, probably written by the French historian Nicolas Fréret (1688–1749). Both authors were atheists but renounced alternative materialist metaphysics as there were fundamental limits to knowledge that did not only apply to theists. Fréret, for example, wrote of the concept of God: "We should leave it at rejecting the chimeras we are told about this subject, and not put ourselves in the embarrassment of substituting another opinion for the one we are dropping."[56] Examples such as these question the value of accepting only Spinoza and Spinozism as the "intellectual backbone of the European Radical Enlightenment everywhere."[57]

Secondly, it can be argued that the metaphysical monism defended by Israel represents a relapse into the dogmatic *esprit de système*, that is, the "spirit of systems" that many enlighteners criticized because of the limits of our knowledge (see 1.2). Is not Hume's skepticism, which emphasizes the finitude, and limitations of reason as well as experience, more radical, and perhaps also more reasonable? (see 2.3).

Thirdly, it is useful to distinguish between radicalism in different areas. In terms of the philosophy of religion, the materialist atheists La Mettrie, d'Holbach, and Helvétius were radical in their anti-religious positions in relation to the society they lived in. In their opinion, religious world views were figments of imagination and human inventions. For them, fanaticism, superstition, and intolerance

---

55 See especially Carlisle, *Spinoza's Religion. A New Reading of the Ethics*, and the article by Wiep van Bunge, Radikalaufklärung neu definiert: eine holländische Perspektive, in: Israel and Mulsow, eds., *Radikalaufklärung*, 121–48.
56 Quoted in Schröder, Radikalaufklärung, 196; see Schröder, Radikalaufklärung, 193–7 on both texts.
57 Israel, *Radical Enlightenment*, vi. See also his *Enlightenment Contested*, 867 and *Democratic Enlightenment*, 950–1. More recently, Israel has tried to qualify this thesis, downplaying the influence of Spinoza and so-called Spinozism; see Israel, *Enlightenment that Failed*, 12–8, 936–8. Yet Israel reaffirms Spinoza's philosophical importance and lasting influence in *Spinoza, Life and Legacy*, Oxford: Oxford University Press 2023.

were not *possible* characteristics or deformations of religion, but its *essence*.[58] Diderot, whom Israel classifies as a materialist atheist, was politically more radical than many other enlighteners and spoke out in favor of sexual emancipation. As far as the status of women and women's rights were concerned, however, Diderot refrained from a radical or forward-looking position, which was occasionally advocated in his time (see 2.1 and 3.2). According to Diderot, women were intellectually inferior to men and should be content with their roles as wives and mothers. This might have been a result of his materialist outlook.[59] In contrast, French philosopher François Poullain de la Barre (1647–1723), "arguably the first modern feminist," was not a Spinozist and materialist monist, but a Cartesian who was convinced of the duality of body and mind. Spinoza, the star, so to speak, in Israel's history of the Enlightenment, "relegates women, like servants [...], to a permanently dependent status," as Israel himself must admit. Apparently, he would like to save Spinoza as a hero of Radical Enlightenment. Thus, he assumes that Spinoza's argument leaves open the possibility that "should women somehow, some day, assert their independence from husbands and fathers, and act as equals to men, they would then be entitled to vote and participate in politics."[60] There are obviously double standards at work here. Those whom Israel assigns to the Radical Enlightenment camp are interpreted more leniently than the supposedly moderate and mainstream enlighteners such as Poullain de la Barre, Hume, or Rousseau. In the case of the latter two authors, it is obvious that they cannot be categorized following the rigid "moderate versus radical" scheme. The same is probably true of the American Revolution and the so-called Founding Fathers (see 4.3. above).[61]

---

58 This position, however, can be challenged with the claim that it (also) amounts to a dogmatic, undifferentiated and intolerant criticism of religions. See for instance, *Toleration in Conflict*, 297–9, Coleman, Religion, 116–7, Kondylis, *Die Aufklärung*, 525, 528–9 and my own essay Auf der Suche nach der eingeschränkten Denkungsart, 42–7.
59 Denis Diderot, Sur les femmes [1771], in: *Œuvres complètes de Diderot*, ed. Jean Assézat, Paris: Garnier 1951, vol. 2, 251–62. See also Jenny Mander, No woman is an island: the female figure in French Enlightenment anthropology, in: Sarah Knott and Barbara Taylor, eds., *Women, gender and Enlightenment*, Basingstoke: Palgrave 2007, 97–116.
60 La Vopa, Intellectual History, 727–8, Israel, *Enlightenment contested*, 557.
61 See Israel, *Enlightenment that Failed*, 928–9, Helena Rosenblatt, Rousseau, the "Traditionalist", *Journal of the History of Ideas*, 77 (2016), 627–35, Joanna Stalnaker, Jonathan Israel in Dialogue, *Journal of the History of Ideas*, 77 (2016), 637–48, and Israel, Rousseau, Diderot, and the "Radical Enlightenment": A Reply to Helena Rosenblatt and Joanna Stalnaker, ibid., 649–77, Jonathan Israel, Schröder, *Radikalaufklärung*, 198–9 on Hume, Wright, Review essay, 6–7 on Rousseau, and ibid., 7 and 15 on the American Revolution.

What is the outcome of my criticism of Jonathan Israel's approach? Firstly, we must abandon the idea that there were "two monolithic Enlightenments locked in an irreconcilable bipolar conflict."[62] It makes more sense to assume a continuum from "moderate" to "radical" and to distinguish between different dimensions of this continuum—such as political, societal, social, religious, epistemological, or economic. Teleological construction should be replaced by an approach that emphasizes the ruptures, discontinuities, complexities and perhaps consequences (intended and unintended) of developments. Texts often have unintended side effects or lead to interpretations that were not intended by the authors in this way. There were obviously also processes of secularization not *against* but *with* religion. Robert Palmer and Alan Kors have shown that some politically "dangerous" conceptions came from Catholic theologians (even if they obviously had quite different intentions). Charly Coleman examined fault lines in 18th century French society that were not exclusively between religious persons and atheists. These fault lines existed between the mainstream of theologians and philosophers, who espoused a notion of identity and personality where one's self related to the world in terms of subject and object, and Christian mystics, radical materialists, and political radicals. The latter groups fought against the "culture of self-ownership, according to which men, and women were thought to possess and stand accountable for themselves and their actions." Although the three groups also had different views, especially in religion, they agreed that people were merely "objects of totalizing forces outside the self": the deity, nature, or the body politic.[63] These complexities of development are probably more typical of the European Enlightenment than Israel's simple narrative of a struggle between "moderate" and "radical." Secularization was not simply a loss of religion, but a dynamic, multidimensional process that started from the religious dimension, but could also continue to include this dimension in a modified form (see 5.4).

When I refer to the radicalization of the Enlightenment in Kant's philosophy, I mean that it was more fundamental than other approaches, i.e. it examined the foundations of cognition, action, belief, and judgment. This does not necessarily mean political or social radicalism. Nor does my thesis mean that Kant's philosophy was necessarily better than others—it was more thorough (in the sense of "getting to the bottom of things"). This form of radicalization can be seen in sev-

---

62 La Vopa, Intellectual History, 726.
63 See the examples in the differentiated analyses of Bunge, Radikalaufklärung, 141–6; Robert Palmer, *Catholics and Unbelievers in Eighteenth-Century France* [1939], New York: Cooper Square Publishers 1961, Alan Charles Kors, *Atheism in France, 1650–1729*, Princeton, NJ: Princeton University Press 1990, Coleman, *The Virtues of Abandon*, 3 and 4; Dan Edelstein, *The Enlightenment. A Genealogy*, Chicago and London: University of Chicago Press 2010.

eral aspects. Firstly, Kant understood self-thinking without restriction as an unconditional right to enlightenment (see 1.1, conception no. 5). This set him apart from many contemporaries who asked, for example, if prejudices could be useful for the common people. German philologist Georg Ludwig Spalding (1762–1811) expressed concerns about "too much" enlightenment in his poem on "contemporary German philosophy." He believed that the fashionable admiration for French philosophy, from Voltaire to the materialists, was debatable and had replaced German "seriousness" and "profundity."[64] Moses Mendelssohn was also worried. He differentiated between "human enlightenment," which was possible in principle, and "civic enlightenment," which had political and social limitations. In certain situations, prejudices were to be tolerated. An "abuse" of enlightenment could weaken "moral feeling" and promote "hardheartedness, egoism, irreligion, and anarchy."[65] German intellectual and politician Friedrich Karl Freiherr von Moser (1723–1798) pointed at the social benefits of prejudice. They supplemented the limited reason of many people and were indispensable for social peace and "the blissful calm and ignorance of a person." Nor would it be desirable for all humans to become freer and wiser. "One has enough trouble getting along with them anyway. A few more granules of general human wisdom would make us very uncomfortable."[66] Finally, Frederick II of Prussia wanted the *Prussian Academy of Sciences* to ask a question about the permissibility of popular deception and the usefulness of errors and prejudices. In his opinion, prejudices were "the reason of the people." Thus, the prize question in 1780: *"Est-il utile au peuple d'etre trompé, soit qu'on l'induise dans les nouvelles erreurs, ou qu'on l'entretienne dans celle où il est?"*[67] ("Is it useful for the people to be deceived, whether they are led into new errors or sustained in those they already have?"). The focus was on usefulness or social utility. This, of course, is where Kant's criticism came in. His key argument was that if questions of truth or enlightenment are involved, utility must take a back seat.

For Kant, enlightenment in the sense of the effort to think for oneself was unconditional or categorical. He saw no "abuse of enlightenment." The strongest argument was provided by his deontological ethics. The question asked about the usefulness of prejudice and deception was the wrong one in the first place.

---

[64] *Berlinische Monatsschrift*, vol. 4 (1784), 50–5. See also Martus, *Aufklärung*, 841–2.
[65] Moses Mendelssohn, Über die Frage: was heißt aufklären?, in: *Berlinische Monatsschrift*, vol. 4 (1784), 193–200, at 197 and 199 and the translation in *Philosophical Writings*, ed. Daniel O. Dahlstrom, Cambridge: Cambridge University Press 1997, 311–17, at 316.
[66] Klaus Reisinger and Oliver R. Scholz, Vorurteil, in: Ritter and Gründer, eds., *Historisches Wörterbuch der Philosophie*, vol. 11, Sp. 1258.
[67] Ritter and Gründer, *Historisches Wörterbuch*, Sp. 1254–5.

What was crucial was the right of every person to cultivate their own thinking and to set out in search of the truth. Kant noted: "Is it also permissible to recommend prejudices or at least to leave them untouched? That means making everything immature." Condoning or even advocating prejudices is paternalistic and elitist, and therefore incompatible with the idea of enlightenment as maturity. People can stand on their own two feet if they are given the opportunity to do so. "The fear that if old prejudices were removed, the long-standing edifice would collapse, is null, and void. A grown man has good feet when you remove his crutches (*Gängelwagen*)."[68] This was an obvious criticism of Moser, but also of the Berlin Academy's *Preisfrage* (competition question)—and indirectly of the king. Finally, Kant claimed that we should not be afraid of undesirable or unpleasant results of the enlightenment process. "For it is quite absurd to expect enlightenment from reason and yet to prescribe to it in advance the side on which it must come out."[69] The process of enlightenment is open-ended. Authorities and guardians often have an interest in ensuring that only certain results emerge. However, this has nothing to do with enlightenment—more accurate terms would be paternalism, coercion, manipulation, or indoctrination.

The second element of Kant's radicalization of the Enlightenment is the enlarged way of thinking and its conditions, above all the public use of reason.[70] Kant's criticism of theories that attempt to justify prejudices was linked to his concept of enlightenment. This could not be reduced, as it were, in the sense of "a little enlightenment yes, but not too much." For Kant, prejudice ultimately arose from the passive use of reason, from the "tendency [...] toward the heteronomy of reason."[71] Kant saw examples of this heteronomy in some proverbs from everyday life, aphorisms, or sayings and maxims in schools. They would all promote the "tendency toward the mechanism of reason instead of spontaneity."[72] They tempt us to slavishly or mechanically repeat them instead of examining and judging (see

---

68 Kant, Refl. 2578–9, in: *Werke*, vol. 16, 426. See also Kant, Religion, in: *Werke*, vol. 6, 188 and On the common saying: That may be correct in theory, but it is of no use in practice (1793), in: vol. 8, 273–313, at 290–1.
69 Kant, *Critique of pure reason*, B 775.
70 The following paragraphs are a summary of my two essays: Denkungsart des Friedens and Auf der Suche nach der eingeschränkten Denkungsart. See also Michael Kubsda, *Selbstreflexion und Emanzipation. Aufklärung als Terminus in Kants kritischer Philosophie*, Würzburg: Königshausen und Neumann 2014, Lawrence Pasternack, Kant's Touchstone of Communication and the Public Use of Reason, *Society and Politics*, 8 (2014), 78–91 and Birgit Recki, An der Stelle [je]des andern denken. Über das kommunikative Element der Vernunft, in: *Die Vernunft, ihre Natur, ihr Gefühl und der Fortschritt*, 111–125.
71 Kant, *Critique of the power of judgment*, vol. 5, 294.
72 Kant, Refl. 2519, 2527, in: *Werke*, vol. 16, 403.

also 2.3 on Rousseau). In the fight against personal prejudice, the effort to think for oneself—or the autonomy of reason—was called for. The second element was the maxim of the enlarged way of thinking. It was the subjective principle of "looking at a situation from a completely different point of view" and comparing one's own judgment with others. This "participatory reason" was the opposite of "logical egoism."[73] Kant regarded this comparison with the judgment of other people as an external criterion of truth (see 3.2). It also presupposed the freedom to use reason publicly.

For Kant, the "egoism of reason" mentioned above coincided with "logical stubbornness," and this was the opposite of *Gemeinsinn*, the general "common human understanding" (*allgemeiner Menschenverstand*) or the *sensus communis logicus*. Kant defined the latter as "a faculty for judging that in its reflection takes account (*a priori*) of everyone else's way of representing in thought, in order *as it were* to hold its judgment up to human reason as a whole and thereby avoid the illusion which, from subjective private conditions that could easily be held to be objective, would have a detrimental influence on the judgment."[74] If we want to test our own judgment, we need a "touchstone" that does not guarantee truth, but is a sufficient condition. We can subject our own judgments to critical scrutiny by submitting them to the judgment of others. In this process of "going public," we can then correct our perhaps erroneous judgments. Narrow-minded persons are not characterized by little or no knowledge but by refusing to transcend the "subjective private conditions" of their own judgments, for whatever reasons.

Kant does not understand personal reason as a monological or subject-centered faculty (a common objection), as it is dependent on other rational beings, on publicity, free expression of opinion, exchange of ideas, controversy, and a republic with a public sphere. This is why Kant called for the "freedom of the pen" and the end of censorship:

> The *logical egoist* considers it unnecessary also to test his judgment by the understanding of others; as if he had no need at all for this touchstone [...]. But it is so certain that we cannot dispense with this means of assuring ourselves of the truth of our judgment that this may be the most important reason why learned people cry out so urgently for *freedom of the press*. For if this freedom is denied, we are deprived at the same time of a great means of testing the correctness of our own judgments, and we are exposed to error.[75]

---

[73] Refl. 2563–66, in: *Werke*, vol. 16, 417–20, *Critique of the power of judgment*, 293–6, *Anthropology*, vol. 7, § 59.
[74] Kant, *Critique of the power of judgment*, 293.
[75] Kant, *Anthropology*, vol. 7, 128–9.

Communication is not only helpful in our search for truth, but also indispensable. Kant combined a subject-centered aspect with a public or communicative aspect. Enlightenment can therefore be jeopardized by political despotism, for example in a dictatorship, because communication, and the public sphere are undermined or destroyed altogether. For precisely this reason, Kant appreciated Frederick II of Prussia, whose domestic policy and censorship policy he described with the words: "*Argue* as much as you will, and about whatever you will, but *obey!*"[76] Yet enlightenment processes can also fail for reasons that have to do with the individual. Selfishness, logical egoism, self-conceit, or arrogance, obtuseness, laziness, or cowardice also jeopardize this enlightenment—or prevent it from getting off the ground in the first place.[77]

The third element of Kant's radicalized enlightenment has to do with the "primacy of practical reason." It was briefly alluded to in the first element. For Kant, enlightenment—like the ideas of human dignity, legal freedom, justice, the republic, truth, or world peace—was not a matter of prudence, but an unconditional moral obligation. Practical reason related to moral action therefore took precedence—primacy—over political prudence. Princes or other heads of state had no right to prevent enlightenment processes "forever" in paternalistic arrogance and in the name of peace and order. At best, there was a provisional entitlement to restrict civil liberties such as freedom of speech, according to the so-called permissive laws, if there was the possibility of the state dissolving into anarchy. Prudential considerations of this kind were justified, but only as long as they did not call into question the fundamental primacy of unconditional legal or moral obligations. The normative yardstick for this criticism of paternalism is the concept of autonomy, which has already been mentioned in earlier sections. Only the respect conception of tolerance, which is based on the recognition, equality, and autonomy of individuals, can provide a justification for tolerance, which has become indispensable in modern pluralistic societies (see 4.2 and 4.3). Its basis is a qualified normative universalism, which Kant thought through more precisely than other enlighteners. Autonomy must not be misunderstood—as is often the case—in the sense that everyone is already autonomous because they are able to post two half-sentences on Facebook or Instagram, for example. In many cases, this has apparently nothing to do with autonomy (or enlightenment), but more with heteronomy as following the widespread assumptions (and prejudices) of mainstream society. According to Kant, autonomy in thought and action is a dis-

---

76 Kant, Enlightenment, vol. 8, 37.
77 See for instance Kant, *Werke*, vol. 24, 874, Logic, vol. 9, 80 and the excellent text by Lutz Koch, Gegen die Unbelehrbarkeit: der Gemeinsinn, in: Heiser and Prieler, eds., *Die erweiterte Denkungsart*, 19–33.

position of every human being that can only be realized in a long and arduous process of cultivation. The potential that is there must be realized, based on the Enlightenment idea of perfection (see 1.2). Unfortunately, these dispositions, which include, but are not limited to, the faculty of reason, can lie fallow for a lifetime. The cultivation of understanding, reason, judgment, will, and moral dispositions coincide with Kant's concepts of emancipation and enlightenment.[78]

Fourthly, the self-reflective late Enlightenment reached its climax with Kant. It was an "enlightenment of the Enlightenment."[79] Those enlighteners who lacked this self-reflective dimension fought against superstition, prejudice, dogmatism and fanaticism (see 3.3). False knowledge had to be eliminated, and ignorance overcome. The aim was to increase knowledge. The reflexive Enlightenment went one step further and turned precisely this knowledge into a problem. In Kant's words, reason had to "take on anew the most difficult of all its tasks, namely, that of self-knowledge."[80] The reflexive Enlightenment sought to enlighten about knowledge; it did not only fight against prejudice and ignorance. Ernst Cassirer described this radicalization of the Enlightenment in Kant's philosophy as follows: "The revolution in the way of thinking consists in the fact that we begin with the reflection of reason on itself, on its presuppositions, and principles, its problems, and tasks; reflection on the objects will follow once this starting point has been secured."[81] There was a danger that naive Enlightenment might promote a new immaturity through an accumulation of knowledge, for example in the sense of "Enlightenment through science" (see 2.3 on Rousseau's criticism). Two purposes of the Enlightenment could be lost in the process: firstly, the reflective dimension of self-knowledge and secondly, the autonomy of thought, namely independent thinking.[82] Kant saw much more clearly than many enlighteners the problem of reason and unreason being interconnected and sometimes overlapping. "Deceptions are rational as such—not only in the sense that they happen

---

[78] For a more profound analysis see Kubsda, *Selbstreflexion und Emanzipation*, especially 109–38.
[79] Axel Hutter, Kant und das Projekt einer Metaphysik der Aufklärung, in: Klemme, *Kant und die Zukunft*, 68–81, at 72. See also Kubsda, *Selbstreflexion und Emanzipation*, and Birgit Recki, Kant und die Aufklärung, in: *Die Vernunft, ihre Natur, ihr Gefühl und der Fortschritt*, 15–38. The following paragraphs rely on *Islam, Aufklärung und Moderne*, 45–9.
[80] Kant, *Critique of pure reason*, A XI.
[81] Ernst Cassirer, *Kant's Life and Thought* [1918], New Haven and London: Yale University Press 1983, 161.
[82] Hutter, Kant, 72 und Herbert Schnädelbach, Über historische Aufklärung, in: ders., *Vernunft und Geschichte*, Frankfurt am Main: Suhrkamp 1987, 23–46, hier 23–6.

to reason, but in the sense that they arise from reason as such. Reason can only be conceived in such a way that it arrives at concepts from within itself, which it is denied from accepting, and which it is also commanded to oppose."[83] One example would be the deceptions in the field of metaphysics, which lead to an illusory knowledge (see also 2.3). Reflective enlightenment also means looking for an implicit, hidden metaphysics even in the harshest critics of metaphysics—especially if this person happens to be oneself.

Again, Kant was able to build upon Rousseau's writings. Rousseau was probably thinking of the *philosophes* in Paris, such as Diderot, and d'Holbach, when he wrote: "I found them all to be proud, assertive, dogmatic (even in their pretended skepticism), ignorant of nothing, proving nothing, mocking one another."[84] In *Émile*, the Savoyard vicar contrasted the endless battles in the field of metaphysics with his own Socratic ignorance. According to the vicar, unreflective, "intellectual [*verständig*] Enlightenment" (Hegel) leads to the desire to "penetrate" and "know" everything. "The only thing we do not know is how to be ignorant of what we cannot know."[85] This knowledge of our own ignorance, an examination of the reasons why we cannot know anything in metaphysics and religion, and our own efforts on the path to this reflexive knowledge are decisive. Kant also thought that "despisers of metaphysics" such as Voltaire, for all their wit, humor, and esprit, could not hide the fact that they too endorsed their own "metaphysical assertions, which they yet professed so much to despise."[86] This was a warning against overestimating one's own reason and a call for Socratic modesty in recognizing the limits of theoretical reason, especially with regard to oneself and one's own philosophy. In the end what matters is what kind of metaphysics we pursue. Kant argued for critical, self-reflective, and practical metaphysics, which revolved around concepts of human dignity, tolerance, the rule of law, and natural religion. Kant recognized a difference between scientific knowledge on the one hand, and philosophy as a doctrine of wisdom (*Weisheitslehre*) on the other, namely the "science of the relation of all cognition to the essential ends of human reason."[87] These

---

83 Dieter Henrich, Vernunft und Selbstaufklärung, in: *Fluchtlinien*, Frankfurt am Main: Suhrkamp 1982, 43–124, at 48. Kant refers to a "conflict of reason with itself" in the *Critique of pure reason*, A 506.
84 Rousseau, *Emile*, 267.
85 Rousseau, *Emile*, 268.
86 Kant, *Werke*, vol. 29, 765 and *Critique of pure reason*, A X. Wolfgang Röd has shown that despite his professed empiricism and agnosticism, Voltaire's writings are full of metaphysical assumptions. See Wolfgang Röd, *Die Philosophie der Neuzeit 2. Von Newton bis Rousseau*, München: Beck 1984, 175–83.
87 Kant, *Critique of pure reason*, B 867. See also La Rocca, Was Aufklärung sein wird and Aufgeklärte Vernunft – Gestern und Heute, in: Klemme, *Kant und die Zukunft*, 100–23.

ends were the above-mentioned concepts of practical reason, such as thinking for oneself, autonomy, or self-legislation, reflective enlightenment, or freedom. It was not the quantity but the quality of knowledge that was important, that is the ability and willingness to make correct use of this cognition in the process of thinking for oneself and making independent judgments.

Finally, Kant's philosophy supports the Enlightenment as an intercultural philosophy and hermeneutics (1.1, concept no. 1 and conception no. 5). Franz Martin Wimmer calls the latter "a continuation of the program of the Enlightenment by other means: not by means of a tradition-free, purely methodologically defined science, and through a rejection of all particular traditions, but through a polylogue of traditions."[88] Wimmer distances himself from a reductionist understanding of the Enlightenment as "enlightenment through science." Intercultural enlightenment is reflexive and adheres to the maxim of an enlarged way of thinking: arguments from different cultures and traditions are considered equal but must undergo an examination before the "forum of reason." In this dialogue among equals, a mutual broadening of horizons "with cosmopolitan intent" is possible.[89]

This intercultural approach according to Kant should be protected from several misunderstandings. Firstly, neither here, nor in Kant's philosophy does the expanded way of thinking imply abandoning one's own position, relativistic pluralism, or epistemological or normative relativism (see 4.5). The concept of truth is not abandoned; instead, dialogue, and a broadening of horizons take their place as a common *search for* truth. Universally valid positions are possible but must first be found in an open communication process "that is as unprejudiced, ideology-critical, and open-ended as possible."[90] Secondly, in line with Kant's critical philosophy, the approach dispenses with assumptions about the essence of other cultures and with culturalism, the assumption that cultures are hermetically sealed units that determine or massively shape the lives of their members. In this

---

[88] Franz Martin Wimmer, Thesen, Bedingungen und Aufgaben interkulturell orientierter Philosophie, *Polylog – Zeitschrift für interkulturelles Philosophieren*, Heft 1 (1998), 5–12, at 12. See also *Interkulturelle Philosophie. Eine Einführung*, Wien: Facultas 2004, 17–20 and 66–73.

[89] Jan Christoph Heiser, *Interkulturelles Lernen. Eine pädagogische Grundlegung*, Würzburg: Königshausen & Neumann 2013, 307. See also Heiser, *Interkulturelles Lernen*, 78, 79, 115, 361, 371, especially 325–45. A useful introduction is Franz Gmainer-Pranzl, Von anderswoher denken: Responsivität als erweiterte Denkungsart, in: Heiser and Tanja Prieler, eds., *Die erweiterte Denkungsart*, 143–66. The phrase "with cosmopolitan intent" refers to an essay by Kant: Idee zu einer allgemeinen Geschichte in weltbürgerlicher Absicht (1784).

[90] Gmainer-Pranzl, Responsivität, 151.

context, Elmar Holenstein has argued that cultures share "many more specific invariants" than was assumed at the beginning of the 20th century (see also 4.2).[91] Thirdly, like the Enlightenment, intercultural philosophy has—or should have—more to do with wisdom than with a reductionist program of training in skills or competences that are considered useful. Unfortunately, this is what is often understood by "intercultural competence," namely optimizing prudence and the intellect, not the formation, or *Bildung* of reason understood as opening to the otherness of others. The cultivation of the way of thinking, impartiality, justice, human dignity, or mutual recognition would fall by the wayside.[92] Intercultural philosophy, in contrast, continues the cosmopolitan thinking that gained momentum in the European Enlightenment (see end of 4.4).

These remarks are not intended to reinforce the cliché of Kant as the philosopher who accomplished, perfected, or crowned the Enlightenment. This hagiography is as superfluous as the veneration of Spinoza, Hume, the radical *philosophes*, Smith, or of the Scottish, or the German Enlightenment.[93] Firstly, Kant—like others—stood on the shoulders of giants. In his case, these were above all the German *Schulphilosophie*, Hume, and Rousseau. Kant allowed himself to be inspired by other philosophers and especially many enlighteners, to adopt their suggestions, and criticism—but these intellectual challenges had to be there in the first place. The 18th century was obviously an extremely fertile ground for philosophical innovation.[94] Secondly, Kant clearly benefited from another external factor: he was granted a long life, dying at the age of 80 at the start of a new century (1804). If Kant had died in the 1770s at the age of fifty—not unusual at the time—there would have been no Kantian criticism or critical philosophy (Gotthold Ephraim Lessing died at the age of 52, Moses Mendelssohn at the age of 57, Georg Forster when he was not yet 40). Kant would have gone down in history as a talented but rather average philosopher. Thirdly, Kant's critical philosophy has clear limitations. Fourthly, Kant's approach can be "radicalized" once more, for example in

---

[91] Elmar Holenstein, *Menschliches Selbstverständnis. Ichbewusstsein – Intersubjektive Verantwortung – Interkulturelle Verständigung*, Frankfurt am Main: Suhrkamp 1985, 125.
[92] Gmainer-Pranzl, Responsivität, 153.
[93] Cassirer and Louden have a strong Kantian orientation. In my opinion, the interpretations of Israel (for Spinoza), Philipp Blom (for the radical *philosophes*) and Pagden (for Hume) tend toward veneration.
[94] See Reidar Maliks, *Kant's Politics in Context*, Oxford: Oxford University Press 2014 as an example how Kant was inspired by, and responded to, other intellectuals.

the context of a responsive phenomenology of interculturality (Bernhard Waldenfels).[95]

5.4 Contemporary Relevance: Between Naturalism, New Atheism, and Dogmatic Fundamentalism

I have already emphasized that although atheistic and materialistic philosophies were developed during the Enlightenment, they were not widespread. They were usually rejected, even if they were probably better known than scholarship has previously assumed. In German-speaking territories of the *Reich*, La Mettrie was regarded as half-mad and a libertine who was not taken seriously due to his radicalism. D'Holbach was shocking but also considered dogmatic and aggressive. Claude-Adrien Helvétius apparently came closest to being accepted in a positive way.[96] In addition to much polemic, there were also fundamental objections. A typical point of criticism was how a society with a widespread materialistic ethic that only allowed pleasure and utility could function. "What hinders me, if I can thereby gain, to thrust the dagger into the breast of my friend, to rob the temples of the gods, to betray my fatherland, or to place myself at the head of a band of robbers; and, if otherwise I have power enough to devastate whole countries, to drown whole peoples in their blood?"[97] This objection by Christoph Martin Wieland did not do justice to Helvétius or d'Holbach, who wanted to establish a new utilitarian ethic. But it showed that materialistic positions could easily be taken further in directions that led to the libertine, writer and pornographer Marquis de Sade (1740–1814), to immorality, arbitrariness, and violence.

What is the significance of enlighteners for present debates about religion? In my opinion, current debates could benefit from the insights of some of the enlighteners. Firstly, participants could and should agree on a "learned ignorance" (*docta ignorantia*), on *scio nescio*, on theoretical agnosticism in the spheres of metaphysics and religion (see 2.3 and 2.4). This would allow them to become aware of the limits of their *own* knowledge; knowledge ends where experience ends. Rousseau has the Savoyard vicar say in his "Creed": "It is not my intention here to engage in metaphysical discus-

---

[95] See Bernhard Waldenfels, *Grundmotive einer Phänomenologie des Fremden*, Frankfurt am Main: Suhrkamp 2006 and Gmainer-Pranzl, Responsivität, 159–66.
[96] Roland Krebs, Die radikale französische Aufklärung im Spiegel der deutschen Aufklärungsliteratur, in: Hofmann, eds., *Aufklärung*, 209–28.
[97] Christoph Martin Wieland, Geschichte des Agathon. Erste Fassung von 1766/1767, in: *Werke in zwölf Bänden*, ed. Gonthier-Louis Fink et al., Frankfurt am Main: Deutscher Klassiker-Verlag 1986, vol. 3, at 109–10.

sions that are beyond my and your comprehension and basically lead to nothing." This leaves room for various forms of belief in the metaphysical realm: from agnostic to atheist, deist, theist, or any form of spiritual belief. The self-reflective motto of all participants would be: "Even my own thoughts without content are empty." The modern separation into different scientific disciplines would be mutually recognized. Italian English lawyer Alberico Gentili (1552–1608) demanded in the early modern period: *"Silete theologi in munere alieno"* ("Theologians, be silent about matters that are outside of your expertise").[98] The same principle would apply reciprocally to scientists from all disciplines.

In recent decades, this form of secularization—namely the separation into different scientific fields or disciplines—has unfortunately been called into question time and again. Some natural scientists, for example, dabble in the field of theology and the philosophy of religion, advocate militant atheism, and believe they can justify it with scientific evidence. The biologist Richard Dawkins is a case in point.[99] Along the same lines, some theologians tamper with the natural sciences and present supposedly scientific arguments for God's existence under the title of "intelligent design." Or it is claimed that modern science has found new evidence for "the invisible," for the essence "behind the phenomena." For instance, theologian and gynecologist Johannes Huber justifies his metaphysical approach with the argument that he does not build walls and "does not put on blinkers."[100] Like other speculative and dogmatic metaphysicians, he does not distinguish between science and faith, between knowledge, and belief.

Secondly, enlightened people could also learn to strive for a greater degree of tolerance in the sense of respect for people with different metaphysical world views and religions—provided they accept the rules and norms of a democratic republic. This would include refraining from insults and abuse. Atheists like Richard Dawkins would restrain themselves from describing religion as a "delusion," a "virus," or a "mental illness," and religious education before the age of 17 as "child abuse." Religious or spiritual persons would not call atheists "unbelievers", a "threat to society", incapable of morality, and bound for hell.

Enlightenment philosophies might help to make contemporary debates more fruitful and sophisticated. Charles Devellennes has argued that thinkers like Bayle, Jean Meslier (1664–1729), d'Holbach and Diderot tried to move from a negative con-

---

98 Quoted in Michael Becker, *Kriegsrecht im frühneuzeitlichen Protestantismus*, Tübingen: Mohr Siebeck 2017, 366.
99 See among others Rudolf Langthaler, *Warum Dawkins Unrecht hat. Eine Streitschrift*, Freiburg und München: Karl Alber 2015.
100 Johannes Huber, *Es existiert. Die Wissenschaft entdeckt das Unsichtbare*, Wien: Edition A 2016, 83.

ception of atheism to a positive one (only two of these authors explicitly defined themselves as atheists). The negative conception simply denies the existence of God. By contrast, the positive conception implies a doctrine or worldview beyond mere anti-theist positions, with moral, political, and social ramifications. Devellennes muses: "Such is the conclusion of the story of Enlightenment atheism in France: atheists may have more in common with like-minded believers than they have with other atheists."[101]

It is very unlikely that a universalist natural religion will become widespread on a global scale. Perhaps that would not even be desirable. However, it might be helpful if some of the Enlightenment's methodological differentiations were to become more widespread, such as Johann Salomo Semler's distinction between theology and religious belief (see 5.2), or between the sphere of experience and that of metaphysics (see 2.3). It would also be encouraging if more than lip service was paid to the moral core of religion. In theory, the common morality thesis (all historical forms of faith contain a core of universal and reasonable religious convictions) is recognized by almost every religious community. Then religious tolerance would have more of a chance.

Perhaps my recommendations are too rational and elitist. There is the sober observation of many enlighteners (often proclaimed with a dose of arrogance) that ordinary people are seldom consistent and reasonable when their minds focus on religious or metaphysical matters. Diderot reports of his friend Didier-François de Montamy (1702–1765), steward to the duke of Orleans:

> He is as well informed as any man I know and as sensible and prudent in his actions … he goes to mass without placing much faith in it, but laughs up his sleeve at the jokes that are made against it, hopes for the resurrection of the dead, without having any very clear ideas about the nature of the soul, and in general is a bundle of contradictory ideas which make his conversation very entertaining.[102]

This might be an apt description of most humans' beliefs globally: "a bundle of contradictory ideas." Enlighteners must be prepared to accept this. And it might even apply to themselves. Which brings us back to familiar topics, such as the fight against superstition, fanaticism, ignorance, dogmatism, and oppressive authority (see 1.1, conceptions no. 3 and 5). Yet without a self-examining and reflective attitude, and without the enlarged way of thinking, this fight might not lead to the intended results.

---

101 Devellennes, *Positive Atheism*, 208.
102 Letter of 26 September 1762, in: Denis Diderot, *Letters to Sophie Volland*, ed. and tr. Peter France, London: Oxford University Press 1972, 123, quoted in Robertson, *The Enlightenment. The Pursuit of Happiness*, 214.

Conclusion
A failed Enlightenment?

> [T]he greatest motive for studying this subject is the awareness
> that the Enlightenment, though distant in time, remains vitally important.
> —Ritchie Robertson, *The Enlightenment. The Pursuit of Happiness*, xxii

Can we argue that the Enlightenment has failed? If so, in what respect? Has it failed completely or partially? First, it is a historical fact that the European Enlightenment came under increasing pressure from movements such as Romanticism after the 1770s, and conservatism after the 1790s. Numerous authors complained that prejudice, superstition, and fanaticism were still the order of the day. It was in 1782 that one of the last witch trials took place in Switzerland (and ended with the execution of the accused). According to one Enlightener, superstition seemed to have "regained new strength in the last ten years." "We are truly in danger of falling back into the previous barbarism and ignorance, and of losing the glory of the Enlightenment if we are not on our guard."[1] The French Revolution was ultimately decisive, especially after the execution of the king and the Reign of Terror, *la Terreur*, from 1793 to 1794. Many distanced themselves from the revolution, among them some enlighteners, and held the Enlightenment —partly or completely—responsible for its excesses. The attempt to export the French Revolution by force via French armies and Napoleon's wars of conquest led to further rejection and discrediting.

It is sometimes argued that the Enlightenment failed because the very concept and its ideas were wrong. In this context, the catchphrase of the so-called "dialectic of Enlightenment" is often used. It goes back to a publication by Max Horkheimer and Theodor W. Adorno (published in 1944; see also the introduction, assumption 4 above). Their main thesis was that enlightened instrumental reason, shaped by the natural sciences, planned to dominate inner, and outer nature. In this context, instrumental reason corresponds to *Verstand* or understanding, which is based on sensory perceptions and focuses on science, calculation, utility and prudence (see 1.1, conception no. 4). The aim of the Enlightenment, understood in this way, was to overcome mythical and traditional worldviews. According to Horkheimer and Adorno, however, a new mythology emerged in modern society, the very opposite of Enlightenment. As already outlined, criticism of this form of Enlightenment also presupposes enlightenment understood as self-

---

[1] Gottfried Christian Voigt, Etwas über die Hexenprozesse in Deutschland, *Berlinische Monatsschrift*, Bd. 3 (1784), 297–311, at 300, and Martus, *Aufklärung*, 681–6 with references.

criticism. Horkheimer and Adorno understood this. Adorno, for example, later referred to the "idea of an autonomous, responsible human being," which Kant had developed in an "unsurpassed" way. "One can only imagine realized democracy as a society of mature people."[2] The "dialectic of Enlightenment" is ultimately not about a blanket rejection of enlightenment per se, but about true enlightenment in the sense of maturity and independent thinking. The one-sided and reductionist enlightenment of the intellect or understanding and enlightenment through science (1.1, conceptions nos. 3 and 4) should be replaced or supplemented by enlightenment as a process of emancipation and the enlightenment of reason (concept no. 1 and conception no. 5). This normative ideal is, in my opinion, unassailable. If it is dropped, the result is a performative self-contradiction (see 2.1).

Many enlighteners can be accused of having made assumptions about results and the future of Enlightenment processes. A common assumption was that free trade would tend to promote world peace and reduce poverty. This assumption has probably not been borne out, at least not in terms of a strict "if-then" logic. Similarly, the emergence of a commercial society, the introduction of compulsory education or the improvement of school systems has not necessarily led to a critical public sphere or an "engaged public sphere" (and if, only partially), "but rather to a privatized consumer culture."[3] It can also be argued that the Enlightenment has outlived itself because it has been successful. Certain demands such as human rights, tolerance, education or hygienic measures, "although in fact repeatedly endangered," have become "self-evident" in several parts of the globe; "some of their postulates have even found their way into the fabric of states through legal reforms."[4] In this context, the *Open Society Barometer. Can Democracy deliver?* of September 2023 is worth noting. Natalie Samarasinghe, one of the co-authors, has argued that despite worldwide cultural, economic, or political diversity, what were originally Western values, ideas, and norms, such as democracy, human rights, religious freedom, pluralism and equality of opportunity, are now widely accepted. "The values of the Enlightenment are not Western, but global." A majority of people all over the world endorse human rights, reject discrimination against homosexuals, or the persecution of people of other faiths.[5] If En-

---

[2] Theodor W. Adorno, *Erziehung zur Mündigkeit*, Frankfurt am Main: Suhrkamp 1971, 107. See Gerhard Schweppenhäuser, Adorno's Negative Moral Philosophy, in: Tom Huhn, ed., *The Cambridge Companion to Adorno*, Cambridge: Cambridge University Press 2006, 328–53 for an introduction.
[3] Louden, *The World We Want*, 10.
[4] Schneiders, *Aufklärung*, 130.
[5] https://www.opensocietyfoundations.org/publications/open-society-barometer-can-democracy-deliver (last accessed October 2, 2025); Veronika Kaufmann, What Problems Are People Around

lightenment is defined using terms such as science and reason, it might have contributed to a stronger orientation toward reason, understanding and science, and to an "argumentative critical faculty that today permeates everyday life as a matter of course (at least as a moral imperative)."[6]

It goes without saying that the modern day differs from the Age of Enlightenment. Yet there are evidently some continuities, and previous chapters have discussed some of them, including concepts of rule of law, toleration, human rights, and cosmopolitanism. I have termed this the "successful Enlightenment" (see 4.3 and 4.4). It may also be argued that some conceptions of the Enlightenment have stayed with us, such as "enlightenment through science" or the emancipatory understanding of the Enlightenment (see 1.1). It could also be suggested that other aspects or characteristics of the Enlightenment have become part of modern societies, in particular the turn toward experience, criticism, the focus on the individual, or the pursuit of happiness. Enlighteners such as Herder and Friedrich von Humboldt helped to establish a new academic discipline, namely linguistics, and the philosophy of language.[7] Enlighteners like Johann Bernhard Basedow (1724–1790) and Rousseau developed novel and forward-looking educational theories that influenced subsequent generations up to the present. Other representatives of the Enlightenment, like Thomas Jefferson, or Condorcet, spoke up in favor of universal public education "without regard to wealth, birth, or other accidental condition or circumstances."[8] German Enlighteners reformed universities such as Halle, Göttingen, and Berlin in the territories of the *Reich*, laying the foundations of the modern university in which teaching and research go hand in hand.[9]

There are additional possible Enlightenment legacies. One legacy can be subsumed under the rubric "individualism, emancipation, freedom, liberalism."[10] One version of liberalism emphasizes the freedom of individuals to pursue their own happiness, with minimal interference from the state. Another version goes beyond a conception of the state which focuses exclusively on the rule of law, maintaining public order, infrastructure, and military defense. Partly influ-

---

The World Most Worried About, https://medium.com/illumination/what-problems-are-people-aro und-the-world-most-worried-about-c798e0692659 (last accessed October 2, 2025).
6 Schneiders, *Aufklärung*, 130.
7 Vicki A. Spencer, *Herder's Political Thought. A Study of Language, Culture, and Community*, Toronto, Buffalo and London: University of Toronto Press 2012, especially 26–95 and Jürgen Trabant, *Wilhelm von Humboldt (1767–1835): Menschen Sprache Politik*, Würzburg: Königshausen u. Neumann 2021, 61–86.
8 Louden, *World We Want*, 27–50, with the quote from Jefferson at 28.
9 Louden, *World We Want*, 46–50.
10 See Robertson, *The Enlightenment. The Pursuit of Happiness*, 745–9.

enced by German conceptions of enlightened absolutism and the paternalistic state, this liberalism sees welfare measures as an integral part of government duties. The key argument is that governments must provide the basic needs for disadvantaged people to enable them to pursue their own well-being and happiness. Debates continue between these two currents of liberalism. Typical labels are "classical liberalism" or "neo-liberalism" versus "social democracy." A forerunner of contemporary neo-liberalism was Wilhelm von Humboldt's *Ideen zu einem Versuch die Grenzen der Wirksamkeit des Staats zu bestimmen* (1792, *Ideas for an Attempt to Define the Limits of the Effectiveness of the State*). Kant, in contrast, though an early liberal like Humboldt, put his faith in a more interventionist state.[11]

Another Enlightenment legacy is the tension between cosmopolitanism on the one hand and patriotism and nationalism on the other. Enlighteners contributed more to cosmopolitan theories than in previous centuries. Many characterized themselves as "citizens of the world." Others formed "patriotic societies." Most apparently did not see a contradiction between moderate patriotism and cosmopolitanism, endorsing what could be termed "cosmopolitan patriotism": intellectuals saw themselves as embedded in their own society, religion, culture, and state, which were often criticized but not necessarily and comprehensively rejected (see 4.4). The French Revolutionary Wars since 1792 turned the tide. Moderate patriotism with cosmopolitan elements was subsequently replaced by aggressive nationalism, in France, Prussia, and elsewhere.[12] The enlighteners laid the philosophical foundations of new forms of cosmopolitanism, among them cultural, juridical, and dynamic cosmopolitanism. Probably the most influential texts on juridical cosmopolitanism, with a focus on an international organization and world peace, were written by the English Quaker and writer William Penn (1644–1718), the French reformer Abbé Charles-Irénee Castel de Saint-Pierre, by Rousseau and Kant (*Zum ewigen Frieden*, 1795).[13] Their ideas underlie the interwar League of Nations and the United Nations after 1945. These enlighteners raised questions that have remained with us to the present: what should an international organization

---

11 Trabant, *Wilhelm von Humboldt*, 27, 43–8 and Allen D. Rosen, *Kant's Theory of Justice*, Ithaca and London: Cornell University Press 1996, 173–208.
12 Robertson, *The Enlightenment. The Pursuit of Happiness*, 750–5, Pauline Kleingeld, Kant's Cosmopolitan Patriotism, in: Sharon Byrd and Joachim Hruschka, eds., *Kant and Law*, Aldershot, Burlington: Ashgate 2006, 473–90.
13 A brief introduction is Robertson, *The Enlightenment. The Pursuit of Happiness*, 754–62. Much longer are Georg Cavallar, *Imperfect cosmopolis: studies in the history of international legal theory and cosmopolitan ideas*, Cardiff: University of Wales Press 2011 and *Kant and the Theory and Practice of International Right*. Second, revised edition, Cardiff: University of Wales Press, 2020.

look like? Does a loose federation of states suffice? Is humanitarian intervention legitimate in cases of serious human rights violations or genocide?

It could also be argued that the Enlightenment has failed because, in principle, ideals cannot be fully realized. In this case, the Enlightenment itself has not failed, but rather its complete realization was always impossible. One problem is often overlooked: Enlightenment in the sense of the attempt to think for oneself (1.1, conception no. 5) must be started again and again with each new generation. It can therefore never come to an end and could fail in the future. An author at the end of the 18th century apparently had this insight. There will only be better readers when there are better writers. But where should better writers come from if not from the readership? "The execution has to start all over again, and the carts that drive away the rubble have to be built bigger and bigger."[14] Enlightenment thus becomes a never-ending battle against a many-headed hydra, where prejudice, half-education, ignorance, superstition, fanaticism, dogmatism, and so on keep growing back. The aim of enlightenment can then only be "to help people not to give up on themselves as rational beings."[15]

It can also be argued that the Enlightenment has not failed, but that the people who do not or have not successfully implemented it are the problem. In other words, the key problem is the people who are unwilling or incapable of enlightenment, not enlightenment itself. The awareness of this kind of failure of the European Enlightenment, or in principle of any attempt at enlightenment, had already emerged in the late Enlightenment. Here are four prominent examples: Voltaire, Lichtenberg, Schiller, and Kant. In his article on fanaticism, Voltaire wrote: "How do you respond to a man who says he would rather obey God than men, and is certain he is going to heaven by cutting your throat?" If we replace the word "God" with "Allah" and think of jihadists, the question remains strikingly relevant, right down to the gruesome detail of beheading. Voltaire only had the usual "weapons" of enlightenment to offer against this kind of fanaticism: Thinking for oneself, critical thinking and questioning intolerance, prejudice, and superstition. However, even the "spirit of philosophy" was perhaps largely powerless against the "foolishness of men."[16] Georg Christoph Lichtenberg wrote in his *Sudelbücher:* "We often speak of enlightenment and desire more light. But, my God, what good is all of this light when people either have no

---

14 Schreiben eines Buchhändlers von der Leipziger Ostermesse, *Berlinische Monatsschrift*, vol. 4 (1784), 63–73, at 72. See also Schneiders, *Hoffnung auf Vernunft*, 179.
15 Schneiders, *Hoffnung auf Vernunft*, 179.
16 Fanatisme, in *La Raison par Alphabet. Septieme Édition* (1773), 285; Besterman et al., *Œuvres complètes de Voltaire* (1994), 36:110, quoted in: *The Quotable Voltaire*, ed. Apgar and Langille, 103. See also Forst, *Toleration in Conflict*, 287.

eyes or deliberately shut those they have?"[17] With this question, Lichtenberg outlines a fundamental problem of any enlightenment movement: what if people simply do not *want* to be enlightened, or are too indifferent?

The simultaneity of the European Enlightenment and the rise of modern barbarism during the French Revolution shocked Friedrich Schiller. "The age is enlightened, that is to say, that knowledge, obtained, and vulgarized, suffices to correct at least our practical principles. The spirit of free inquiry has dissipated the erroneous opinions [...]. Reason has purified itself from the illusions of the senses and from a mendacious sophistry [...]. Why is it then that we are still barbarians?"[18] Friedrich Schiller asked this question in 1795, when word had spread of the crimes during the Reign of Terror and Robespierre's tyranny. The French Revolution, initially greeted with enthusiasm by intellectuals throughout Europe, had ended in a bloodbath (and later in a military dictatorship and military aggression). Why was that? The European Enlightenment obviously found its logical continuation in the *Declaration of Human Rights* of 1791, but perhaps Schiller was too naive in believing that the age had already been enlightened and that "reason" had triumphed. French historians Reynald Secher and Pierre Chaunu, and the French jurist Jacques Villemain have argued that the War in the Vendée (1793–1796) included the first modern genocide on European soil.[19]

As early as 1783, in his famous essay on the Enlightenment, Kant saw character and moral deficiencies as possible causes of the failure of the Enlightenment as a historical phenomenon. "It is because of laziness and cowardice that so great a part of humankind, after nature has long since emancipated them from other people's direction [...], nevertheless gladly remains minors for life, and that it becomes so easy for others to set themselves up as their guardians. It is so comfortable to be a minor!"[20] The passage is often overlooked but has retained its relevance. Anyone involved in education knows how difficult it is to encourage and motivate young people to think for themselves. Perhaps it is naive to underestimate the potential of human laziness, cowardice, narrow-mindedness, or sheer stupidity. It is probably realistic to assume that enlightenment is more likely to fail than succeed. It is problematic to understand enlightenment as a process

---

[17] Lichtenberg, *Philosophical Writings*, 171. Schneiders, *Hoffnung auf Vernunft*, 161 mentions additional examples, namely Frederick II. of Prussia, Mendelssohn and Johann Jakob Engel.
[18] Friedrich Schiller, Letters on the Aesthetical Education of Man [1795], 8th letter, in: *Aesthetical and Philosophical Essays*, ed. Nathan Haskell Dole, Boston: Francis A. Niccolls and Company 1902, vol. 1, 28.
[19] For an introduction, see Jacques Villemain, *Vendée, 1793–1794. Crime de guerre? Crime contre l'humanité? Génocide? Une étude juridique*, Paris: Les éditions du Cerf 2017.
[20] Kant, What is Enlightenment?, vol. 8, 35.

that can be finished once and for all, to reduce it to the model of "Enlightenment through science," to reduce rationality to understanding, pragmatism, and prudence. It is probably arrogant to regard one's own age as "enlightened" in its entirety. Reflective enlightenment as thinking for oneself will likely remain a minority program. In the words of a disillusioned Enlightener: "All the sciences and arts, of whose influence on the education of the mind and the spirit so much is spoken, seemed to me mere trash; all men an incurable heap of fools."[21]

Gottfried Christian Voigt (1740–1791), a town syndic from Quedlinburg in the Holy Roman Empire, is an outstanding example of how the Enlightenment may be endangered or even ruined by its own representatives. Voight reacted to what was apparently the last witch trial in Europe in the 1780s. In what must have been a sincere effort to help the Enlightenment triumph over superstition, religious fanaticism, prejudice, bogus knowledge, barbarism, and myth, he promoted the very things he was fighting against, namely prejudice, and bogus knowledge—and founded a new popular myth. Based on shaky evidence and with some arbitrariness, he calculated that since the time of Constantine the Great, about nine million witches must have been burned in Europe (research today assumes 40,000 to 50,000 victims). Wolfgang Behringer calls this an "outrageous extrapolation," but the numbers have been widely disseminated right up to the present. The fictitious numbers—Behringer refers to the "nine million theory"—have been used with no critical attitude to the present, among others by 19th-century culture warriors, National Socialists, anti-Christian, and neo-pagan polemicists, contemporary feminists, and sensationalist journalists.[22] A popular myth, prejudices, and laziness have dominated instead of references to sources, historical facts, and critical thinking. What Voigt presented in the name of popular Enlightenment (*Volksaufklärung*)—and probably with the best of intentions—has nothing to do with "enlightenment through science" or "enlightenment of the understanding" and has certainly nothing to do with the self-reflective enlightenment of thinking for oneself. As an irony, it should also be noted that Voigt published in the most

---

21 Die Wallfahrt zum Monddoktor in Berlin, *Berlinische Monatsschrift*, vol. 1 (1783), 368–385, at 385.
22 Wolfgang Behringer, Neun Millionen Hexen. Entstehung, Tradition und Kritik eines populären Mythos [1998], https://langzeitarchivierung.bib-bvb.de/wayback/20190716084950/https://www.historicum.net/themen/hexenforschung/thementexte/rezeption/artikel/neun-millionen/ (last accessed October 2, 2025). See also Behringer's *Hexen und Hexenprozesse in Deutschland*, München: Deutscher Taschenbuch-Verlag 2000, *Witches and witch-hunts: a global history*, Cambridge: Polity Press 2004, *Hexen: Glaube, Verfolgung, Vermarktung*, 5th ed., München: Beck 2009, especially 92–8 and Wolfgang Behringer et al., eds., *Späte Hexenprozesse: der Umgang der Aufklärung mit dem Irrationalen*, Bielefeld: Verlag für Regionalgeschichte 2016.

famous journal of the German Enlightenment in which most of Kant's shorter essays and the debates on the question "What is Enlightenment?" were published. It is almost ridiculous that, after 1945, even people who had massively distanced themselves from National Socialist ideology continued its polemics and narrow-minded way of thinking. We are dealing here with a piece of failed Enlightenment.

Two examples are often cited in the context of an allegedly failed Enlightenment. One is associated with American diplomat and statesman Thomas Jefferson, one of the Founding Fathers and the third president of the United States, the other with Rousseau. Jefferson, the primary author of the *Declaration of Independence* with its key passage that "all men are created equal," owned more than 600 slaves and had a relationship with his slave Sarah Hemings (around 1773–1835), with whom he had four children. Although Jefferson criticized the international slave trade, for various reasons he only freed two of his own slaves during his lifetime.[23] Rousseau became famous with *Émile* (1762), a book on the ideal education of a hypothetical boy of this name. In real life, Rousseau sent his own children to the Paris Foundling Hospital, again for a variety of reasons, among them financial problems.[24] Both Jefferson and Rousseau are usually assigned to the camp of enlighteners and labeled hypocrites. Yet we may also ask if they really betrayed the Enlightenment or "Enlightenment ideals." Perhaps it is fairer to say they failed the test of self-contradiction and universality.

It is possible that enlightenment, in the sense of the various meanings mentioned in the first chapter, is also, and perhaps especially, endangered by those who profess it; it need not only be threatened from the outside, by religious fanaticism, or modern ideologies, for example. I cited one such example from the 18th century at the beginning of this section, namely the Enlightenment philosopher Gottfried Christian Voigt and his daring theses on the history of witch hunts.

Examples of a failed Enlightenment can also be found in the present. I think a case in point is Steven Pinker's book *Enlightenment Now. The Case for Reason, Science, Humanism, and Progress*. Pinker, a Canadian American cognitive psychologist, defends the Enlightenment against its various alleged enemies, such as "faitheists," theists, brands of Counter-Enlightenments, nationalisms, or postmodern philosophy. The first problem is Pinker's superficial definition of the En-

---

23 For introductions to this ongoing controversy, see Henry Wiencek, *Master of the Mountain. Thomas Jefferson and His Slaves*, New York: Farrar, Straus and Giroux 2012 and M. Andrew Holowchak, *Rethinking Thomas Jefferson's Writings on Slavery and Race: [God's] justice can not sleep for ever*, Newcastle upon Tyne: Cambridge Scholars Publishing 2020.
24 For an introduction, see David Potts, Were Rousseau's Children Victims of His Moral Theory?, posted on June 28, 2015, *Policy of Truth*, https://irfankhawajaphilosopher.com/2015/06/28/were-rousseaus-children-victims-of-his-moral-theory/ (last accessed October 2, 2025).

lightenment. He identifies it with "reason, science, humanism, and progress."[25] This study has shown that the issue is somewhat more complex. A second, related problem is that Pinker posits a comprehensive "Enlightenment project" based on these four ideas. Following binary patterns of thought, Pinker contrasts the good, and progressive Enlightenment of the 18th century with various subsequent Counter-Enlightenments, lumping together diverse authors such as Rousseau, Herder, Nietzsche, Heidegger, Adorno and Foucault, and movements and ideologies such as Nazism, Bolshevism, Stalinism, Italian Fascism, "theoconservatism" or "Trumpism." Other enemies in this Manichaean worldview are pessimism, "progressophobia," lack of faith in modernity, and cynicism.[26] Thirdly, key concepts like reason, or progress are never properly defined and differentiated. Sometimes, the Enlightenment seems to coincide with science, scientific progress, liberalism, generic humanism, or parts of European modernity. Fourthly, the book abounds with psychological speculations, polemics, and sweeping generalizations. For instance, a chapter begins with the statement: "Intellectuals hate progress. Intellectuals who call themselves "progressives" *really* hate progress."[27]

The best parts of the book are Steven Pinker's attempts to summarize data, statistics and evidence to show that, as a result of the Enlightenment, life has improved for most people over the last two centuries. According to Pinker, this progress is demonstrated in areas such as life expectancy, health, wealth, the environment, democracy, equal rights, but also in quality of life and happiness. These are global trends over long periods. Yet even here crucial questions remain. Can we trace these markers of progress back to "the Enlightenment"? How do we define and how do we measure happiness and human flourishing? Is there a causal connection or a mere correlation between wealth and happiness? Is utilitarianism, the greatest happiness for the greatest number, really the only ethical theory based on alleged "Enlightenment ideals"?

Finally, despite his commitment to reason and science, Pinker blurs the difference between correlation and causality. It is not obvious that the European Enlightenment was the key or only cause of technological or societal progress. Other plausible factors include, among others, the Industrial Revolution, capitalism, European expansion and colonialism, trade, technological changes, the Renaissance, the Protestant Reformation, or institutional changes.[28] Any one-sided,

---

[25] Steven Pinker, *Enlightenment Now: The Case for Reason, Science, Humanism, and Progress*, New York: Random House 2018, 8.
[26] Pinker, *Enlightenment Now*, 443–9 and 39–52 (on progressophobia).
[27] Pinker, *Enlightenment Now*, 39.
[28] Succinct criticisms are Gary Guttling, Never Better: Steven Pinker's Narrow Enlightenment, *Commonweal*, vol. 145 (2018), 20 ff. and John Gray, Unenlightened thinking: Steven Pinker's em-

polemical, and undifferentiated defense of the European Enlightenment is bound to fail.

Steven Pinker claims that the Enlightenment "has *worked*—perhaps the greatest story seldom told. And because this triumph is so unsung, the underlying ideals of reason, science, and humanism are unappreciated as well."[29] Pinker, this "evangelist for science" (John Gray),[30] follows the "Enlightenment-as-science" conception, yet it is a simplified version, and Pinker fails to see its endemic philosophical problems. Pinker's narrative is embarrassingly triumphalist and prone to mystification. Enlighteners like Diderot or Rousseau are more sophisticated, more critical, more self-reflective, or—to put it bluntly—more enlightened and enlightening.

Why enlightenment at all? Commitments to and pleas for the Enlightenment have continued to the present day. Israeli German historian Dan Diner, for example, sees the Enlightenment as indispensable in a present in which, due to globalization, and different traditions, societies, and cultures have much more contact with each other than in previous centuries. This leads to an "ever-growing commonality of a universal humanity", "behind which no longer any return to particularities is possible." Diner claims that the tradition of enlightenment is "an orientation, guideline, and ethical measure for people. All attempts to talk the enlightened consciousness out of the Enlightenment are counter-Enlightenment and therefore anti-universal."[31] I am skeptical. I doubt whether there really can no longer be a "return to particularities." There are even signs that this reversion is already taking place in some societies. It is questionable and perhaps even arrogant to refer to an "enlightened consciousness" in general terms. The European Enlightenment had characteristics that can be considered universal in the sense of "cross-cultural." Yet it does not make sense to simply equate the Enlightenment with universality. Here—as in the first chapter—we need to ask: to which Enlightenment are we referring? Dan Diner appreciates the Scottish Enlightenment and the moderate "Anglo-Saxon tradition." He criticizes the French *philosophes* as too extreme, as they gave absolute importance to Reason and constructed an irreconcilable opposition between Reason and Religion.[32] Diner therefore does not simply

---

barrassing new book is a feeble sermon for rattled liberals, *The New Statesman*, February 22, 2018, https://www.newstatesman.com/culture/books/2018/02/unenlightened-thinking-steven-pinker-s-embarrassing-new-book-feeble-sermon (last accessed October 2, 2025).
29 Pinker, *Enlightenment Now*, 6.
30 Gray, Unenlightened thinking. He concludes: "With its primitive scientism and manga-style history of ideas, the book is a parody of Enlightenment thinking at its crudest."
31 Dan Diner, *Aufklärungen: Wege in die Moderne*, Ditzingen: Reclam 2017, 82.
32 Diner, *Aufklärungen*, 45–59, 73 and 47–8.

mean "the tradition of the Enlightenment," but a specific historical variant of the Enlightenment, namely the Anglo-Saxon, and especially the Scottish brand. Can this really lay claim to universality? This and similar pleas for the Enlightenment often raise more questions than they answer.[33]

There is enough to do in terms of enlightenment and thinking for oneself. Even minimal human rights standards regarding torture, state arbitrariness, or slavery, for example (see 4.3 and 4.4), are still not taken for granted worldwide, even in states that see themselves in the tradition of the European Enlightenment.[34] We witness a new, global terrorism that is religiously legitimized by its followers. In industrialized countries with functioning healthcare systems, children are dying because their parents give them home remedies instead of consulting a doctor.[35] Over 150 Serbian professors, scientists, doctors, and theologians signed a petition in May 2017, demanding the introduction of the biblical doctrine of creation in school lessons at the expense of Darwin's theory of evolution. The petition claimed that "globalists and atheists, who occupy the most influential positions in the world today, are financing the spread of the theory of evolution." The doctrine that humans and apes have common ancestors was seen as an "insult to all believers."[36] This looks like a conspiracy theory, with prejudices, and a missing methodological separation between science and faith. In return, the Enlightenment might become a polemical concept for its defenders. It is what others do not have or even cannot have as a matter of principle: the non-Europeans, the Muslims, the reactionaries, the religious people. The Enlightenment serves as a demarcation in an alleged "clash of civilizations."

"Purely rational enlightenment cannot compete against teachers of salvation and miracles."[37] This observation by Werner Schneider in 1990 is more pertinent than ever in times of fake news, filter bubbles, "alternative facts," echo chamber

---

[33] In Diner's case, this also has to do with a vague or undifferentiated concept of Enlightenment (see chapter 1 above and Diner, *Aufklärungen*, 11 and 14). Something similar is probably also true of Pagden, *Enlightenment*, especially 315–51.

[34] Keywords are Abu Ghraib, Guantanamo and the so-called Torture Memos. See the references in *Islam, Aufklärung und Moderne*, 135–40. On the subject of state despotism, see for example Daniel Berehulak, They Are Slaughtering Us Like Animals, *The New York Times*, December 7, 2016 on Philippine President Duterte's "extended" war against drug dealers.

[35] Examples: Michael E. Miller, The anti-vaccine couple facing prison over the death of their toddler from meningitis, *The Independent*, 18 March 2016, Learn the Facts – Cases of Childhood Deaths due to Parental Religious Objection to Necessary Medical Care (masskids.org), 27.12.2023.

[36] Pete Baumgartner, Adam & Eve Challenge Darwinism in Serbia, Radio Free Europe, https://www.rferl.org/a/serbia-creationism-vs-darwinism-petition-education/28487414.html (last accessed October 2, 2025).

[37] Schneiders, *Hoffnung auf Vernunft*, 172.

effects in social networks, rampant conspiracy theories of all kinds and the tunnel vision of contemporary digital tribes.[38] Enlightenment can also not compete because it can become boring and tedious, never comes to an end and, due to its critical, and sometimes destructive aspects, perhaps takes more than it can give. In this context, it is important to recall examples of successful enlightenment processes (see 4.3 and 4.4).

Attacks on the Enlightenment are not a contemporary phenomenon. One of the most celebrated works on the European Enlightenment is the study by Ernst Cassirer of 1932. Cassirer was a German philosopher with Jewish roots and had a philosophical as well as a political goal: the defense of the Enlightenment as self-liberation, thinking for oneself, and critical thinking in times of darkness, dominated by the rise of totalitarian ideologies such as Stalinism and, above all, National Socialism in Germany. Cassirer saw himself as an Enlightener who took a stand against Heidegger's new metaphysics or fundamental ontology. This was evident in the famous discussion during the Davos University Days in 1929, where Cassirer answered the question about the task of philosophy as follows: "Philosophy has to make man as free as he can be."[39] This was directed against Heidegger's existentialism, but also against the dogmatic, anti-Enlightenment world view (or rather ideology) of the National Socialists and their philosophical helpers—which also included Heidegger. In 1933, after Hitler had become German chancellor, Cassirer lost his chair at the University of Hamburg and went into exile.

Since this is a philosophical introduction to Enlightenment, I want to continue with philosophical issues that are difficult to solve. I assume that some cannot be solved as a matter of principle.

Presentism and historicism, condemnation, or defense. Ritchie Robertson argues that the Enlightenment as a historical phenomenon or movement "demands a double optic." On the one hand, historians are obliged to study it with objectivity, detachment, and distance. The problem with this approach—which might be called "historicism" or an antiquitarian understanding of the past—is that it puts people, ideas and conflicts "into a historical deep freeze."[40] And it is suggested that these ideas and conflicts have nothing or little to do with the present. They are in the distant past, like a foreign culture one has difficulties understanding. On the other hand, the Enlightenment can also be presented as a move-

---

38 See for instance John David Seidler, *Die Verschwörung der Massenmedien. Eine Kulturgeschichte vom Buchhändler-Komplott bis zur Lügenpresse*, Bielefeld: Transcript 2016.
39 Quoted in Gerald Hartung, Einleitung, in: Ernst Cassirer, *Die Philosophie der Aufklärung* [1932], Hamburg: Felix Meiner 1998, vii–xxiii, at xvi.
40 Robertson, *The Enlightenment. The Pursuit of Happiness*, 41.

ment "that still speaks urgently to the present." "Enlightenment values" are invoked, and they range from secularism to positivism, democracy, human rights, cosmopolitanism, and belief in modern science. Representatives of this approach are, among others, Anthony Pagden, Steven Pinker, Jonathan Israel, Robert Louden, and Susan Neiman.[41] In some cases, these Enlightenment values are vehemently defended against their deadly enemies, such as the representatives of various branches of the Counter-Enlightenment. This second position—the opposite of historicism—is presentism. Present day concepts, perspectives, values, and ideas are used in the interpretation of the past, thereby perhaps distorting it. In the case of the Enlightenment, this might amount to "interpreting it too much in the light of the present."[42] I may also be guilty of the charge of presentism, although I have tried to present a rich historical tableau.

Another possible fallacy is the abuse of hindsight. During and after the French Revolution, conservative critics accused the enlighteners of having prepared or even caused this revolution, including, of course, the Reign of Terror. This went hand in hand with making them responsible for the ills and horrors of the Revolution. Another abuse of hindsight is projecting 19th-century European arrogance and narratives such as "Oriental despotism" back onto the 18th century (see 4.4).[43]

Condemnation or defense is an issue related to the fallacy of presentism. If we evaluate the Enlightenment in the light of the present, should we defend or condemn it, or do both? Should a balanced view be the proper goal? What would it look like? Can we avoid falling into the trap of either condemnation or defense, or even glorification? Many scholars resort to binary thinking, assuming there was a good and a bad Enlightenment (see Introduction, Assumption 7). Can we really escape this reductionism?

I can offer only one remedy, described above as a change of perspective, the enlarged way of thinking, a skeptical attitude, and the fight against one's own prejudices and dogmatism (3.2 and 3.3). And I can only hope that I have followed this remedy. How can we exclude our own preferences and personal judgments? Is this impossible? Or perhaps not even desirable? This leads to the second philosophical problem.

Scholars who interpret the Enlightenment following their own assumptions. The German American historian Peter Gay (1923–2015) wrote the highly influential two-volume *The Enlightenment: An Interpretation* (1966 and 1969). The

---

41 Susan Neiman, *Moral Clarity: A Guide for Grown-up Idealists*, London: Vintage 2009 and *Why Grow Up? Subversive Thoughts for an Infantile Age*, London: Penguin 2016.
42 Robertson, *The Enlightenment. The Pursuit of Happiness*, 41. See also Robertson, *Enlightenment*, xx, xvi, xxi for the following.
43 See Osterhammel, *Unfabling the East*, 2–5, 33 and 183, 283, 358–77.

first volume, subtitled "The Rise of Modern Paganism," asserts that the enlighteners were a group of radical anti-religious and anti-Christian intellectuals, driven by a single passion, namely "the passion to cure the spiritual malady that is religion, the germ of ignorance, barbarity, filth, and the basest self-hatred" (see also Introduction, Assumption 6).[44] I have argued that there is no historical evidence for this sweeping claim, over-generalization and cliché (see 5.1 and 5.2). This invites an obvious question: is it possible that Gay's personal convictions influenced his interpretation? Yes, this was almost certainly the case. In his autobiography, he wrote that "[m]y parents made me into a village atheist, and, with a few psychological refinements, I have remained one [...] My upbringing was not simply irreligious; it was antireligious. My father, bluff, and outspoken, left no doubt where he stood in the historic battle between reason and unreason. With his bellicose view of past and present, he was a true son of the Enlightenment."[45] Gay rehearses the cliché of the anti-religious Enlightener, and of the identification of Enlightenment with reason (or perhaps "Reason"; see Assumption 3). The argument follows a binary pattern: atheism stands for reason, religion for unreason. The follow-up question is: did Peter Gay ever seriously challenge his own atheist worldview or faith? In line with the "Enlightenment of the intellect:" challenging one's own possible prejudices, clarifying concepts (like "the Enlightenment"), and fighting against one's own lack of understanding (1.1, conception no. 3).

We might arrive at the following conclusion: We tend to see only what we want to see in the Enlightenment. We are inevitably biased, at least to some extent. And only later generations will find out. Yet this is just an assumption that may be wrong. See the limitations of our knowledge (2.3).

A narrow-minded way of thinking can be avoided. I take the example of English philosopher Claire Carlisle. In her book on Spinoza's enlightened religiosity, she notices that in the past, Spinoza was often attacked and condemned as an atheist (which he was not). In the 20th century, this assessment was turned on its head. Secularist readers "championed Spinoza as an early pioneer of their own worldview."[46] So Carlisle is fully aware that our own personal beliefs may cloud or deeply influence what we think about an author—or an entire movement, like the Enlightenment. She is familiar with divergent and mutually incompatible interpretations of Spinoza's philosophy of religion over the last 350 years, apparently mostly or often based on interpreters' own personal preferences (see

---

44 Peter Gay, *The Enlightenment: An Interpretation*, vol. 1: *The Rise of Modern Paganism*, New York: Norton 1966, 373.
45 Peter Gay, *My German question. Growing up in Nazi Berlin*, New Haven and London: Yale University Press 1998, 48 and 50.
46 Carlisle, *Spinoza's Religion*, 5.

also 5.2). "So I wonder whether, in refusing to categorize Spinoza's religion, I am any different from other scholars who interpret Spinoza in their own assumption." This self-reflective and undogmatic caution is admirable. Carlisle writes: "I have until quite recently felt rather tentative and uncertain about my relationship to [religious] questions."[47] I think this open-minded, undogmatic, reflective and tentative attitude follows the spirit of enlightenment (3.2).

Now, having condemned, and praised other Enlightenment scholars, it is time to show a self-critical attitude to my own approach. There is an obvious argument against my own interpretation. In the Introduction, I stated that it is a highly questionable approach only to take out of the Enlightenment era what we currently need or consider valuable, as if in a supermarket. I have also claimed that we should not construct a "monolithic European Enlightenment." However, critics might wish to accuse me of having done exactly that in this book. It could be argued that the passages on tolerance, the rule of law, slavery and human rights (4.3 and 4.4) are anachronistic and presentist, and that I attempt to distill a moral message from the wealth of different positions, in the sense of: "Be tolerant! Stand up for human rights! This is the proper enlightened frame of mind," and so on.

This means, among others, that as an author, I also have a philosophical orientation that can perhaps be characterized—or labeled— using terms such as liberal, highly Kantian, lenient with religions, and with a cosmopolitan orientation. And that a particular Enlightenment narrative has flowed from this orientation. In Jonathan Israel's terminology, I am a moderate Enlightener. My book is not a mere historiographical analysis. Like Cassirer and many others after him, I am also making an ideological plea.

The limits of knowledge. This is the third philosophical problem. It relates to epistemology and pops up in various areas. Here is a brief overview. Firstly, like other historians, I have struggled with the Enlightenment's "unity in diversity." There is obviously a lot of diversity and pluralism in the Enlightenment, and some have referred to different national Enlightenments, for instance. Ultimately, I have argued for the Enlightenment's overarching unity with qualifications (see especially 1.2). One key argument in favor of its unity is that it was a pan-European phenomenon. If we add the American Enlightenment and the Catholic Enlightenment in Spanish America and elsewhere, it was even global in reach. There is a second, more pragmatic argument in favor of the Enlightenment's unity. Nathaniel Wolloch argues "that the pluralizing tendency in intellectual history, if taken to the extreme, risks undermining any type of generalization, and verges on a postmodernist rejection of historiographical debate. So, for a historical

---

47 Carlisle, *Spinoza's Religion*, 16.

study, the question of where pluralization ceases and generalization begins inevitably arises."[48] According to the pragmatic argument, we simply need concepts, conceptions, and generalizations, otherwise we would not have a coherent story to tell. In the end, we must draw a line between legitimate pluralization and unavoidable generalization. But where exactly do we draw this line? Perhaps this problem cannot ultimately be solved.

Secondly, it is difficult to assess, for instance, to what extent the Enlightener's professions of faith in Christianity, in their denomination, or natural religion were mere lip service, hypocrisy, self-censorship, compromises with state censorship, or sincere statements (see 5.2). For example, interpreters of Spinoza have variously argued that he deceived his readers to keep out of trouble and used the word "God" for pragmatic reasons, but without philosophical conviction.[49] I have argued above that these arguments should be met with enlightened skepticism. Claims of this kind are just that: assumptions that are very difficult, perhaps even impossible, to prove. There is no access to an author's intentions, and arguments of this sort often amount to psychobabbles. Why not let the text speak for itself, while also considering its context? Put more polemically, why not leave an author's alleged hidden intentions to the metaphysicians? Yet it is evident that most of us want to know about a person's intentions. Is this not legitimate?

A third epistemological problem relates to the principle of causality (see 2.3). Consider the following questions: What caused the Enlightenment? The Reformation and the ensuing denominational pluralism in Europe? The Scientific Revolution? A generic process of secularization? What German sociologist Max Weber later called the "disenchantment of the world"? A deliberate effort of brave and predominantly White Western males to "make the world a better place, and increase happiness"? The impulses of the late 17th century Netherlands, with relatively free publishing, many freethinkers, and a revolutionary called Spinoza? Was the "revolution in print" decisive? Or a mixture of these and other factors?[50]

Similar questions arise regarding Spinoza and his impact on the Enlightenment (and modernity), an impact stressed by Jonathan Israel and challenged by his critics (see 5.3). There are other issues. Why did the witch craze start? Why did it end? Was it skepticism endorsed by authors like Michel de Montaigne and Thomas Hobbes? How did enlighteners contribute? How and why did "educat-

---

48 Nathaniel Wolloch, *Moderate and Radical Liberalism. The Enlightenment Sources of Liberal Thought*, Leiden and Boston: Brill 2022, 131. See also Robertson, *The Enlightenment. The Pursuit of Happiness*, 40–1 and 779.
49 See Carlisle, *Spinoza's Religion*, 10–11. A similar tendency can be found regarding Kant's philosophy of religion; see Wood, *Kant and Religion*, 210.
50 Robertson, *The Enlightenment. The Pursuit of Happiness*, 38–9 and 42–84.

ed elites" cease "to believe in witchcraft"?[51] Or we take the all-time favorite of Enlightenment studies relating to the problem of causality: Did the Enlightenment lead to, and was it responsible for, the French Revolution? Should we exclusively blame the French *philosophes*, because they were so radical? Do we argue that other factors were more crucial, such as demographic changes, namely a youth bulge in France, the agrarian crisis, extreme poverty, and hunger, the failure to reform the state, the financial crisis, the rise of the urban middle class or *bourgeoisie*, or the incompetence of King Louis XVI, to name just a few?[52] Here, as in related cases, monocausal explanations should be replaced by multicausal ones. It is implausible that one single entity such as "the Enlightenment" singlehandedly caused a historical phenomenon like the French Revolution. Discussions should focus on the Enlightener's direct or indirect contributions in the context of a plurality of possible causes. But this is probably not a very profound insight.

A fourth epistemological problem relates to teleological constructions. In a book that criticizes utopian thinking in the modern world, English philosopher John Nicholas Gray claims the following:

> The role of the Enlightenment in twentieth century terror remains a blind spot in Western perception. [...] The communist regimes were established in pursuit of a utopian ideal whose origins lie in the heart of the Enlightenment. Though the fact is less widely recognized, the Nazis were also in some ways children of the Enlightenment. They had only scorn for Enlightenment ideals of human freedom and equality, but they continued a powerful illiberal strand in Enlightenment thinking and made use of an influential Enlightenment ideology of 'scientific racism'.[53]

The message is clear: "Somehow" the Enlightenment values and its alleged "project" led to Stalinism, the Gulags, National Socialism, the Holocaust, and the deaths of millions. The condemnation follows a familiar pattern: the heterogeneity of the Enlightenment is thinned down to a reductive homogenization (which in turn the Enlightenment is said to have imposed on the world).[54] Nuances are omitted, generalizations triumph (see Introduction, Assumptions 3–5). The various currents of the Enlightenment are reduced to two clichés: the rationalist and the scientific Enlightenment, with its poisonous branch, scientific racism (see 1.1).

---

51 Robertson, *The Enlightenment*, 14–21.
52 Outram, *The Enlightenment*, 130–46 offers a succinct introductory answer to this complex question.
53 John Gray, *Black Mass: Apocalyptic Religion and the Death of Utopia*, London: Penguin 2007, ch. 2: Enlightenment and Terror in the Twentieth Century. See also the section Nazism and the Enlightenment.
54 Robertson, *The Enlightenment. The Pursuit of Happiness*, 769–70.

This is a familiar "defense" of the Enlightenment against its critics. Here I want to focus on one aspect, namely teleology: A teleological construction of history claims that it is purposeful and directed toward a goal. One version is Whig historiography, the belief that history is the march from an evil, dark, oppressive, ignorant, and unenlightened past to a liberal, glorious, enlightened, and happy present.[55] This progressive narrative has a teleological structure. The same structure applies to Nicholas Gray's pessimistic narrative, with a reversed content. It is —like its counterpart, Whig historiography—a view "from above," a philosophical history that can be interesting and stimulating by offering new perspectives, but it is always speculative and fanciful (see 2.3). The teleological constructions are not based on historical evidence, but are its flaky, very far-fetched interpretations. They blur the difference between correlation and causality. Eventually the enlighteners are caught in a kind of Catch-22: whatever they wrote, did, or said is used against them.

Jonathan Israel, in the seventh and last volume of his monumental project on the Radical Enlightenment, is more pessimistic than Steven Pinker. This is indicated in the title of his book: *The Enlightenment that Failed. Ideas, Revolution, and Democratic Defeat, 1748–1830*. He rehearses familiar claims about Radical Enlightenment and its enemies. Radical Enlightenment, he asserts, "offers a superior alternative to either traditional religion or an enfeebling, ultimately absurd Postmodernism." In spite of its alleged superiority, Radical Enlightenment is, or appears to be, "stalling if not in full retreat."[56] Israel's key thesis in this last volume is that after the 1830s, the Enlightenment was replaced by new ideologies such as nationalism and imperialism, but also, and more importantly, by socialism/Marxism, "which was essentially a new tendency without real eighteenth-century roots or predecessors." Why did Radical Enlightenment fail? According to Israel, because it was unable "to sufficiently close the gap between the concepts it offered and the loyalist thinking and religious assumptions of the great majority." According to Israel's interpretation, socialism was philosophically deficient, as it had no room for philosophy, democracy, or freedom of expression, whereas the Radical Enlightenment was apparently too elitist (though Israel avoids this negative term). Karl Marx started out as a radical Enlightener yet turned to socialism in the decade after 1838.[57] Israel detects two additional camps—and enemies— that ultimately helped to bring down Radical Enlightenment. The first was the con-

---

55 See especially Herbert Butterfield, *The Whig Interpretation of History* [1931], New York, London: Norton & Company 1965.
56 Israel, *Enlightenment that Failed*, 942.
57 Israel, *Enlightenment that Failed*, 25, 32, 916, 898–917.

servative Counter-Enlightenment (see Introduction, Assumption 4), the second was "Robespierreisme," a populist, anti-philosophical, Rousseauist, antifeminist, authoritarian, and unenlightened variant of the Counter-Enlightenment (evidently, Robespierre is another bad guy in Israel's story).[58]

My arguments concerning Israel's narrative of the failed Enlightenment link up with my previous criticism (see again 5.3). Israel's framework is too narrow, sweeping generalizations tend to downplay complexities, causal relations are asserted rather than justified, alternatives to the Radical Enlightenment are polemically presented as insufficient and philosophically weak, and so on. I subscribe to Israel's thesis that Enlightenment currents continued up to the 1830s (and did not die a sudden death around 1800). Yet I am skeptical whether narratives about the impact, success, or failure of the European Enlightenment, no matter if radical, or moderate, pass the test of critical scrutiny.

A qualified endorsement of the Enlightenment (first, third, fourth, fifth conceptions) makes sense. Conceptions number 6 and 7 will remain contested. Even today, the texts of the European Enlightenment remain "our best starting point for serious reflection on improving the human condition by peaceful and open means."[59] A starting point means that we can and should go beyond these texts at any time, in accordance with the understanding of enlightenment as a constant willingness to think for ourselves and change perspectives. It is an exhausting task, but worth it. This mode of thinking might be subversive, yet not necessarily so. It is self-reflective and relies on scientific expertise and knowledge. It avoids the pitfalls of *excessive* thinking, where people are in principle "rebellious and recalcitrant, notoriously suspicious of everything they are presented with."[60]

A qualified endorsement of the Enlightenment gives rise to the modest optimism that is formulated at the end of Voltaire's satire *Candide* (1759). Candide says to Pangloss, who is once again spouting theses about the "best of all possible worlds": "That is well put, [...] but we must cultivate our garden."[61] Anyone who has ever worked in a garden knows that this work can be demanding. But it can also be fulfilling, because a garden can stand for life in bloom. The symbolism of the garden is multifaceted and includes typical Enlightenment themes: the cultivation of one's talents, the idea of the perfection or *perfectibilité* of individuals and societies, the hope of a better future. People who believe in enlightenment work

---

58 Israel, *Enlightenment that Failed*, 7, 457, 491, 929. The crucial chapter is chapter 16 (457–96).
59 Louden, *The World We Want*, 223.
60 Christoph Paret, Der Reiz des unverhohlen Illegitimen, in: Markus Kotzur, ed., *Wenn Argumente scheitern. Aufklärung in Zeiten des Populismus*, Münster: mentis 2018, 53–69, at 68 and Frick, *Mutig denken*, 30, 33–5.
61 Voltaire, *Candide and Other Stories*, 88.

on their inner and outer nature and cultivate it. They do not wait for something to happen but do something themselves. They want to improve an imperfect world and believe that this endeavor is an end in itself. But they also endure imperfection, namely that of the world, their fellow human beings and, above all, their own. The assumption of working in the garden can represent all of this.

For urban people who do not have their own garden and have adopted a postmodern attitude, a different motto may be more suitable. They may see the assumption of cultivating a garden as just another totalizing and repressive discourse of mainly white Western males. They may find the symbolism of gardening too loaded. Voltaire's novel contains other answers at the end. "So what should one do?" Pangloss asks a dervish, a representative of ascetic, and spiritual Sufism. He answers—long before Wittgenstein—with a curt "Be silent." When Pangloss wants to philosophize with him about God and the world, about the soul and "pre-stabilized harmony," the Sufi simply slams the door in his face. The companion and world-weary philosopher Martin suggests: "Let's get down to work and stop all this philosophizing […]. It's the only way to make life bearable."[62] Others might agree with Walter Sobchak, who says to his friend the Dude after a rather unsuccessful funeral by the sea: "Let's go bowling."[63]

---

62 Voltaire, *Candide and Other Stories*, 87 and 88.
63 The quote is from the movie *The Big Lebowski* (USA 1998, Joel and Ethan Coen). For an introduction see Emily Dill and Karen Janke, New Shit Has Come to Light: Information Seeking Behavior in The Big Lebowski, *Journal of Popular Culture*, 46 (2013), 772–88.

Explanation of important terms

Anthropocentrism: Humans see themselves as the center of the world. From a normative point of view, this advocates the thesis: "Human beings are the measure of all things" (Protagoras). Opposing positions would be theocentrism (God or deities are at the center), or physiocentrism (nature as the center).

Causality: Refers to the relationship between cause and effect. Hume assumes that thinking in causal contexts is a matter of custom, habit, and belief. For Kant, the causal principle is part of the understanding (*Verstand*) and one of the synthetic judgments *a priori*; see also transcendental.

Criticism: Kant used this term to describe his transcendental philosophy. Criticism in epistemology asks about the "conditions of possibility" of experience and knowledge in the subject.

Determinism: All events without exception are fixed and determined by preconditions. Determinists deny the possibility of free will.

Deism: The belief in an aloof and impersonal deity that does not interfere in human affairs. Tricoire distinguishes between a moderate deism endorsed by the English deists and Rousseau and a radical wing, with Voltaire as the most prominent representative.

Dogmatism: Dogmatists are convinced that they can arrive at knowledge in all areas, also in the realm of metaphysics. They hold this knowledge to be true. Opposing positions include skepticism, epistemological relativism, perspectivism, and Kantian criticism.

Empirical: Related to experience or empirical knowledge.

Empiricism: A philosophical, epistemological school of thought which assumes that all knowledge must be based on sensory experience. The methodical collection of data can also be described as empiricism. It overlaps with positivism. Opposing positions would be rationalism, constructivism, or Kant's criticism.

Essentialism: Thinking in terms of "essences," i.e. the conviction that it is possible to know, for example, the essence of being, of humans, of the universe, or of the Enlightenment.

Fatalism: The view that fate (*fatum* in Latin) predetermines our lives. Human will is seen as weak or even defenseless. Fate can be understood as a personal (deity) or impersonal, cosmic power. Fatalism is close to => Determinism.

Fideism: The philosophical doctrine that faith (Latin *fides*) should take precedence over reason. According to fideism, reason is unable to arrive at knowledge in matters of faith or religion.

Hermeneutics: A theory that endeavors to interpret and understand cultural products, especially texts, as appropriately as possible.

Materialism: Explains all phenomena as products of matter and its laws. Opposing positions are idealism and dualism. See also Naturalism.

Metaphysics: one of the disciplines of philosophy. It investigates the foundations, structures, and laws of being and the nature or essence of things. See also essentialism.

Methodology: The (study of) procedures in scientific disciplines. Methodological determinism claims: "*As far as experience goes*, there is no freedom of will, only determinism." Ontological or metaphysical determinism asserts: "There is no freedom of will, only determinism."

Naturalism: A philosophical theory that interprets the world as an exclusively natural event. If the concept of nature coincides with physical nature, the result is a materialistic philosophy; see also Materialism.

Neology: An 18th-century movement within Protestant theology that was positively disposed toward the Enlightenment and strove for a modern, humanistic Christianity.

Orthodoxy: Refers to a prevailing or traditional doctrine. Religious orthodoxy in the 18th century differed from Neology, natural religion, or the religion of reason.

Rationalism: An epistemological position that regards reason as the (only) source of knowledge. Opposing positions would be empiricism, criticism, irrationalism, or fideism.

Religion, natural: in the 18th century, it usually referred to those aspects of religion that could be understood by humans without the help of divine revelation.

Religion, positive: Here "positive" means "existing"; positive religions would be Christianity or Buddhism, for example, in contrast to the idea of natural religion.

Secularization: Has several dimensions of meaning: 1. the separation of religious and political spheres; 2. the differentiation of scientific disciplines and their emancipation from theology; 3. the privatization of religion; and 4. the loss of religion.

Spirit of systems, *Systemdenken*, *esprit de système:* Thinking within the framework of a => metaphysical system. It asserts a metaphysical system based on theses that are independent of experience and cannot be proven. Many Enlightenment thinkers rejected the *esprit de système* and preferred the *esprit systématique,* i.e. systematic thinking, instead.

Teleology: The assumption that actions and developments are purposeful and goal oriented. A teleological construction of history claims, for example, that it is purposeful, and directed toward a goal.

Transcendent or beyond experience: Everything that goes beyond the realm of experience. This can refer to the nature of things, metaphysics, or religion. See also Essentialism and Metaphysics.

Transcendental: That which lies in the mind, the understanding, or in reason, such as the laws of logical thinking.

Utilitarianism: A philosophical school of thought that holds that only (or above all) utility counts. Utilitarianism is a form of => Teleological ethics. According to Jeremy Bentham, "the greatest happiness of the greatest number" is the decisive moral standard.

Select bibliography

Comprehensive bibliographies are included in Martus, *Aufklärung*, 961–1012, Ritchie Robertson, *The Enlightenment. The Pursuit of Happiness*, 893–925, and Haakonssen, *The Cambridge History of Eighteenth-Century Philosophy*, 1237–1341.

Avis, Paul, *Theology and the Enlightenment. A Critical Enquiry into Enlightenment Theology and Its Reception*, London: T&T Clark 2023.

Beutel, Albrecht, *Kirchengeschichte im Zeitalter der Aufklärung*, Göttingen: Vandenhoeck & Ruprecht 2009.

Bellaigue, Christopher de, *The Islamic Enlightenment. The Struggle Between Faith and Reason, 1798 to Modern Times*, New York: Norton 2017

Bielefeldt, Heiner, *Menschenrechte in der Einwanderungsgesellschaft. Plädoyer für einen aufgeklärten Multikulturalismus*, Bielefeld: transcript 2007.

Blom, Hans, John Christian Laursen, and Luisa Simonutti, eds., *Monarchisms in the Age of Enlightenment: liberty, patriotism, and the common good*, Toronto: University of Toronto Press 2007.

Brewer, Daniel, ed., *The Cambridge Companion to the French Enlightenment*, Cambridge: Cambridge University Press 2014.

Broadie, Alexander, and Craig Smith, eds., *The Cambridge Companion to the Scottish Enlightenment*, 2nd ed., Cambridge: Cambridge University Press 2019.

Bulman, William J., and Robert G. Ingram, eds., *God in the Enlightenment*, New York: Oxford University Press 2016.

Carlisle, Clare, *Spinoza's Religion. A New Reading of the Ethics*, Princeton and Oxford: Princeton University Press 2021.

Carroll, Ross, *Uncivil Mirth. Ridicule in Enlightenment Britain*, Princeton and Oxford: Princeton University Press 2021.

Cassirer, Ernst, *The Philosophy of the Enlightenment* [1932], updated edition, Princeton: Princeton University Press 2009.

Cavallar, Georg, *The Rights of Strangers: Theories of international hospitality, the global community, and political justice since Vitoria*, Aldershot: Ashgate 2002.

Cavallar, Georg, *Imperfect cosmopolis: studies in the history of international legal theory and cosmopolitan ideas*, Cardiff: University of Wales Press 2011.

Cavallar, Georg, *Theories of Dynamic Cosmopolitanism in Modern European History*, Oxford: Peter Lang 2017.

Cavallar, Georg, *Islam, Aufklärung und Moderne*, Stuttgart: Kohlhammer 2017.

Cheneval, Francis, *Philosophie in weltbürgerlicher Bedeutung. Über die Entstehung und die philosophischen Grundlagen des supranationalen und kosmopolitischen Denkens der Moderne*, Basel: Schwabe 2002.

Coleman, Charly, *The Virtues of Abandon. An anti-individualist History of the French Enlightenment*, Stanford, Calif.: Stanford University Press 2014.

Curran, Andrew S., *Diderot, and the Art of Thinking Freely*, New York: Other Press 2019.

Devellennes, Charles, *Positive Atheism. Bayle, Meslier, d'Holbach, Diderot*, Edinburgh: Edinburgh University Press 2021.

Diner, Dan, *Aufklärungen: Wege in die Moderne*, Ditzingen: Reclam 2017.

Ducheyne, Steffen, ed., *Reassessing the Radical Enlightenment*, Abingdon: Routledge 2017.

Edelstein, Dan, *The Enlightenment. A Genealogy*, Chicago and London: University of Chicago Press 2010.
Faber, Richard, and Brunhilde Wehinger, eds., *Aufklärung in Geschichte und Gegenwart*, Würzburg: Königshausen & Neumann 2010.
Ferrone, Vincenzo, *The Enlightenment. History of an Idea*, translated by Elisabetta Tarantino, Princeton and Oxford: Princeton University Press 2015.
Fillafer, Franz Leander, *Aufklärung habsburgisch. Staatsbildung, Wissenskultur und Geschichtspolitik in Zentraleuropa 1750–1850*, Göttingen: Wallstein Verlag 2020.
Fitzpatrick, Martin et al., eds., *The Enlightenment World*, London: Routledge 2004.
Förschler, Silke, and Nina Hahne, eds., *Methoden der Aufklärung. Ordnungen der Wissensvermittlung und Erkenntnisgenerierung im langen 18. Jahrhundert*, Paderborn: Fink 2013.
Frazer, Michael L., *The Enlightenment of Sympathy. Justice and Moral Sentiments in the Eighteenth Century and Today*, Oxford: Oxford University Press 2010.
Frick, Marie-Luisa, *Mutig denken. Aufklärung als offener Prozess*, Ditzingen: Reclam 2020.
Forst, Rainer, *Toleration in Conflict. Past and Present*, Cambridge: Cambridge University Press 2013.
Fulda, Daniel, Sandra Kerschbaumer, and Stefan Matuschek, eds., *Aufklärung und Romantik. Epochenschnittstellen*, Paderborn: Fink 2015.
Fulda, Daniel, and Jörn Steigerwald, eds., *Um 1700: Die Formierung der europäischen Aufklärung. Zwischen Öffnung und neuerlicher Schließung*, Berlin and Boston: de Gruyter 2016.
Garrard, Graeme, *Counter-Enlightenments. From the eighteenth century to the present*, New York: Routledge 2006.
Geier, Manfred, *Aufklärung. Das europäische Projekt*, 2nd ed., Reinbek bei Hamburg: Rowohlt 2012.
Gilead, Tal, ed., *A History of Western Philosophy of Education in the Age of Enlightenment*, London, New York and Dublin: Bloomsbury Academic 2021.
Goldie, Mark, and Robert Wokler, eds., *The Cambridge History of Eighteenth Century Political Thought*, Cambridge: Cambridge University Press 2006.
Gründer, Karlfried, and Karl Heinrich Rengstorf, *Religionskritik und Religiosität in der deutschen Aufklärung*, Tübingen: Max Niemeyer 2011.
Haakonssen, Knud, ed., *The Cambridge History of Eighteenth-Century Philosophy*, Cambridge, UK: Cambridge University Press 2006.
Hanley, Ryan Patrick, *Love's Enlightenment. Rethinking Charity in Modernity*, Cambridge: Cambridge University Press 2017.
Hanley, Ryan Patrick, and Darrin M. McMahon, eds., *The Enlightenment. Critical Concepts in Historical Studies*, 5 volumes, London and New York: Routledge 2010.
Hardtwig, Wolfgang, ed., *Die Aufklärung und ihre Weltwirkung*. Göttingen: Vandenhoeck & Ruprecht 2010.
Hofmann, Michael, ed., *Aufklärung. Epoche, Autoren, Werke*, Darmstadt: Wissenschaftliche Buchgesellschaft 2013.
Hulliung, Mark L., *Enlightenment in Scotland and France. Studies in Political Thought*, New York: Routledge 2019.
Israel, Jonathan, *Radical Enlightenment. Philosophy and the Making of Modernity 1650–1750*, Oxford: Oxford University Press 2001.
Israel, Jonathan, *Enlightenment Contested. Philosophy, Modernity, and the Emancipation of Man 1670–1752*, Oxford: Oxford University Press 2006.
Israel, Jonathan, *A Revolution of the Mind. Radical Enlightenment and the Intellectual Origins of Modern Democracy*, Princeton: Princeton University Press 2009.

Israel, Jonathan, *Democratic Enlightenment. Philosophy, Revolution, and Human Rights 1750–1790*, Oxford: Oxford University Press 2011.
Israel, Jonathan, *The Enlightenment that Failed. Ideas, Revolution, and Democratic Defeat, 1748–1830*, Oxford: Oxford University Press 2019.
Israel, Jonathan and Martin Mulsow, eds., *Radikalaufklärung*, Berlin: Suhrkamp 2014.
Jacob, Margaret C., *The Secular Enlightenment*, Princeton and Oxford: Princeton University Press 2019.
Kates, Gary, *The Books that Made the European Enlightenment. A History in 12 Case Studies*, London et al.: Bloomsbury Academic 2022.
King, Margaret L., ed., *Enlightenment Thought. An Anthology of Sources*, Indianapolis and Cambridge: Hackett Publishing Company, Inc. 2019.
Klemme, Heiner, ed., *Kant und die Zukunft der europäischen Aufklärung*, Berlin/New York: de Gruyter 2009.
Klemme, Heiner F. and Manfred Kuehn, eds., *The Dictionary of Eighteenth-Century German Philosophers*, London and New York: Continuum 2010.
Kondylis, Panajotis, *The Enlightenment within the framework of modern rationalism* [1981], ed. Jörn Garber and Ulrich Kronauer, Hamburg: Felix Meiner 2002.
Kors, Alan Charles, ed., *Encyclopedia of the Enlightenment*, 4 volumes, Oxford and New York: Oxford University Press 2003.
Lacorne, Denis, *The Limits of Tolerance. Enlightenment Values and Religious Fanaticism*, transl. C. Jon Delogu and Robin Emlein, New York: Columbia University Press 2019.
Laursen, Chris, and María José Villaverde, eds., *Paradoxes of Religious Toleration in Early Modern Political Thought*, Lanham et al.: Lexington Books, 2012.
Lehner, Ulrich, *Enlightened monks. The German benedictines 1740–1803*, Oxford: Oxford University Press 2011.
Lehner, Ulrich and Michael Printy, eds. *Brill's Companion to the Catholic Enlightenment in Europe*, Leiden: Brill 2010.
Lehner, Ulrich and Jeffrey Burson, eds. *Enlightenment and Catholicism in Europe. A Transnational History*, University of Notre Dame Press 2014.
Genevieve, Lloyd, *Enlightenment Shadows*, Oxford: Oxford University Press 2013.
Louden, Robert B., *The World We Want: How and Why the Ideals of the Enlightenment Still Elude Us*, Oxford: Oxford University Press 2007.
Martus, Steffen, *Aufklärung. Das deutsche 18. Jahrhundert – ein Epochenbild*, Berlin: Rowohlt 2015.
Matytsin, Anton M., and Dan Edelstein, eds., *Let There Be Enlightenment. The Religious and Mystical Sources of Rationality*, Baltimore: Johns Hopkins University Press 2018.
Meyer, Annette, *Die Epoche der Aufklärung*, Berlin: Akademie Verlag 2010.
Mosher, Michael, and Anna Plassart, eds., *A Cultural History of Democracy in the Age of Enlightenment*, London et al.: Bloomsbury Academic 2021.
Mulsow, Martin, *The Hidden Origins of the German Enlightenment*, transl. by H. C. Erik Midelfort, Cambridge: Cambridge University Press 2023.
Neugebauer-Wölk, Monika and Holger Zaunstöck, eds., *Aufklärung und Esoterik*, Hamburg: Felix Meiner 1999.
Neugebauer-Wölk, Monika, Renko Geffarth, and Markus Meumann, *Aufklärung und Esoterik: Wege in die Moderne*, Berlin, Boston: de Gruyter 2013.
Osterhammel, Jürgen, *Unfabling the East. The Enlightenment's Encounter with Asia*, translated by Robert Savage, Princeton and Oxford: Princeton University Press 2018.

Outram, Dorinda, *The Enlightenment*, 4th ed., Cambridge: Cambridge University Press 2019.
Pagden, Anthony, *The Enlightenment, and Why it Still Matters*, Oxford: Oxford University Press 2013.
Parekh, Surya, *Black Enlightenment*, Durham and London: Duke University Press 2023.
Parkin, Jon, and Timothy Stanton, eds., *Natural Law, and Toleration in the Early Enlightenment*, Oxford: Oxford University Press 2013.
Pocock, John Greville Agard, *Barbarism and Religion*, 6 vols., Cambridge: Cambridge University Press 1999–2015.
Rubiés, Joan-Pau, and Neil Safier, eds., *Cosmopolitanism, and the Enlightenment*, Cambridge: Cambridge University Press 2023.
Robertson, John, *The Enlightenment. A Very Short Introduction*, Oxford: Oxford University Press 2015.
Robertson, Ritchie, *The Enlightenment. The Pursuit of Happiness, 1680–1790*, London: Penguin 2022.
Röd, Wolfgang, *Die Philosophie der Neuzeit 2. Von Newton bis Rousseau*, München: Beck 1984.
Schmidt, James, ed., *What is Enlightenment? Eighteenth Century Answers and Twentieth Century Questions*, Berkeley, Los Angeles, London 1996.
Schneider, Ulrich Johannes, *Die Erfindung des allgemeinen Wissens: Enzyklopädisches Schreiben im Zeitalter der Aufklärung*, Berlin: Akademie Verlag 2013.
Schneiders, Werner, *Hoffnung auf Vernunft. Aufklärungsphilosophie in Deutschland*, Hamburg: Meiner 1990.
Schneiders, Werner, ed., *Lexikon der Aufklärung. Deutschland und Europa*, München: Beck 1995.
Schneiders, Werner, *Das Zeitalter der Aufklärung*, 3rd ed., München: Beck 2005.
Sharpe, Matthew, *The Other Enlightenment. Self-Estrangement, Race, and Gender*, Lanham, Boulder, New York, London: Rowman & Littlefield Publishers 2023.
Sommer, Andreas Urs, *Sinnstiftung durch Geschichte? Zur Entstehung spekulativ-universalistischer Geschichtsphilosophie zwischen Bayle und Kant*, Basel: Schwabe 2006.
Sorkin, David, *The Religious Enlightenment. Protestants, Jews, and Catholics from London to Vienna*, Princeton: Princeton University Press 2008.
Tomaszewska, Anna, ed., *Between Secularization and Reform. Religion in the Enlightenment*, Leiden and Boston: Brill 2022.
Tomaszewska, Anna, and Hasse Hämäläinen, eds., *The Sources of Secularism. Enlightenment and Beyond*, Palgrave Macmillan 2017.
Tricoire, Damien, *Die Aufklärung*, Köln: Böhlau 2023.
Tunstall, Kate E., ed., *Self-Evident Truths? Human Rights and the Enlightenment*, New York: Bloomsbury 2012.
Vartija, Devin J., *The Color of Equality. Race and Common Humanity in Enlightenment Thought*, Philadelphia: University of Pennsylvania Press 2021.
Warman, Caroline, et al., eds., *Tolerance. The Beacon of the Enlightenment*, Cambridge: Open Book Publishers 2016.
Wetzel, Dietmar J., ed., *Perspektiven der Aufklärung. Zwischen Mythos und Realität*, München: Wilhelm Fink 2012.
Winterer, Caroline, *American Enlightenments: Pursuing Happiness in the Age of Reason*, New Haven: Yale University Press 2016.
Wood, Allen, *Kant and Religion*, Cambridge: Cambridge University Press 2020.

Author Index

Abduh, Muhammad   41
Adorno, Theodor   6–8, 18f., 22, 177f., 185
Ali, Ayaan Hirsi   65f., 69
Aquinas   24, 157
Aristotle   8, 44, 75
Ash, Timothy Garton   66
Atran, Scott   67, 95
Augustine of Hippo   24
auto-da-fés   76

Bahrdt, Carl Friedrich   21
Barbeyrac, Jean   24
Barre, François Poullain de la   164
Basedow, Johann Bernhard   21, 45, 179
Basseporte, Madeleine Françoise   46
Baudeau, Abbé Nicolas   32
Bayle, Pierre   9–12, 14, 25–27, 29, 35, 38, 42, 53–55, 63–65, 163, 175
- *Philosophical Commentary*   10f., 14, 26, 53f.
Beccaria, Cesare   15f.
Behringer, Wolfgang   183
Bentham, Jeremy   7f., 16f., 199
Berlin, Isaiah   2, 4–6, 8, 10, 13, 15, 22, 28f., 33, 40f., 43f., 65, 78, 81, 84f., 150, 152, 157, 160–162, 167, 179, 183, 190
Berman, Harold J.   148
Bevilacqua, Alexander   71
Bielefeldt, Heiner   10, 41, 46
Biester, Johann Erich   4f., 29, 152
Bolingbroke, Henry St. John Viscount   153
Bossuet, Jacques-Bénigne   11, 25, 38

Carlisle, Claire   154, 163, 190–192
Cassirer, Ernst   2, 34f., 50, 145f., 150, 154, 170, 173, 188, 191
Charles III., king of England   11, 12
Cherbury, Lord Edward Herbert of   154
Cloots, Anacharsis   33, 35
Collins, Anthony   28, 67, 95
Condorcet, Marie Jean Antoine Nicolas de Caraitat, Marquis de   22, 32f., 35, 179
Constant, Henri-Benjamin   151f.
Cook, Captain James   43, 93

d'Alembert, Jean Le Rond   33f., 43, 54–56, 82, 151
d'Argens, Marquis   135
Darnton, Robert   5f.
Dawkins, Richard   67, 175
Devellennes, Charles   35, 175f.
d'Holbach, Baron   33, 35, 55, 59, 90f., 146, 161, 163, 171, 174f.
Diderot, Denis   12, 17–19, 22, 25, 32f., 35f., 42–44, 49, 54–56, 59, 71, 78–80, 88f., 151, 161, 164, 171, 175f., 186
- *Jacques le fataliste et son maître*   80
- *Rameau's Nephew*   42, 44
Diez, Heinrich Friedrich von   84f.
Diner, Dan   186f.
Dreams of a Spirit-Seer, Illustrated by Dreams of Metaphysics   81f.

Eldar, Akiva   68
Emcke, Carolin   53, 97f.
Erasmus of Rotterdam   30
Essay "What is Enlightenment?"   4, 5, 184

Ferguson, Adam   38
Ferrone, Vincenzo   2, 19, 38, 41, 45f.
Forster, Georg   5, 17f., 35–38, 40, 43f., 173
Frederick II. of Prussia   182
Fréret, Nicolas   163
Freud, Sigmund   1f., 78

Garrard, Graeme   9f., 12f., 20f., 25
Gay, Peter   14, 25, 145, 148, 154, 189f.
Gedicke, Friedrich   74, 92
Gellert, Christian Fürchtegott   7, 35, 43, 49
Gentili, Alberico   175
Gibbon, Edward   38, 71
Goethe, Johann Wolfgang von   15, 50, 77f., 152
- *Faust*   15
- *The Sorrows of Young Werther*   50, 77
Goldsmith, Oliver   38
Gottsched, Johann Christoph   31, 47, 49

Gottsched, Luise Adelgunde Victorie, born Kulmus 47
Gouges, Olympe de 4f., 32, 40, 43, 47
– *Réflexions sur les hommes nègres* 4
Gray, John Nicholas 185f., 193f.
Grégoire, Abbé Henri Jean-Baptiste 32, 34, 39
Günderrode, Karoline von 13f.

Habermas, Jürgen 1, 22, 24, 41
Hamann, Johann Georg 8, 45, 152
Hardenberg 3, 152, 154
Hardenberg, Georg Philipp Friedrich Freiherr von 3
Hegel, Georg Wilhelm Friedrich 18f., 21, 171
Heidegger, Martin 2, 19, 185, 188
Helvétius, Claude-Adrien 7, 55, 59f., 163, 174
Herder, Johann Gottfried von 8, 10, 12, 35, 38, 41, 45, 152, 179, 185
Hilker, Annette 79
Himmelfarb, Gertrude 15f.
Hippel, Theodor Gottlieb von 47, 84
Hobbes, Thomas 7, 58–60, 192
Holst, Amalia 46
Horkheimer, Max 6f., 18f., 22, 177f.
Humboldt, Wilhelm von 40, 179f.
Hume, David 7, 11, 17, 27, 31, 35, 38, 54, 80, 90, 94, 146f., 155, 157, 163f., 173, 197
Hutcheson, Francis 35, 49, 80

Iselin, Isaak 36
Israel, Jonathan 9, 16f., 24–26, 33, 46, 147, 152, 161–165, 173, 189, 191f., 194f.
– *The Enlightenment that Failed. Ideas, Revolution, and Democratic Defeat, 1748–1830* 17, 194

Jacobi, Friedrich Heinrich 9f., 152
Jaucourt, Chevalier Louis de 18
Jefferson, Thomas 29f., 179, 184
Jerusalem, Johann Friedrich Wilhelm 160
Joseph II., Emperor of the Holy Roman Empire 10
Julie ou la nouvelle Héloïse 35
Justi, Johann Heinrich Gottlob von 1, 31, 37
– *Comparisons of the European with the Asiatic and Other Supposedly Barbaric Governments* 37

Kant, Immanuel 2–5, 7–14, 17–19, 22, 24, 27–30, 32f., 36–42, 44, 58, 60–66, 81–83, 87f., 90, 92, 94, 148, 151–153, 155, 157, 160f., 163, 165–173, 178, 180–182, 184, 192, 197
– *Critique of Pure Reason* 33, 62–64, 81, 87, 157
Kondylis, Panajotis 8, 26, 30, 59f., 164

La Mettrie, Julien Offray de 59, 146, 163, 174
La Roche, Marie Sophie von 47
Lavater, Johann Caspar 148f.
Leechman, William 61
Lehner, Ulrich L. 24, 149
Lepaute, Nicole-Reine 46
Lessing, Gotthold Ephraim 7, 9, 27f., 82, 85f., 89, 92, 152, 155, 173
– *Nathan the Wise* 27
– *The Education of the Human Race* 82
Ley, Michael 67f.
Lichtenberg, Georg Christoph 75, 78, 82, 181f.
– *Sudelbücher* 75, 181
Linné, Carl von 36
Locke, John 17, 24f., 27–30, 41, 44, 53f., 61–63, 65f., 73, 90–92, 94, 154
Louden, Robert 13, 15f., 21, 26, 33, 36, 44, 146, 150, 154f., 158, 161, 173, 178f., 189, 195
Louis XIV, king of France 4, 23, 25, 55f., 73, 91

Macaulay, Catharine 47
Maistre, Joseph de 8, 10
Mandeville, Bernard de 7, 80
Manemann, Jürgen 70
Marion, Élie 73
Martus, Steffen 15f., 21, 30, 32, 42f., 46f., 75, 78, 84, 90, 150, 166, 177
Marx, Karl 19, 194
May, Karl 14, 53, 187
Meier, Georg Friedrich 88
Mendelssohn, Moses 6, 20, 24, 28f., 37, 63, 80f., 92, 149, 152, 155, 166, 173, 182
Meslier, Jean 35, 175
Molainville, Barthélemy d'Herbelot de 71
Montagu, Lady Mary Wortley 38

Montamy, Didier-François de   176
Montenoy, Charles Pallisot de   80
Montesquieu, Charles-Louis de Secondat   3, 12, 15f., 32, 37f., 71, 78, 83, 89, 149–151
– *Persian Letters*   3, 37, 78, 83, 89, 151
– *The Spirit of the Laws*   15
Moser, Friedrich Karl Freiherr von   166f.
Mozart, Wolfgang Amadeus   43
Murray, Judith Sargent   46

Nicolai, Christoph Friedrich   7, 29, 77f., 84

Osterhammel, Jürgen   1, 16, 31f., 37, 189

Pagden, Anthony   33, 38, 145–147, 173, 187, 189
Paine, Thomas   17, 32, 155
Penn, William   180
Pestalozzi, Johann Heinrich   15
Pezzl, Johann   38
Pinker, Steven   19, 184–186, 189, 194
Price, Richard   20
Priestley, Joseph   20
Pufendorf, Samuel Freiherr von   15, 17, 24

Quesnay, François   22

Raddatz, Hans-Peter   69f.
Raynal, Abbé de   17f., 22, 56
– *Histoire des deux Indes*   18
Reimarus, Hermann Samuel   82, 155
Reland, Adriaan   71
Robertson, Ritchie   5f., 8, 17f., 23f., 26–38, 42, 45, 47, 50f., 62, 71, 73, 86, 150f., 176f., 179f., 188f., 192f.
Robespierre, Maximilien   40, 182
Rohan-Chabot, Chevalier Guy Auguste de   4
Rousseau, Jean-Jacques   3, 9f., 12, 20, 32f., 35f., 38, 43, 45f., 49f., 52, 56, 58, 60, 85–87, 94, 151, 154f., 164, 168, 170f., 173f., 179f., 184–186, 197
– *Émile*   58, 171, 184

Sade, Marquis de   174
Saint-Pierre, Charles-Iréné Castel, abbé de   33, 180
Sale, George   71

Schiller, Friedrich   11–13, 42, 181f.
– *Don Carlos*   11f.
Schmidt, Helmut   2
Schmidt, James   25
Schneiders, Werner   6, 11, 20, 26, 29, 33, 42f., 52, 55f., 60, 90, 92, 94, 96, 146f., 152, 178f., 181f., 187
Semler, Johann Salomo   160, 176
Shaftesbury, Anthony Ashley Cooper, third Earl of   3, 7, 35, 49, 73–75, 80f., 94
Smith, Adam   5f., 11, 23, 35f., 49, 51, 83f., 86, 151, 173
– *The Theory of Moral Sentiments*   51, 86
Sobchak, Walter   196
Spalding, Georg Ludwig   166
Spalding, Johann Joachim   37, 151
Spinoza, Baruch de   24, 27f., 34, 53, 63, 65, 152–154, 161–164, 173, 190–192
Swedenborg, Emanuel   81
Swift, Jonathan   78f.
– *A Modest Proposal*   78f.

Taylor, Charles   148, 164
Thomasius, Christian   6, 24, 30, 32f., 74, 90, 94, 153
Traité sur la tolérance   4, 27
Tricoire, Damien   3, 5, 8, 20, 22, 31f., 37, 39, 46, 56, 59, 154, 162, 197

Usbek   3, 83, 89

Vattel, Emer de   17, 33
Vico, Giambattista   8, 10, 38, 45
Voigt, Gottfried Christian   183f.
Voltaire   4f., 12, 16, 19, 27f., 34, 38, 54–56, 65f., 71, 75–79, 146, 151, 154f., 158f., 166, 171, 181, 195–197
– *Candide*   76, 78f., 195f.

Wallace, George   32
Wehler, Hans-Ulrich   2, 13
Wieland, Christoph Martin   85, 92, 174
Wilberforce, William   32
Wimmer, Franz Martin   172
Wolff, Christian   7f., 17, 30f., 33, 36, 54, 63, 83f., 88, 153

Wollstonecraft, Mary 43, 51
– *A Vindication of the Rights of Woman* 47f., 51
Wright, Kent 31, 38, 162, 164

Zertal, Idith 68
Žižek, Slavoj 69

Subject Index

Abolition, abolitionist   129–30
Absolutism   10, 15
- Enlightened absolutism   17, 180
- French absolutism   55
African Americans   19
Allah   41, 66, 70, 95f., 181
American Revolution   38, 115–18, 164
Anthropology   8, 24, 35f., 40, 146, 164, 168
A priori   9, 14, 40, 53, 62, 168, 197
Asia   17, 37, 84
Assertion   25, 44, 58f., 61, 67, 79, 81, 171
Assumption   1–3, 5, 10f., 13–19, 22, 31f., 34, 37–40, 42, 44, 46, 54f., 58, 62, 66, 72, 98, 145, 150f., 153f., 157f., 169, 171f., 177f., 189–196, 199
Atheism, atheist   13, 14, 35, 55, 59, 63, 66–7, 86, 90, 107, 126–7, 140, 150, 151, 152, 155, 161, 174–6, 190
Autonomy   10, 20, 32, 42, 146, 169f., 172
- autonomy of reason   168
- moral autonomy   1, 7

Berlinische Monatsschrift   4f., 29, 166, 177, 181, 183
Bible   6, 18, 24, 39, 56, 75, 149, 153, 155
Binary   5, 9, 31, 66, 69, 72, 84, 146, 148, 162, 185, 189, 190
bourgeoisie   42, 193
Brandt, Susanna Margaretha   113

Calas, Jean   102f., 113
Camisards   73, 94
Capitalism   6, 12, 69, 185
- Global capitalism   69
Carnivalization   79
Catholic   4, 25, 27f., 30, 32, 34, 39, 56, 60, 71, 73, 76, 84, 146, 151, 165
Causality, causal
- Causal assumption   2
- Causal relation   195
- principle of causality   62, 65, 68, 70, 192
Censorship   55f., 78, 153, 168f., 192
Change of perspective   12, 25, 82, 86, 88, 189

Chiliasm   92
China, Chinese
Christ   11
Christianity, Christian   1,15, 30, 35, 63, 65f.,68, 71, 77, 85, 122, 128, 146, 148–152, 153–155, 160, 161, 192
Church   3, 25, 56, 61, 75, 84, 93, 146, 148–150, 154, 159–161
- Catholic Church   55f., 66, 75, 77
- state church   146, 153
Citizen, citizens   40, 115, 117, 121, 123, 127, 128, 134, 135, 180
Citizens of the world   180
Civilization   6, 17–19, 39, 49
- Clash of civilizations   46, 66, 187
Cliché   14, 32, 40, 145, 148, 173, 190
Colonialism   10, 16f., 19, 31, 185
Common human understanding (*allgemeiner Menschenverstand*)   168
Common sense   15, 17, 41, 51, 74f., 87
Community   11, 15, 26, 33, 35f., 58, 73f., 80f., 148, 179
- Religious community   89, 151, 154, 158, 176
Compassion   1, 7, 32, 39, 81
Concept   6–10, 13–16, 18–22, 25f., 28–30, 32f., 35–38, 41f., 44f., 49, 51, 55, 59, 62, 87, 90, 92, 94, 96, 147, 151f., 154, 157f., 162f., 169–172, 177–179, 185, 187, 189f., 192, 194, 198
Conception   2f., 5, 10, 16f., 20–25, 27–30, 32, 35, 37f., 41, 43–46, 56, 58, 60, 65f., 80f., 87, 89, 94, 96, 147f., 150, 158, 165f., 172, 176–181, 186, 190, 192, 195
Condemnation   51, 67, 188f., 193
Conscience   1, 3, 6, 9, 24, 27, 29, 86, 160
Conservatism   8, 177
Constitution   17f., 20, 44
Constitutionalism   115
- Modern constitutionalism   115
Construction   147
- teleological construction   147, 162, 165, 193f., 199

Contradiction, contradictory   46, 53, 56, 59, 60, 61, 78, 96, 111, 112, 116, 180
– see performative self-contradiction
Correlation   185, 194
Cosmopolitanism, cosmopolitan
– cultural cosmopolitanism   35
– dynamic cosmopolitanism   33, 36 f., 148, 160, 180
– economic or commercial cosmopolitanism   35
– epistemological or cognitive cosmopolitanism   37
– Juridical or legal cosmopolitanism   180
– moral cosmopolitanism   35
– political cosmopolitanism   33
– religious cosmopolitanism   33, 36, 158
Counter-Enlightenment see Enlightenment
Creation   1, 16, 24, 36, 155, 187
Criticism   3, 6, 10–12, 20 f., 26, 29, 31–34, 39–41, 43 f., 52, 56, 58, 60, 63, 67, 75, 77, 79, 81, 89 f., 92, 98, 146, 153, 162–167, 169 f., 173 f., 177–179, 185, 195, 197, 199
– Age of criticism   33, 151
Crutches (*Gängelwagen*)   167
Cultivation   37, 46, 58, 170, 173, 195
Cynicism   73–75, 185

Declaration of Human Rights   182
Declaration of Independence   17, 20, 37, 184
Deism   14, 24, 28, 55, 150, 154, 197
Democracy   1, 18–20, 25, 96, 98, 178, 185, 189, 194
– social democracy   180
Denomination   5, 22 f., 27, 73, 83 f., 146, 150, 153, 155 f., 158, 192
Determinism, deterministic   24, 55, 58, 59, 152
Dialectic   6, 18, 177 f.
– "dialectic of Enlightenment"   6, 116, 178
dignity   9 f., 14, 16, 18, 29, 32, 40 f., 46, 155, 169, 171, 173
diversity   18, 22, 25 f., 36, 39, 47, 150, 152, 160, 178, 191
Dogmatism, dogmatic   12, 32, 66, 82, 89–94, 96, 170, 176, 181, 189
Duty, duties   28, 43, 106, 107, 112, 118, 123
– Moral duty   8

Dynamic   20, 25, 33, 36 f., 44, 49, 69, 80, 97, 158, 165
– Dynamic cosmopolitanism   134, 180

écrasez l'infâme   75
Edict of Nantes   6, 15, 23, 25, 28, 73
edicts of tolerance   23
education   2 f., 21, 24, 26, 28 f., 33, 44 f., 84, 87, 95, 160 f., 175, 178, 181–184, 187
egoism   12, 166, 168 f.
– egoism of reason   36, 168
Emancipation, emancipatory   42, 45, 70, 85, 116, 123, 137, 164, 170, 178, 179
Emotion   1, 5, 22, 32, 35, 40, 42 f., 49, 51, 53
Empiricism, empirical   11, 34, 55, 56 61, 62, 65 112, 138, 139, 157
empiricist   11, 58–60
Encyclopédie   23, 25, 33 f., 43, 54–57, 90, 151
Encyclopedists   21, 32
Enlarged way of thinking   5, 24, 37, 58, 72 f., 82, 84, 86 f., 167 f., 172, 176, 189
Enlightenment   1–47, 49–53, 55 f., 58–60, 62–68, 71–73, 75, 78–81, 83 f., 86–91, 94, 96, 98, 145–155, 158 f., 161–167, 169 f., 172–195, 198 f.
– assumptions about the Enlightenment   1–19
– British Enlightenment   15
– Catholic Enlightenment   14, 24, 149, 191
– Concept of enlightenment   20, 22, 46, 167, 187
– Counter-Enlightenment   8–13, 20 f., 25, 184–186, 189, 195
– Criticism of the Enlightenment   8 f., 13
– Currents of the Enlightenment   20–25
– Emancipatory conception of the Enlightenment   22
– Enlightenment and religion   145–76
– "enlightenment of the Enlightenment"   170
– Enlightenment of the intellect   21, 24, 30–32, 45, 178, 190
– Enlightenment Project   1, 6, 22, 44, 185
– Enlightenment thinking   6 f., 55, 186, 193
– Enlightenment through science   21 f., 24 f., 31, 41, 56, 58, 60, 98, 170, 172, 178 f., 183
– European Enlightenment   1–3, 5 f., 8–16, 18, 20–22, 25–27, 29–31, 33–35, 38 f., 42, 44–46, 54–56, 59, 63, 66, 68, 71, 75, 80,

83, 91, 95, 145 – 147, 151 f., 154, 160, 165, 173, 177, 181 f., 185 – 188, 191, 195
- "failed Enlightenment" 19, 177 – 96
- French Enlightenment 15, 29, 56, 90, 146, 164
- Intellectual [*verständig*] Enlightenment (Hegel) 171
- Jewish Enlightenment 20, 24, 28, 149
- Moderate Enlightenment 16, 161
- Popular Enlightenment (*Volksaufklärung*) 97, 183
- Process of Enlightenment 29, 39, 85, 167
- Protestant Enlightenment see Neology
- Radical Enlightenment 9, 16, 25 f., 47, 84, 161 – 164, 194 f.
- Reflective enlightenment 11 f., 147, 171 f., 183
- religious Enlightenment 20, 22, 24, 145 f., 148, 151
- secular Enlightenment 24, 58
Enthusiasm 10, 40, 43, 50 f., 61, 63, 74, 85, 89 – 92, 94, 149, 182
- fanatical enthusiasm 74
- noble enthusiasm 94
- religious enthusiasm 61
Epistemology, epistemological 40 – 72, 100, 124, 134 – 5, 139, 165, 172, 191
Equality 16 f., 25 f., 34, 40 f., 44, 47, 51, 74, 169, 178, 193
- legal equality 21, 39
Essentialism 26, 65 f., 198 f.
Ethics 1, 6 – 11, 13 f., 27, 35, 39, 43, 50, 84, 87, 154, 163, 199
- deontological ethics 9, 166
- virtue ethics 6 f., 9, 90
Eurocentric 10, 16 f., 45
Europe, European 2, 10, 21, 26, 52, 67, 69, 78, 84, 97, 104, 114, 121, 124, 147, 148, 150, 182, 183, 192
Evolution 17, 187
- Darwin's theory of evolution 187
Exclusion 18 f., 46
Experience 4 f., 13 – 15, 18, 21 f., 25 f., 30 – 36, 40 f., 45, 49, 54, 58, 61 f., 70, 77, 79, 82 f., 85, 92, 94 f., 150, 163, 174, 176, 179, 197 – 199

faith 2 – 4, 14, 22, 24 – 27, 30, 40 f., 55 f., 65 – 67, 73, 76, 83, 90 f., 95, 145 – 147, 152 – 155, 158, 175 f., 178, 180, 187, 190, 192, 198
- Christian faith 24, 30, 56, 150
Fake news 95, 97, 187
Fanaticism 10, 14, 19, 23 f., 27, 29, 40, 62 f., 71, 73 f., 76, 78, 89 f., 92 – 96, 146 f., 150, 153, 155, 163, 170, 176 f., 181, 183 f.
Fascism 8, 185
Female 32, 47, 85, 164
fideism 26, 64, 198 f.
Filter bubble 95, 97, 187
Formation (*Bildung*) 3, 15, 21, 26, 95, 148, 173
Founding Fathers 8, 16, 20, 159, 164, 184
France 6 f., 15, 23, 25 – 28, 31, 39, 50, 55 f., 83, 89, 149, 155, 162, 165, 176, 180, 193
Freedom 6, 13, 15 – 17, 19 – 23, 25, 27, 29 f., 37, 40 f., 60, 62, 73 f., 149, 159, 168 f., 172, 178 f., 193 f., 198
- freedom of the pen 168
Freedom of thought 11, 25
- Political freedom 33
- Sexual freedom 36
French Revolution 10, 13, 15, 19, 52, 75, 90, 177, 182, 189, 193
Fundamentalism 1, 9, 66
- Dogmatic fundamentalism 174

Gender see sex 46, 47, 70, 84
Generalization 2, 9, 17, 26, 70, 150, 185, 190 – 193, 195
- principle of generalization (Kant) 87
German Idealism 21, 65, 152
Germany 7, 14, 27, 29, 35 f., 84, 92, 95, 162, 188
God 2 f., 8 f., 22, 24, 28 – 31, 34, 37, 41 f., 51, 55, 59, 61 – 63, 66, 77, 79, 89, 92, 148, 151 – 155, 157 f., 160, 163, 174 – 176, 181, 184, 192, 196 f.
Grace 30, 55

Haitian Revolution 33
Happiness 5 – 9, 13 f., 17 f., 20, 23 f., 26 – 38, 43, 45, 47, 50 f., 71, 73, 79, 86, 150 f., 157, 176 f., 179 f., 185, 188 f., 192 f., 199
- "pursuit of happiness" 37
Haskalah 24

Heart 3, 18, 33, 41, 43, 50, 81, 85–87, 155, 193
Heresy, Heretic 59, 76, 122, 151
Hermeneutical, hermeneutics 96, 138, 139, 172
Heteronomy 10, 167, 169
Hindsight 76
– Abuse of hindsight 189
Historicism 188f.
Historiography 14, 20, 25
– Whig historiography 194
History 3f., 6, 9f., 16–19, 21, 24–28, 31, 33, 35–41, 47, 50f., 54, 65, 67f., 71, 83, 89, 146f., 149, 152f., 158, 160, 164, 173, 180, 183f., 186, 194, 199
– Cultural history 11, 18, 21, 42
– Intellectual history 6, 21, 162, 164f., 191
– turn towards history 138f.
Holy Roman Empire 6, 15, 30, 45, 55, 183
Huguenot 6, 12, 23, 25f., 30, 55, 73, 91
Humanism 8, 19f., 27, 35, 42, 44, 46, 66, 184–186
– elitist humanism 45
Humanity 2, 8, 16f., 19, 21–23, 35f., 44, 57, 70, 74, 145, 148, 186
Humor 73–75, 78, 80, 171
Hypocrisy 44, 153, 192

Ignorance 14, 20f., 45f., 54, 63, 67, 96, 145, 166, 170f., 176f., 181, 190
– learned ignorance (*docta ignorantia*) 58, 174
Immanence, immanent 21, 26, 56
Impartiality, impartial 5, 86, 99, 107, 108, 109, 123, 124, 134, 173
Impartial observer or spectator (Smith) 86, 124
Imperative 13, 152, 179
– Categorical imperative (Kant) 9, 13f., 157
Individual 1, 5, 10, 13, 16–18, 21f., 24–26, 28f., 35–37, 39, 42–45, 49, 53, 55f., 61–63, 70, 85, 95f., 149, 169, 179, 195
Individualism 19, 24, 179
Intellect 8, 14, 22f., 27, 32, 35, 40–43, 45, 50, 54, 79, 173
Intellectus 7, 18, 22, 32, 42
Interest 3f., 7f., 10, 18, 29, 31, 37, 43, 56, 65, 74, 167

Intolerance 6, 14, 23–29, 53, 75, 78, 89, 146f., 150, 153, 155, 163, 181
Irish 35, 38f., 78f.
Islam 1f., 16, 25, 36, 65–72, 95f., 147, 170, 187
Islamic state 95f.
Islamism 8

Jews, Jewish 20, 24, 27, 28, 104, 126, 135, 137, 149, 188
Jihad, jihadist 70, 95f., 181
Judaism 6, 27, 71, 85, 149
Judgment 9, 14, 16, 26, 28, 33, 35f., 40f., 53, 56, 58, 61f., 71, 76, 81, 86f., 91, 146, 161, 165, 167f., 170, 172, 189, 197
– Practical judgment 14, 58
Justice 3, 9, 11, 14, 16, 20, 25, 37, 44, 49, 59, 70, 150f., 155, 160, 169, 173f., 180, 184
– Global justice 16

Kantian 6, 9, 11, 14, 173, 191, 197
Knowledge 2, 16, 21–23, 26–30, 32–34, 37, 41, 43, 54, 56–58, 60–63, 65f., 87, 92, 94–96, 146, 152, 154, 156f., 160f., 163, 168, 170–172, 174f., 182f., 190, 195, 197–199
– Lack of knowledge 54
– Limits of knowledge 61, 191
– Scientific knowledge 31, 58, 171

Law 1f., 4, 8f., 11, 13, 15–17, 25, 30, 34, 36f., 46, 49, 55, 59, 96, 148, 169, 180, 198f.
– Laws of nature 22
legacy, legacies 10, 179
– Enlightenment legacies 179
Levellers 20
Liberalism 6, 18, 152, 179f., 185, 192
– classical liberalism 180
liberty 15, 17, 32, 37, 53

Male 17, 32, 44–47, 192, 196
Materialism, materialist 24, 55, 59, 140, 151, 152, 161
Maxim (Kant) 8, 13f., 29, 71, 86, 90, 167f., 172
Metacritique 11

Metaphysics   8, 13, 16, 41, 53 f., 62, 66, 77, 79, 81 f., 147, 154, 157, 163, 171, 174, 176, 188, 197–199
– Dogmatic metaphysics   59, 63, 82
Middle Ages   16, 27, 71, 92, 148
Minority (*Unmündigkeit*)   6, 22 f., 27, 147, 183
Mockery   74 f., 78, 81, 84
moderate   12, 18, 24 f., 30, 42, 55, 61, 84, 95, 154, 161–165, 180, 186, 191 f., 195, 197
Modernity   1 f., 6–9, 12, 15 f., 18 f., 26, 35, 42, 59, 66, 72, 147, 161 f., 185, 192
– Enlightenment and modernity   1 f., 6
– European modernity   5, 185
Monocausal   69 f., 72, 193
monolithic   39, 66, 165, 191
Morality   1–3, 7–11, 15, 20, 22, 28 f., 35, 40–44, 46, 50, 56, 60, 63, 65, 94, 151, 157, 161, 175
– Foundations of morality   3, 6
Morals   1 f., 8, 11, 13, 49
– Public morals   21
Moral universalism
– Qualified moral or normative universalism   107–13, 169
Murder   2–4, 11 f., 14, 30
Muslim, Muslims   1, 2, 65, 66, 68, 69, 83, 89, 95 f., 123, 124–6, 151, 187

Napoleon   15, 177
Narrative   1–3, 5 f., 8, 12, 14, 16, 18 f., 24, 27, 30, 32 f., 35–38, 66, 77, 96, 145, 147, 153, 165, 186, 189, 191, 194 f.
Nationalism   8, 52, 180, 184, 194
National Socialism   6, 52, 67, 188, 193
Native Americans   19
Naturalism   24, 44, 174, 198
Natural law   7, 15–17, 21 f., 24 f., 32, 35, 150
Nature   3 f., 9, 11, 14, 16, 18 f., 21–23, 26 f., 31, 34, 36, 40, 45, 59, 72, 75, 82, 92, 94, 151, 154, 165, 176 f., 182, 196–199
– Human nature   7, 24, 44
– Law of nature   5
Nazism   8, 185, 193
Neology, neologians   14, 15, 24, 148, 150
New Atheism   66 f., 174
Novel   14, 18, 35, 37, 41, 43, 50 f., 58, 76–80, 159, 179, 196

Obligation   8 f., 11, 157, 169
– Unconditional moral obligation   169
Opposition   32, 38, 45, 63, 154, 186
– Binary opposition   5, 9, 31, 66, 146, 148
Order   33, 37, 94, 153 f., 161, 168 f., 177, 179
– Natural order   8, 20, 22, 46
Organization   180
– international organization   180
Orthodoxy   24, 63, 65, 158, 198

Palestine   68 f.
Palestinian   68 f.
Panentheism   154
Pangloss   79, 195 f.
Pantheism   14, 158
– Pantheism Controversy   152
Parody   73, 78, 186
Party   11, 19, 60 f.
– Religious party   55 f., 60
Passion, passions   14, 49, 108, 109, 135, 190
Patriotism, patriotic   134, 137, 180
– cosmopolitan patriotism   36, 180
Patronage   56
perception   8, 13, 19, 22, 54, 60–63, 71, 92, 97 f., 147, 157, 177, 193
Perfectibility, perfection   37, 105, 106, 115, 160
– Idea of perfection   17, 37, 170
Performative self-contradiction   2, 41, 60, 178
Perspective   1 f., 24, 36 f., 41, 43, 45, 49, 56, 72, 78, 83 f., 86, 90, 98, 145, 160, 162, 189, 194 f.
Philosophes   14, 22, 30, 55 f., 58, 80, 151, 159, 171, 173, 186, 193
Philosophy   3, 5–9, 11–13, 16, 18, 21 f., 26 f., 30, 33 f., 38–42, 44 f., 52, 54–56, 60 f., 63, 65, 68, 71, 82 f., 85 f., 90, 92, 146, 150–154, 161, 163, 165 f., 170–173, 178 f., 181, 184, 188, 194, 197 f.
– Intercultural philosophy   172 f.
Pietism, pietist   83, 94, 148
Pluralism   54, 172, 178, 191 f.
– Religious pluralism   23
Polemics   14, 26, 61, 150, 184 f.
Pope   19, 26, 28
Popular   4, 15, 20, 27, 36 f., 40, 166, 183, 196
Positivism   6, 8, 189, 197
Postmodernism   9, 19, 33, 83, 194

Pragmatic   18, 30, 79, 158, 191 f.
Predestination   55
Prejudice   2, 4, 10, 12, 15, 21, 28, 30, 32 f., 39 f., 45, 83, 86, 89–91, 94–98, 145, 147, 153, 166–170, 177, 181, 183, 187, 189 f.
Presentism   188 f.
Principle   3, 8, 11, 14–18, 20, 23, 26, 28–30, 32, 34–36, 40, 44, 49, 53, 55, 61 f., 71, 79, 83 f., 86 f., 92, 162, 166, 168, 170, 175, 181 f., 187 f., 195, 197
– Moral principle   1 f., 4, 9–12, 40, 77, 79
Progress   18 f., 25, 31, 35, 69, 145, 147, 152, 184 f.
Promise   13 f., 20, 28
Proselytism   89, 150
Protestantism, protestant   71, 73, 102, 119, 121, 128, 159, 185
Providence   151, 161
– Divine providence   24, 30
Prudence   1, 8, 13, 18, 23, 30 f., 40, 65, 95, 169, 173, 177, 183
psychobabble   2, 44, 192
Public sphere   46, 81, 97 f., 168 f., 178

Quaker   89, 148, 180
Quran   71, 96

racism, racist   11, 16 f., 129, 137, 193
– scientific racism   193
radicalism, radical   126, 163 f., 165, 174
ratio   7, 18, 22, 27
Rationalism   3, 6, 27, 54, 64, 94, 197, 199
Reason   2 f., 5–11, 13–19, 22 f., 25–29, 31–37, 39–45, 49, 51–54, 56, 58, 60–63, 65–69, 75–77, 79–82, 87 f., 90, 92, 94, 145–147, 150–152, 155, 157 f., 161, 163, 166–173, 178 f., 182, 184–186, 190, 192, 198 f.
– Age of Reason   32, 37, 155
– Belief/believing in reason   2, 34, 40–45, 62, 65
– ideas of reason   32
– instrumental reason   22, 177
– limits of reason   26 f., 40, 53, 62, 64–66, 81
– public use of reason   167
– "tyranny of reason"   44
Reasoning   9, 11, 27, 31, 34, 36, 41, 151
– Moral reasoning   10

Reform   7, 13, 15–17, 21, 40 f., 45, 52, 74, 85, 146, 148–151, 161, 178, 180, 193
– Judicial reforms   15
Relativism   17, 42, 83, 86, 172, 197
– Moral relativism   1–3, 10, 35, 39 f., 98
Religion   3, 5, 7, 9–11, 13–15, 21–33, 35–38, 46, 53–55, 60, 62 f., 65–68, 71, 73, 76 f., 83–87, 89, 91 f., 96, 145–152, 154–158, 160 f., 163–165, 167, 171, 174–176, 180, 186, 190–194, 198 f.
– Natural religion   7, 15, 24, 86, 150–155, 171, 176, 192, 198 f.
– Philosophy of religion   31, 157, 163, 175, 190, 192
– Religion and science   31
Republic   12, 29 f., 33, 46, 71, 168 f., 175
Republicanism   18, 25, 46, 161 f.
Revealed religion   155
Revelation   7, 10, 30, 41, 61 f., 89, 91 f., 94, 155, 157, 161, 199
Revolution   13, 17, 30, 36, 46, 87, 95, 97, 148, 152, 155, 170, 177, 185, 189, 192, 194
Right, rights   55, 70, 88, 94, 117, 119 f.,121, 122, 124, 130, 161,
166, 167, 169
– Human rights   10, 16–19, 21 f., 25, 31 f., 35, 41, 45 f., 149, 152, 162, 178 f., 181, 187, 189, 191
– Natural rights   21 f., 32, 74
Romanticism, Romantic era   3, 5, 8, 12 f., 40, 50, 65, 94, 152, 178
Rule of law   11, 15, 17 f., 23, 32, 44, 46, 171, 179, 191

Satire   73–75, 77 f., 80 f., 92, 195
School of Salamanca   22
Science, scientific   185
Second Scholastic   22
Secularist   147, 190
Secularization, secular   8, 13, 14, 16, 24 f., 38, 58, 66, 69, 71, 94, 108, 113, 115, 119, 123, 140, 145–150, 162
Self-knowledge   170
Self-reflective   13, 41, 59, 79, 81 f., 170 f., 175, 186, 191, 195
Semantics   17, 158
– New temporal semantics   38

Sensibility   30, 32, 34f., 42, 45, 49, 51, 60f.
– A sea change in sensibility   35, 42
Sensualism   55
sensus communis   74, 87, 168
Sex   45f.
Sexes   45f.
Simplifications   9, 147
Skepticism   14, 54, 58, 63, 65, 82f., 86, 88, 150, 153, 163, 171, 192, 197
Slavery   4, 16–18, 20, 31–33, 37, 40, 51, 78, 184, 187, 191
Slave trade   17, 20, 31f., 51, 78, 184
Social contract   15, 52
Social media   97
Sophism, Sophists   99, 182
Species   17, 44, 74
– Human species   2, 26, 36f., 44
Spinozist   16, 21, 26, 147, 162, 164
Spirit of systems (*Systemdenken, esprit de système*)   34f., 59, 163, 199
State   3, 5, 10, 14–16, 18f., 22, 25, 28–30, 33, 35f., 39, 43, 55, 75, 81, 83f., 145, 150f., 153, 159, 169, 178–181, 187, 192f.
– modern state based on the rule of law (*Rechtsstaat*)   16
Stoicism, stoic   51, 106
Stories see Narrative
Sufism   196
Superstition   5, 21, 24, 26–29, 31, 35, 40, 45, 59, 63, 71, 80, 89f., 92–96, 98, 146f., 149, 154f., 163, 170, 176f., 181, 183
System   3, 15f., 29, 32f., 37, 41, 44, 51, 56, 59, 63, 66, 69, 82, 154, 178, 187
– Metaphysical system   34, 82, 199
– Systematic thinking (*esprit systématique*)   34, 199
Systemdenken   34, 82, 199

Teleology, teleological   142, 147, 162, 165, 193, 194
terreur, French Reign of Terror   12, 19, 177, 182, 189
Terrorism   67–69, 95, 187
Test of Ridicule   73f.
Theism, theistic   35, 63, 152

Theology   5, 9f., 16f., 21, 24, 26, 30f., 38f., 42, 44, 55f., 63, 145f., 149–151, 153f., 157, 160, 175f., 198f.
– Critique of theology   153
Theory   6f., 10f., 17f., 20f., 33, 38–40, 49, 59f., 63, 68f., 88, 98, 155, 167, 176, 180, 183–185, 187, 198
– British moral sense theory   35, 49
– four stages theory   39
– moral theory   35, 184
Thesis   11f., 14f., 53, 68, 148, 161, 163, 165, 177, 194f., 197
– common morality thesis   154, 176
Thinkers   4f., 8, 12, 14f., 23, 29, 31, 38, 40, 44, 60, 62, 65, 89, 94, 145–147, 149–151, 154, 175, 199
– dogmatic metaphysical system thinkers   77
Thinking   6–9, 13, 16–18, 22, 25f., 28f., 32–36, 39, 44f., 51, 58, 62, 66, 69–71, 82–89, 92, 94, 96, 98, 146, 158, 166f., 170–173, 178, 181, 183–186, 188, 190, 193–195, 197–199
– Binary thinking   66, 72, 189
Thinking for oneself   3, 27f., 87, 172, 181, 183, 187f.
Tolerance, toleration   120–128
– conception of tolerance   22f., 25, 27, 29f., 41, 169
– Justifications for tolerance   15f., 25
– Permission conception of tolerance   121, 127
Totalitarianism, totalitarian   1, 8, 12, 19, 66, 188
Transcendence, transcendent   13, 30
transcendental   13, 197, 199
Travel report   36
Trump, Donald   96–98, 185
Truth   2, 7, 9f., 19f., 26f., 29, 31f., 37, 39–41, 53, 59f., 62, 75, 84f., 88–90, 96, 98, 166–169, 172, 184
– search for truth   28, 96, 169, 172

understanding (*Verstand*) see intellect
Unhistorical   6f., 38, 147
United Nations   180
Unity   25f., 56, 191
Universality, universalism, universalist   137–144
– Moral universalism   2, 39
– religious universalism   155

Universalizability, universalization 112
– test of abstraction and universalization 14, 112
universal moral grammar 40
university 3, 5f., 8–10, 13–20, 22, 24–41, 49–51, 56, 59, 65, 71, 74–76, 83f., 86f., 89, 94, 146–149, 152, 154f., 157f., 161–163, 165f., 170, 173, 176, 178–180, 188, 190
Utilitarianism, utilitarian 22, 79, 107, 111, 137, 158, 186

Value, values 1, 2, 3, 66, 99, 118, 127, 135, 178, 189, 193
– European values 3
Vendée 182
verification 58, 92
Verstand see intellect
Violence 6, 9, 11, 18, 25, 40, 53, 67–71, 95f., 174
– Islamist violence 67
Virtue 1, 3, 6–11, 13, 15f., 24f., 27, 29, 35, 42–44, 46, 50, 58f., 74, 83, 94, 146, 154, 157, 165
– Civic virtue 46
– Moral virtue 23

Western 2, 4, 6, 16, 21, 46, 51, 66, 69, 71, 148, 178, 192f., 196
Western see Western Enlightenment
Wisdom 3, 5, 18, 20, 30, 43, 55, 153, 166, 173
– doctrine of wisdom (*Weisheitslehre*) 171
witchcraft 193
witch, witches 90, 104, 149, 183
Worldview 5, 8, 10f., 21, 29, 33, 42, 65, 79, 95–97, 176f., 185, 190
– Scientific worldview 90

www.ingramcontent.com/pod-product-compliance
Lightning Source LLC
Chambersburg PA
CBHW061939220426
43662CB00012B/1957